František Kupka

1871-1957

A RETROSPECTIVE

This project is supported by a grant from the National
Endowment for the Arts, Washington, D.C., a Federal Agency

The Solomon R. Guggenheim Museum, New York

Published by The Solomon R. Guggenheim Foundation, New York, 1975
Library of Congress Card Catalogue Number: 75-27339
© The Solomon R. Guggenheim Foundation, 1975
Printed in the United States

TABLE OF CONTENTS

LENDERS TO THE EXHIBITION

Dr. Altmayer, Paris
Lucy Delmarle
Mr. and Mrs. Solomon Ethe
Karl Flinker
Mr. and Mrs. Andrew P. Fuller
Gallien Family
Peter Gimpel
Mr. and Mrs. M. A. Gribin
Wilhelm Hack, Cologne
Joseph H. Hazen
Mr. and Mrs. Alexander Liberman
McCrory Corporation
P. P., Paris
Camille Renault, Paris
Mr. and Mrs. Daniel G. Ross
Mr. and Mrs. Arnold A. Saltzman, Great Neck, New York
Nancy Schwartz
Mr. and Mrs. G. E. S., New York
Mr. and Mrs. Joseph Randall Shapiro
Theodoros Stamos
Richard S. Zeisler, New York
William Zierler

The Cleveland Museum of Art
Los Angeles County Museum of Art
The Metropolitan Museum of Art, New York
Musée National d'Art Moderne, Paris
The Museum of Modern Art, New York
Museum des 20. Jahrhunderts, Vienna
Národní Galerie, Prague
Philadelphia Museum of Art
The Solomon R. Guggenheim Museum, New York

Louis Carré et Cie
Margit Chanin, Ltd.
Royal S. Marks Gallery, New York
Stephen Mazoh & Co., Inc.
Galerie Denise René, Paris, New York
Spencer A. Samuels and Company, Ltd.

František Kupka has gained a secure place in the history of modern paint-ing, for he was among those very few authentic innovators who, early in the second decade of this century, dared to cross the threshold which at the time separated representational from non-objective painting. Like his fellow Slavs, Vasily Kandinsky and Kasimir Malevich, or the Frenchmen Robert Delaunay and Francis Picabia (Piet Mondrian and the Dutch Neo-Plastic movement came somewhat later), Kupka demonstrated that painting, like music, has a capacity to convey its meanings entirely through formal means. He supported this radical proposition with a prolific output that, again like Kandinsky's, ran its full course from illustration and representation through Fauvist attenuations and, from there, to organic and geometric abstraction.

The creative impulses that motivated this Czech-born French émigré, the influences that may have shaped his style, whether derived from Eastern Slav, Central European Czech and Austrian, or finally from French sources, are the explicit subject matter of Kupka's retrospective exhibition at the Guggenheim Museum and that of this accompanying catalogue. Apart from the thought-provoking sequences and the supportive documentation that underlie this double-pronged venture, apart indeed from Kupka's well-founded claim to having originated fundamental stylistic departures, we are confronted in the current show with close to 200 paintings, watercolors, drawings and graphics of compelling visual power that may or may not coincide with moments of stylistic innovation. The tenuous and complex relationship between the new and the vital clearly mirrored in this show provides Kupka's oeuvre with its particular tension and significance. It affords to the viewer an often merging, sometimes parallel, twofold avenue that leads toward an understanding and enjoyment of Kupka's art.

The organization of the current retrospective required an awareness of Kupka's composite nationality with all its implications, as well as a degree of familiarity with Czech and French sources, circumstances and with the location of works. The existing literature about Kupka, as well as the artist's own writings is primarily in Czech and French, while the German and English bibliography, except for translations, remains marginal. Correspondingly, many of the most important loans were secured from European sources—Czechoslovakia and France above all—before we approached other continental countries and the still limited group of American lenders who have acquired paintings and works on paper of primary importance. On both sides of the Atlantic, the response of museums, collectors and galleries was exemplary, and our gratitude toward those cited in this catalogue's list of lenders (as well as toward others who have chosen to remain anonymous) is correspondingly great.

The Guggenheim's deepest indebtedness, acknowledged here in behalf of the large public for whom this exhibition is created, must go to the Národní Galerie in Prague and to its director, Professor Dr. Jiří Kotalík. The comprehensive survey of František Kupka's life work could not have been arranged without the massive loan of almost thirty works from this particular source. We are as indebted to the Musée National d'Art Moderne in Paris, the other largest repository of Kupka's oeuvre. Without the generous commitment of Dominique Bozo, then Acting Director of the Collections, for a loan enacted by Pontus Hultén and Germain Viatte, this exhibition could not take place.

It should also be stressed that this retrospective could be selected and presented only after exhaustive preparation which depended upon the participation of extraordinarily talented and qualified individuals within and outside of the Guggenheim Museum. Neither Margit Rowell, the Guggenheim's Curator of Special Exhibitions, nor Meda Mladek, who was asked to be a Consultant, could have achieved the result as it stands without the complementary capacities of the other. Miss Rowell, as curator of the exhibition, brought to the task of selection and presentation her penetrating and original research and tested knowledge of exhibitions as well as her wide experience with technical aspects of exhibition and catalogue production. Mrs. Mladek's deep involvement with Kupka's entire oeuvre, one that goes back to the artist's lifetime, her rich store of painstakingly gathered information, and her command of the Czech language were an extremely important factor in the successful completion of both catalogue and exhibition. Miss Rowell and Mrs. Mladek have also made valuable contributions in their respective and highly personal essays.

Throughout the preparatory phase, other Kupka specialists, aware of crucial art historical issues that still surround his problematical art, joined in an extended de facto symposium thereby adding new information. Kupka experts who have provided us with extraordinary assistance are Denise Fédit and Ludmila Vachtová. The scholars Lilli Lonngren, Virginia Spate and Yvonne Hagen, as well as the museum officials, Jiří Kotalík and Dominique Bozo, and the gallery directors, Louis Carré (aided by Mme. Diane Foy) and Karl Flinker have also helped us greatly. Special gratitude is also due the artist's stepdaughter Mme. Andrée Martinel-Kupka who has encouraged and aided the Guggenheim's efforts from the outset. Finally, the patient efforts of the Guggenheim's staff require grateful acknowledgement although they must necessarily remain largely anonymous. Among those who may be named in this context besides Margit Rowell, the sustained and effective work of her assistant Karen Lee and the Museum's editor, Carol Fuerstein, call for prominent mention and special gratitude.

The František Kupka presentation at the Guggenheim will be followed early in 1976 by a single European showing at the Kunsthaus Zürich. We therefore salute Dr. R. Wehrli and Dr. Felix A. Baumann, respectively the departing and the incoming directors of this institution, who have both given us their generous professional help and cooperation.

The mounting costs that have become part of our daily lives have reached and limited museums in many areas of their functioning. The programming of ambitious shows and the publication of valuable catalogues have suffered more than other museum activities from these inhibiting factors. Therefore, the aid extended to museums throughout the country by the National Endowment for the Arts assumes crucial significance as it fills otherwise insurmountable financial gaps. The František Kupka retrospective depended to an important degree upon National Endowment funding which is acknowledged here with every gratitude on behalf of the trustees and the staff of The Solomon R. Guggenheim Museum.

Because of increasing difficulties of every kind and description that are now inherent in the organization of major modern exhibitions, it is safe to predict that a long time, probably decades, will pass before a comparable effort can be extended on behalf of František Kupka's work by any New York museum. It is our sincere hope therefore that this full review of the Czech master's central contribution to modern art will result in the desired benefits for scholars and the public at large.

THOMAS M. MESSER, DIRECTOR
The Solomon R. Guggenheim Museum

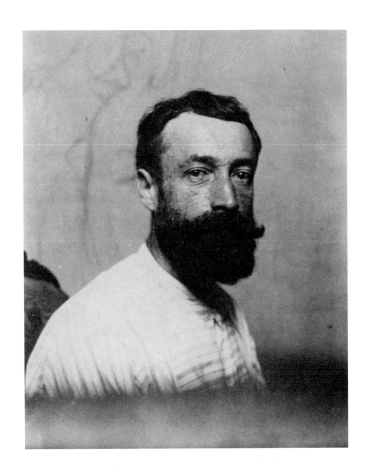

CENTRAL EUROPEAN INFLUENCES

Meda Mladek

In 1912, at the *Salon d'Automne* in Paris, František Kupka exhibited what he called "his painter's credo," *Amorpha, Fugue* and *Warm Chromatics*. French critics were indignant, enraged. Almost unanimously they rejected the paintings, mainly because they were incompatible with French tradition and taste. Protests against the barbaric invasion of the Paris art scene by Slavs and Americans reached the steps of the French Parliament.

In 1966, however, the Musée National d'Art Moderne in Paris organized a one-man show of Kupka's works. The French catalogue indicated that, without question, Kupka had by now been accepted into the Paris school. In it Bernard Dorival states that: "Kupka, already awakened by a few French Realist and Impressionist paintings shown in Bohemia, passed through the stage of Art Nouveau, which he discovered in Paris and not in Vienna, as has often been written, hesitated between a docile symbolism and the lesson given by Odilon Redon, traversed the expressionism of Toulouse-Lautrec and Fauvism, was influenced by the praxinoscope of Reynaud and chronophotography of Marey...."[1] Denise Fédit, in the same catalogue, insists that: "Kupka could not bring to light his essentially original creations without the French contribution, which taught him that a pictorial work lacks value if it does not observe certain laws.... His encounter with the French painters, Realist and Impressionist, opened new horizons before his eyes. From then on he wished to handle familiar themes as they did...."[2] The only credit ascribed to Prague is the academic training which gave Kupka "excellence in drawing" and "the metaphysical and occultist anxieties"[3] which the painter presumably brought from his country of origin. Vienna's influence is dismissed altogether for a rather surprising reason: "Kupka, as a good Czech hostile to Germanism, could not allow

[1] Bernard Dorival, *Kupka,* Paris, Musée National d'Art Moderne, 1966, p. 11.

[2] Denise Fédit, Ibid., p. 27.

[3] Ibid., p. 34.

himself to be influenced by the intellectual or spiritual manifestations that he noted there."[4] An obvious question comes to mind. Who was right in interpreting the art of Kupka? The French critics of 1912 who thought it outrageously alien to their Latin taste and tradition, or the critics of 1966 who thought that it was essentially a product of French influence? This question is important not because of any intrinsic significance of the 1966 catalogue, but because the thesis of its authors has been docilely adopted by many writers on Kupka, including several Czech art historians.

Fourteen years had elapsed between Kupka's arrival in Paris in 1896 and the time he began to work on his "painter's credo," *Amorpha, Fugue* and *Warm Chromatics*. The temptation to conclude that these fourteen years were fully responsible for Kupka's discovery of non-objective art proved irresistible to French art-historians when, after some fifty years, they understood and recognized the significance of his work, and he was explained as a product of French formalistic evolution. However, what was not considered was that Kupka had reached Paris after many years of deep involvement with art and art philosophy. Nor was it considered that the famous "law"[5] to which Denise Fédit refers must have been known to Kupka before his arrival in Paris. He had spent six years at the Academies of Prague and Vienna, where this theory was expounded by the Nazarenes. It was through the application of this law that he was guided into abstraction.

Neither was it considered that Kupka's Symbolist art could have had its origin elsewhere than in Paris. By 1966 it was generally accepted that Symbolism, like Impressionism, was born in France. "Let us repeat it: born in France,"[6] and that the Manifesto,[7] from which Symbolism supposedly originated, reached Germany via a circuitous route through Belgium only ten years later—that is in 1896 when Kupka was already in Paris. New trends in the history of art suggest that Impressionism is not the source of Symbolism, and that German Symbolism had existed independently since the beginning of the nineteenth century. Indeed, the Nazarenes were Symbolists. By 1967, Werner Hofmann, in his introduction to the catalogue of Kupka's exhibition at the Museum des 20. Jahrhunderts in Vienna recognized as I do, that Kupka gained from his immigration to Paris in several respects, but he also made it clear that Kupka might have reached the abstract phase of his development years earlier than he actually did, had he remained in Vienna.

It seems appropriate to investigate Kupka's formative years spent in Bohemia and in Vienna in order to probe the various degrees to which he was influenced by Central European thought and culture. These influences have not been taken into account by French critics since little of Kupka's background is known in France.

Bohemia

While Kupka' artistic education and intellectual environment in Prague and Vienna are crucial determinants of his concepts, knowledge of his childhood also throws light on his personality.

The land around Opočno and Jaroměř in eastern Bohemia, where Kupka spent his boyhood, preserved a high concentration of Baroque monuments

4 Dorival, Ibid.

5 The "law" was formulated in France by Maurice Denis in the 1890's precisely as an antithesis to the Realist and the Impressionist doctrines. "We must repudiate this academic naturalism, insisting that one should paint what one sees. . . . we must repudiate the realism of Impressionism whose purpose still is to imitate nature. . . . Realism, one of the errors which we encounter invariably during the worst epochs of art, at times of decadence and sterility. . . . It should be remembered that a picture . . . is essentially a flat surface covered with colors which are assembled in a certain order." Published in *Art et Critique,* August 13, 1890.

6 Jean Cassou in *Les Sources du vingtième siècle,* Paris, 1961, p. 54. Cassou was director of the Musée National d'Art Moderne in Paris, and professor of nineteenth and twentieth-century art at the Ecole du Louvre. He is also the author of many texts on modern art and his views have exercised considerable influence in France.

7 Jean Moréas, "Un Manifeste littéraire, 1886," in Guy Michaud, *La Doctrine symboliste,* Paris, 1947, p. 23.

and art, in which the boy showed an early and lively interest. Yet, the area was one of the poorest in Bohemia, and Kupka's father, although a municipal official, could not afford to send his children to high school, not even the most talented child, Frank. In accordance with his father's decision, he was apprenticed in a local saddler's workshop to learn a craft he quickly grew to hate. Having missed secondary school, Kupka could not enroll in a university to study the two subjects in which he was most deeply interested —philosophy and history. His lack of a formal education—except for painting—was a source of anguish and humiliation, and it led to tremendous efforts at self-education on his part, especially during his stay in Vienna. It also led to a continuous search for the company of learned and intellectually prominent men.

The family climate surrounding Kupka's boyhood was not happy. He lost his mother at a young age, and his stepmother showed little understanding for his first attempts to draw and paint. The boy withdrew into himself and developed a strong tendency to indulge in dreams. He lived, indeed, two lives, one based on reality, the other on fantasy. This tendency seems to have been strengthened by his early encounter with spiritualism. The saddler to whom Kupka was apprenticed was a well known spiritualist and head of a secret sect. He held regular seances at his house, to which he brought the supersensitive boy, and it was not long before Kupka became a much appreciated medium.

Prague, the old city celebrated by Apollinaire, the city which inspired Franz Kafka's writings and deeply impressed André Breton, was also destined to leave strong impressions on young Kupka. It stirred his imagination, but it also confirmed his inclination toward daydreaming, despite the fact that his dreams were constantly shattered by the poverty in which he lived and by his growing disappointment with the social order. In Prague, Kupka indulged again in spiritualism, which, at least, had a practical reward—he earned money as a successful medium. But it also had a serious effect on his mental stability, and he suffered several breakdowns. For the rest of his life, he was subject to depressions which robbed him of much of his vitality.

The factors that directly influenced Kupka's artistic orientation are, in order of time, if not of importance: his involvement with folk art; his professional training and education in Bohemia which steeped him in the Nazarene tradition; his preoccupation with two particular Czech painters, Josef Mánes (1820-1871) and Mikuláš Aleš (1852-1913) who were educated in Nazarenism and influenced strongly by folk art and music; his contact with the Viennese intellectual and artistic milieu which deepened his inherent tendencies, stimulated his talents and determined his future choices.

Kupka first encountered folk art in his early youth, when as a journeyman saddler, he wandered to Domažlice in south Bohemia, a region well known for its rich folklore. He spent six months there. Many pages in his diary, written at that time, are covered with drawings of folk costumes of the same type as those used by Aleš. Both artists were more interested in the decorative details that in the costumes and figures themselves. At that time, it was not yet a matter of Kupka's being inspired by Aleš, but rather of an

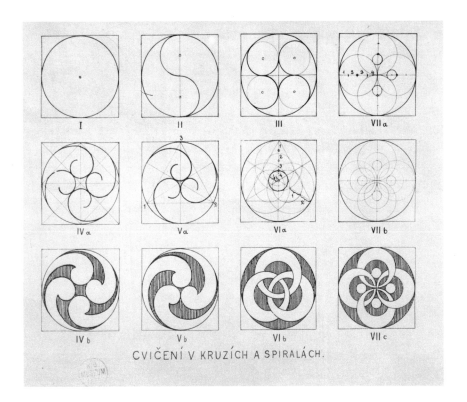

CVIČENÍ V KRUZÍCH A SPIRALÁCH.

fig. 1
Studnička, Exercises: circles and spirals
from *Český Kreslíř*, 1885-88.

fig. 2
Decorating a Czechoslovakian country
house.

interest that the two painters, brought up in the same environment, had in common.

When Kupka was seventeen, he received his first professional artistic education at the Crafts School in Jaroměř. Its director and Kupka's professor, Alois Studnička (1842-1927), was a prominent teacher of drawing, a well-known connoisseur of folk art, a specialist in ornamentation and a defender of the ornamental abstract concept. He was also an admirer of the great Czech painters of the Nazarene school. Kupka emphasized his gratitude to Studnička throughout his life, crediting him with having given him a solid foundation in drawing and introducing him to Mánes.[8] From a professional review called *Český Kreslíř* [Czech Draftsman], which Studnička published for three years (1885-1888) for drawing teachers, we may detect elements of his long-forgotten didactic method, very different from that of the Academy where students had to copy from a model. Studnička's students were trained to draw simple and complicated geometric lines, spirals, ovals, circles and curves. "There is no other way to see better the unskillfulness of a draftsman than in the drawing of a circle" was a leitmotif of his teaching.[9] He taught his students his own method of drawing these basic elementary forms and curves until they reached perfection. He insisted that they draw curves in one continuous line. Lines made out of small strokes he rejected, as did his teachers the Nažarenes. Studnička's students also had to learn how to use color in ornamentation. They had to study not only Newton's color theory but also those of Dr. Wilhelm Bezold *(Die Farbenlehre),* Quido Schreiber *(Die Farbenlehre)* and Rudolf Adams *(Die Farbenharmonie).* Thus the ornamentation that Kupka had first observed as a young journeyman he now studied professionally. He learned about

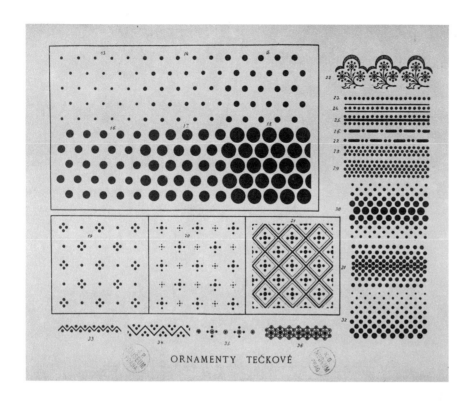

fig. 4
Studnička, Ornamental studies derived from dots, *Český Kreslíř*, 1885-88.

fig. 5
Decorated Czechoslovakian country house.

fig. 6
Kupka, Study for *Quatre histoires de blanc et noir,* 1925, gouache and india ink.

ornament of different periods and cultures, especially that of Islam which influenced Czech and Slovak folkloric motifs. Kupka's diary reveals his deep interest in ornamentation. In it he copied verbatim pages from *Český Kreslíř* about color mixtures. He also specifically noted two books, widely discussed in the review, Dr. Ernest Brucke's *Die Psychologie der Farben* (Leipzig, 1866) and A. Anděl's *Das Polychrome Flachenornament* (Vienna, 1880). In Brucke's book, Kupka learned, probably for the first time, about the invented colors of oriental art, particularly that of Moorish Spain, which Brucke considered superior to all others. In his study, Brucke rejects the inspiration of colors from nature, which affect us more by virtue of association than by the perfection of harmony between color and form, and advocates that the artist use invented colors in decorative paintings.

Kupka never ceased to be interested in the psychology of color, eventually devoting a great part of his research to it. In his book *Tvoření v Umění Výtvarném* [Creation in Plastic Art], published in 1923 in Prague, he developed a theory very similar to that of Brucke in a chapter entitled "Meaning and Feeling of Color." "The aesthetic of color in art is not the same in nature, they differ substantially"[10] wrote Kupka.

Even more important for Kupka than theories of color and ornament must have been Studnička's rejection of realism. "Whenever natural forms were imitated, art was in decadence or at a very low level of development. Yet an artist must not violate nature by using shapes which are truly opposite of nature. Unnatural shapes cannot be satisfactory, as the eye immediately recognizes their impossibility and incompatibility. A real artist should collect all beautiful elements he finds in particular forms of the same kind and fuse them into one sole shape."[11] Although Studnička's conception

10 *Tvoření v umění výtvarném,* Prague, 1923, p. 97.
11 *Český Kreslíř,* Jr. 1, no. 2, p. 30.

of abstract art was probably quite remote from Kupka's "painter's credo" of 1912, Kupka's painstaking effort to realize the *Amorpha, Fugue* is reminiscent of his teacher's advice.

Kupka's Nazarene education at the Prague Academy has generally gone unnoticed and yet the Nazarenes[12] played a decisive role in the formation of modern Czech art in general and of Kupka's art in particular. The original Nazarenes advocated the return of painting to the spiritual orientation of the late Middle Ages in Germany. Contemplation remained the main source of creative art for their followers. Poetic and philosophical thought was the real subject matter of art. They believed that "all beauty is allegory. Because they are inexpressible, the highest things can only be said allegorically."[13] The Nazarenes wanted to produce with their paintings an effect parallel to that of church music or religious songs. As the effect often had to appeal from a great distance, they realized that they must revive monumental art, namely fresco painting. This in turn, led them to adopt a particular style, and a fine, simplified, melodic and decorative linear technique became their hallmark. They realized that if they wanted to disseminate their ideas rapidly, they must reorganize the teaching system, and this led to the establishment of "master classes," consisting of a very few particularly gifted students, who were able "to keep their natural, unaffected, freely developed individualism and independence."[14]

Among the followers of the original Nazarene group which moved from Vienna to Rome in 1810 were painters from Prague, all of whom would eventually exercise an important role in the development of painting in Prague and Vienna. Kupka's professor in Prague, František Sequens (1836-1896), spent five years at the Munich Academy before he became director of the Academy in Prague. He seems to have followed the usual pedagogical method; strict initial training in drawing, geometry and perspective the first year; drawing from life models, composition and introduction to painting in the second; in the third, students chose a direction according to their talent. The very talented students were accepted into the "master class," where they drew cartoons for Sequens' murals and stained glass windows in Bohemian churches, but they also painted independently. Kupka's Czech biographers describe in some detail how poor Kupka suffered under the exacting and allegedly uncongenial teacher—a Nazarene who "kept forcing him to draw plaster copies of sculptures and cartoons for murals, while the young man, enamoured of the Baroque sculpture of his native land, longed for Mánes."[15]

Indeed, Kupka may well have "suffered" under Sequens, but evidently not enough to choose to leave his teacher for one of the alternative schools then flourishing in Prague. When Kupka came to Prague in 1888 there were three independent schools at the Academy: the school of religious painting, headed by the Nazarene Sequens; an important landscape school, led by a disciple of the Barbizon School who conducted his classes in the open air and enjoyed great popularity; and the equally popular school of genre painting. Students were encouraged to switch direction in any year, to "find a professor whose style expresses their own artistic talents."[16] This raises an interesting question: Why did Kupka stay with Sequens during all his

12 In 1809, a group of painters founded, at the Vienna Academy, a brotherhood modeled on the medieval *Bruderschaften*. After moving to Italy, they became known as the Nazarenes. In about the middle of the century, the Nazarenes occupied nearly all the important German and Central European academies and exercised a great influence over the development of art in that part of the world. Of particular interest is the Academy in Munich where Peter von Cornelius (1783-1867) was director from 1825. (His student P. Lenz became director of the famous Benedictine school of Beuron, where Paul Sérusier learned about the use of the Golden Section and brought it to Paris in 1897.) During his leadership, the influence of the Munich Academy became so important and the style of its painters so distinct that the members soon became known as the "Munich School," whose impact can be likened to that of the Ecole de Paris in the twentieth century. Another recognized center was Dusseldorf under the directorship of Wilhelm Schadow (1788-1862). But, whereas Cornelius in Munich accepted only the grand style of primarily monumental but always simplified and idealized forms, Schadow eventually allowed the introduction into Nazarene art of small sentimental paintings, which originated in the genre art of France and Holland.

13 Peter von Cornelius quoted in Fritz Novotny, *Painting and Sculpture in Europe: 1780-1880*, Baltimore, 1960, p. 68.

14 A. Kuhn, *Peter v. Cornelius*, Berlin, 1921, p. 252.

15 Emmanuel Siblík, *František Kupka*, Prague, 1928, p. 5.

16 *Almanac of the Prague Academy*, Prague, 1926, p. 46.

fig. 7
Mánes, Detail from *Rukopis Královehradecký* [Manuscript], Prague, 1857-60.

fig. 8
Aleš, Ornamental border for poem, "Záboj" from *Rukopis Královehradecký,* [Manuscript], Prague, 1884.

17 *Josef Mánes,* Prague, Národní Galerie, 1971, exhibition catalogue.
18 Letter to Machar, January 2, 1902.

four years at the academy, when he could have turned, for example, to the flourishing modern landscape school? The obvious answer is that Kupka had a deeper affinity for Nazarenism and found little attraction in landscape painting. There is no complaint in his diary, where we find a note of June 15, 1889: "In the lap of good fortune, I am in the Academy of Painters in Prague!" The diary further shows that he studied Italian in preparation for a future in Rome, the dream of every Nazarene. In his short autobiography of 1902, despite a few condescending remarks about the Academy, he records: "Every year I won school prizes and was presented as an example of diligence to the other students at the Academy. The director had a great liking for my compositions in Mánes' style." This quotation reveals beyond any doubt that Sequens let his pupil follow the example of his idol Mánes.

A powerful and lasting influence on Kupka's life and art was Josef Mánes. He died the year Kupka was born. Mánes had studied at the Prague Academy for many years with an original Nazarene, and spent three years in Munich. During his stay in the Bavarian capital, Hegelian nationalism was quickly gaining ground in Germany, and Mánes soon returned to Prague to stress the validity of a Czech culture less dependent on foreign patterns. As a result of his new-found purpose, Mánes made many trips into the countryside to study the people and their art. These trips provided him with an experience that would have lasting consequences on his style. In 1971 Jiří Kotalík reevaluated Mánes' work on the occasion of an exhibition at the Národní Galerie in Prague.[17] He stresses the romantic substance of Mánes' contribution, which finds its most remarkable expression in his symbolism. Mánes personifies the ideals of Nazarenism by his stress on composition based on melodical line and by his "global and metaphorical perception of nature and its poetic interpretation." Kupka's admiration for Mánes, dating back to his early years, continued throughout his life. After six years of experience in France, he still believed in Mánes' approach to art: "Professor Studnička revealed Mánes to me, and when he was bidding me farewell he urged me to seek in Mánes all an artist can express. His words fell on fertile soil. Mánes impressed and moved me powerfully and fatefully."[18] Kupka treasured Mánes' illustrations for a collection of old Czech poems entitled *Manuscripts,* and Mánes' photograph hung on his studio wall until the end of his life.

Mánes' most prominent follower was Mikuláš Aleš whose art further influenced Kupka. Aleš popularized the Manesian concept. He had a genuine decorative talent which the Nazarene's reverence for Dürer could only strengthen. He believed that he could express his ideas only by monumental art. A painter of robust and powerful talent, reminiscent of Delacroix in his warmth of color and direct expressiveness, he abandoned paintings on canvas and turned to the preparation of monumental frescoes. His surviving cartoons show him at work on flat surfaces, evidencing his understanding of the use of surface in architecture. Even more than Mánes, he stressed the globality and integration of vision in symbols. Regrettably, his two-dimensionally conceived pieces ran up against the local taste of that time. Aleš sought consolation in communion with folk art and was seduced by its rhythm and melody. He went beyond Mánes' style in emphasis upon ornament, integrating figures and all other elements into ornamental space, in opposition to the prevailing taste for realism. Aleš showed his generation the beauty, melodiousness, harmony and symbolism of folk art ornamentation. The strongest manifestation of his interest in folk art was in his extensive illustrations of Czech folk songs. His decorative paintings for the exterior and interior of buildings and on furniture demonstrate his disregard for the strict division between high and applied art, and represent an early expression of the Czech Secession. In the years Kupka spent at the Czech Academy, Aleš lived in Prague, rediscovered and celebrated by a younger generation of painters. We do not know if Kupka knew Aleš personally, but it is not unlikely that he did. Kupka's close friends, Siblík[19] and Jíra[20] confirm his great admiration for Aleš' work. Kupka's encounter with Aleš' illustrations for folk songs was important. These illustrations represent a masterful synthesis of the musical and the pictorial and found their echo in Kupka's later desire to fuse painting with music.

During Kupka's study at the Prague Academy, the year 1891 was particularly significant in Czech art because of the *Jubilee Exhibition*. This soon revealed itself as a manifestation of Czech cultural independence. On this occasion a number of aspects of Czech creativity were exhibited simultaneously. The "out-of-date" school of the Nazarenes was prominently represented. The modern trend of realistic and genre painting was shown in a separate exhibit, and, for the first time, genuine examples of Czech folk art were prominently featured. In addition, another group of paintings, "the first result of a great effort to find a new, genuinely Czech style"[21] was recognized as what we call today the style of the Czech Secession. This exhibition was the best possible opportunity for Kupka to observe opposite trends: the realism of Dusseldorf and France and the idealism of the Nazarenes. Nowhere could he better understand the ornamental, melodic and symbolic art of the Czech Secession than when juxtaposed with its original sources, the Nazarenes and Czech folk art. And it may have been here that he made his choice. His feeling for Mánes deepened and he spent that summer in Valašsko, eastern Moravia, a region rich in folk art, in order to "immerse himself in the vital source of folk art, following Mánes' example."[22] Back in Prague in the fall of 1891, he was accepted in the master class of Sequens and painted compositions in the style of Mánes and Aleš and under the influence of folk art. Before entering the Vienna Academy in the autumn of 1892 he spent his last vacation near Znojmo in southern Moravia, another district steeped in the tradition of folk art. Unfortunately, none of Kupka's paintings created during this period, when he was most directly stimulated by Mánes, Aleš and folk art, have so far been recovered and we have only sparse information about them. In 1900 Kupka sent some drawings to a Prague review, *Zlatá Praha*, which he described as an ornamental head for which he used motifs from Czech folk art. In 1901 he wrote in a letter to Machar from a region in the mountains of Slovenia that he was no longer interested in painting peasants in the national costumes they were still wearing in that region. But he added a significant statement: "Maybe I will paint them again, but not the way it has been done to date."[23] And indeed, the melodic new visions of Kupka's dancing girls in *Amorpha*,

19 Siblík, *Kupka*, p. 7.

20 Jaroslav Jíra [Frant. Kupka as Artist and as Man], *Národní Osvobozeni*, no. 261, Prague, 1931, pp. 1-2.

21 *Zlatá Praha*, Prague, 1891; reprinted in *Dilo*, Prague, 1903, p. 102.

22 Siblík, *Kupka*, p. 8. It is not without interest that two of the most important artists of the Viennese Secession, the painter Adolf Hoelzel (1853-1934) and the architect Josef Hoffmann (1870-1956) were born and spent their childhoods in the same region.

23 September 13, 1901.

Fugue, and *Lines, Planes, Spaces* could not have been possible without Kupka's "concealed recollection" which Carl Jung describes as : "A musician who has heard a peasant tune or popular song in childhood . . . finds it cropping up as the theme of a symphonic movement that he is composing in adult life. An idea or an image has moved back from the subconscious into the conscious mind."[24]

Vienna

With the single exception of Werner Hofmann cited above, art historians either completely overlook Kupka's four years in Vienna, or, at most, downgrade their importance. But, thanks to records preserved at the Academy and to the letters written by Kupka between 1894 and 1914 to his friends, especially Arthur Roessler, his time in the Austrian capital can now be reliably reconstructed. The importance of Kupka's stay in Vienna rests not so much on the advancement of his painting technique as on his exposure to the ideas which were current in Vienna at that particular time. These were strongly formative years for Kupka's personal philosophy and for his concept of art.

Kupka came to Vienna in the summer of 1892, when he was twenty-one. He was accepted directly into the master class of Professor A. Eisenmenger (1830-1907), a Nazarene and a specialist in fresco painting. As in Prague, Kupka took no notice of the very successful schools of landscape and genre painting. As in Prague, Kupka was obliged to support himself and, in order to earn money, he seems to have served again as a medium in spiritualist seances.[25] But he was unable to pay for the master class and during the second semester was struck from the register of the Academy "for inability to pay." He was readmitted, however, and relieved of the school fee during the third semester. Although he did not receive the Rome Prize, which he always claimed he had been promised, he was instead awarded a special prize of two hundred florins from the Academy exhibition fund. In a state of terrible disappointment he announced his withdrawal from the Academy on December 20, 1893 and began to paint his colossal work *The Last Dream of the Dying Heine,* commissioned by the Viennese Kunstverein.[26]

Vienna, the capital of the monarchy, City of Dreams, and the "Proving-Ground for World Destruction,"[27] was, at that time, a very busy cultural center. It is surely not a coincidence that modern architecture, abstract painting, legal and logical positivism, the beginning of twelve tone music, psychoanalysis and art history were all in simultaneous evidence in Vienna around the turn of the century. In the field of the fine arts, Alois Riegl (1858-1905), professor of art history in Vienna during the period of Kupka's study, published his *Stilfragen,*[28] in which he recorded his opposition to Gottfried Semper's materialistic dictum that form follows function and recognized that the fundamental intent of a work of art is to give form to the inner life of man. He saw ornament as the purest and most lucid expression of artistic volition. Kupka would, at a later date, emphasize again and again, in his book, in his articles and in interviews, his concept and belief that "it is necessary for an artist to seek and find a means by which he may express the material likeness of all movements and states of his inner life and

24 Carl Jung, *Man and His Symbols,* New York, 1964, p. 37.

25 In later years Kupka always referred to these earnings from his activities as a medium as coming from lessons given in religion.

26 This painting was made purely for financial reasons and was repeatedly condemned by Kupka in later years.

27 Karl Kraus, *Die Fackel,* Vienna, no. 400, 1914, p. 2.

28 Alois Riegl, *Stilfragen: Grundlegungen zu einer Geschichte der Ornamentik,* Berlin, 1893. Wilhelm Worringer (1881-1928) built his own thesis as published in *Abstraktion und Einfühlung,* Munich, 1908, on the foundation of Riegl's theories. Worringer compared abstraction and naturalism and recognized abstraction as an essential formulative principle of art. See also T. Lipps, *Aesthetik,* Hamburg, 1903-06. Lipps was Worringer's teacher at the University of Munich.

through which he may capture all abstractions"[29] and that "ornament should be revived."[30]

It was Otto Wagner (1841-1918), the famous Viennese architect, who became a defender of simple geometric structure. In an inaugural lecture at the Viennese Academy in 1894 he argued that "what is practical may also be beautiful," as against the German Jugendstil thesis that "what is beautiful can if necessary also be practical." His lecture as well as his book[31] were very successful. Many talented students at the Academy became Wagner's followers and, later, the creators of a new architecture and decorative style called Viennese Secession. Arguments for and against ornamentation soon began to excite Viennese artistic circles.

At about the same time, Viennese poets and intellectuals became conscious of the limitations of language. The young poet, Hugo von Hofmannsthal (1874-1924) and the Bohemian-born critic and philosopher, Fritz Mauthner (1894-1923)[32] were highly skeptical about the range of thoughts and feelings susceptible to communication by words. Kupka would later reach the same conclusion about painting: "Because no two people have the same intellect and senses, we cannot find the truth in representing things as we see them; they will always be distorted."[33]

Kupka's compatriot, Eduard Hanslick (1825-1904), professor of music at the University of Vienna, maintained in his much debated book *Von Musikalisch Schönem*[34] that beauty was entirely self-contained and rejected literary ideas as subjects for musical composition. According to Hanslick, music was essentially "logic of sound in motion . . . The important law is the primordial law of harmonic progression by means of which themes are developed and transformed."[35] Around 1909 Kupka made a series of pastels and drawings depicting progression of movement according to the laws of music which seemed to him to be applicable to painting.

Kupka participated very actively in the intellectual ferment of Vienna. His Czech friend Miloš Meixner, with whom he shared an apartment for two years, was educated in philosophy. The two young men spent much of their time together in feverish reading and discussion. As Kupka wrote, "Days, evenings, nights we spent together in turning the world upside down and I started to make up for what I had missed in my education. My studio was a meeting place of many German intellectuals and I tried to penetrate Kant's metaphysical knots."[36]

Kupka's interest in spiritualism and esoterica brought him into contact with Austrian and German Theosophists. Theosophy at that time was for Kupka an ideal practical philosophy that helped him to deepen his knowledge, brought him into contact with Eastern philosophy and sustained him in the belief that life never dies. He was familiar with the writings of Paracelsus and Calvin and studied many philosophers from Plato to Nietzsche. Eastern philosophy only reaffirmed the Nazarene doctrine of contemplation as a source of artistic inspiration. However, as a painter, he emphasized the need for communicating experience to others. "Contemplation is a virtue if we recognize the truth but it becomes a vice if we don't communicate it to others."[37]

29 *Tvoření v umění výtvarném*, p. 123.

30 Notes for *Tvoření v umění výtvarném*.

31 Otto Wagner, *Moderne Architektur*, Berlin, 1896.

32 Fritz Mauthner, *Beitrage zu einer Kritik der Sprache*, 3 vols., Stuttgart, 1901-03, vol. 1, p. 111.

33 *Tvoření v umění výtvarném*, p. 42.

34 Eduard Hanslick, *Von Musikalisch Schönem*, Leipzig, 1854. This book was so popular that by 1910 there had been eighteen editions. Hanslick returned from the University in 1895 but continued to write for the *Neue Freie Presse* in Vienna.

35 Eduard Hanslick, *The Beautiful in Music,* Indianapolis and New York, 1957, p. 51. English translation by Gustav Cohen.

36 Letter to Machar, January 2, 1902.

37 Letter to a sect brother, December 8, 1894. Collection Wiener Stadtbibliothek, Vienna.

In 1894 Theosophy brought Kupka into contact with the Nazarene artist Karl Diefenbach (1851-?), a somewhat extravagant and extremely controversial painter and philosopher who was called everything from "Kohlrabi Apostle" and swindler to "pioneer of a New Age." Diefenbach came to Vienna from Munich in 1892, the same year as Kupka. He believed that most contemporary human behavior and its resultant social conditions were contrary to the laws of nature and thus the source of human misery. Diefenbach used his art to argue for the return of man to nature, peace and humanity, referring to himself as *ein Ideen Maler* and *ein Protest Künstler* (an idea painter, a protest artist). He painted prodigiously, primarily in cycles on religion, pedagogical and scientific themes such as *Thou shalt not kill* and *paradise regained,* mostly left in sketches or finished by his pupils, such as his most devoted disciple, Fidus (Hugo Hoppener, [1868-1948]), because his philosophical and moral preoccupations absorbed much of his time. After spending several weeks in a Munich prison because of his habit of taking a daily air bath in the nude in his garden, he moved to Vienna where he hoped to pursue a quieter life.

Soon after his arrival, which was accompanied by great publicity, Diefenbach became Kupka's idol: "I dreamt about him for two years and now I spend a lot of time with him." Kupka will say in a letter in 1894: "He is a moralist, a musician, a painter, a poet . . . he imagines his happiness *[Glückseligkeit]* as Nirvana. But I found out that he doesn't know enough about esoterica . . . The basis of his thoughts is probably Aristotle, Plutarch, Plato and Schiller. Paracelsus or Agrippa von Nettesheim are unknown to him—he is a *Naturphilosopher*.[38] In 1894, the twenty-three year old Kupka moved to Diefenbach's isolated cottage in Hütteldorf and spent several months there. It was a kind of a commune where Diefenbach lived with his children, their teachers and several pupils who followed the precepts of his practical philosophy: vegetarian life with daily air bath and exercise in the nude, philosophical discussions, contemplation, music and painting. Diefenbach believed in a certain analogy between painting and music and in the mutual influence of the two. Many musical soirées were held, and a pianist, or preferably a violinist, accompanied Diefenbach and his students while they worked.[39] It is unlikely that Kupka became a better painter because of Diefenbach's teaching, but many characteristics of his lifestyle and philosophy of art are so similar to Diefenbach's that his influence cannot be ignored. Kupka was greatly addicted to daily physical exercise in the nude in his garden in any weather, summer or winter, to which he ascribed a vital importance and which he continued to practice until a very old age. He drew conclusions about the influence of one's physical condition, ascetism, the consumption of wine, nicotine and caffeine on the perception of color. He developed his theory at length in his chapter on color in his book:

I have discovered for myself the sensations of splendid sensitivity to color, aroused exclusively by hygienic care. After my morning shower, I exercise, summer and winter, entirely naked in the garden. It is also a manner of hardening the body. It is like a prayer with which I turn to the rising sun, the great fireworks in the beautiful seasons accompanied by birdsongs, my entire body penetrated by the fragrances and the rays of light. Thus I experience magnificent

38 Ibid.

39 Karl Diefenbach, *Ein Beitrag zur Geschichte der Zeitgenössichen Kunstpflege,* Vienna, 1895.

moments, bathed by hues flowing from the titanic keyboard of color. The principle of harmonized forces is the best answer to all questions as to enrich and grasp the picturesqueness of the colorist.[40]

Just as Diefenbach ordered piano and violin music for his painting sessions with his pupils, Kupka writes in his book particularly about the violin and its capacity to unfold a specific chromatism. We know from his postwar correspondence with Jindřich Waldes and from the testimony of many of his friends the degree to which music was indispensable to him, and the fact that the radio was always playing music in his Paris studio.

In 1895, through Diefenbach, Kupka met the future art critic Arthur Roessler (1877-1955). They became good friends and saw each other very often, and for a time Roessler lived in Kupka's apartment. At that time Roessler was a student of philosophy and history of art at the University of Vienna and was therefore in touch with the ideas current in the intellectual world. Kupka was six years older than Roessler, which gave him a certain superiority in experience and spared him his usual complexes, which stemmed from his lack of a classical education. We sense in Kupka's letters a tone of assurance which enabled him to express and formulate his thoughts boldly. It was at that time that Kupka realized that a "subject" is unnecessary in painting, that one can experience a great joy just in seeing colors and lines. He speaks of "spots of color and lines moving in his head"[41] and signs most of his letters to Roessler "color symphonist," which is what he was called by his Viennese friends. While difficult to prove, the assumption is not farfetched that Kupka influenced his friend Roessler's ideas on abstraction as expressed in the introduction to his book *Neu Dachau,* published in 1905, as well as in his call to painters to use simultaneous color contrast in abstract ornament. But at that time in Vienna, Kupka wished to express more than an emotion, a state of mind; like so many Central Europeans, his concern was to give form to the metaphysical anxiety that tormented him. These philosophical concerns are reflected in his paintings of the Viennese period such as *Quam ad causam sumus?* (Why are we here?), *Hymn to the Universe* and *Towards Luminous Heights.* Unfortunately these three paintings are now lost.

We do not know how many of Roessler's friends in Vienna were also Kupka's friends. Roessler's correspondence with many Czech and Austrian painters may, in the future, open the door to a new study of this Viennese period in the history of art, now so very much neglected—the history of the Secession. A part of this history is Kupka's participation in the movement. For decades his evident Secessionist morphology has been ascribed to his origins and to his stay in Vienna. The Czech critics have treated these elements of his style with a certain embarrassment, and the French have rejected these characteristics as traces of his early, non-French taste, *"Le goût si différent du nôtre—hélas!"*[42] With the changing of public taste, Kupka's Secessionist verticals, horizontals, squares and circles are currently being reevaluated, but ascribed to the influence of French Art Nouveau; this hypothesis is based on the false ideas that French Art Nouveau, German Jugendstil and Viennese Secession are essentially the same style and that the Viennese Secession did not begin as a movement until April 3, 1897. It is

40 *Tvoření v umění výtvarném,* pp. 90, 94.

41 Letter to Roessler, September 11, 1895.

42 Ed. Déverin, "F. Kupka," *L'Art décoratif,* July 1909.

important to understand the basic conceptual and formal differences between Art Nouveau, which originated with French Post Impressionism and Jugendstil, whose origins are in the unrealistic, idealistic paintings of the Nazarenes. Jugendstil reached Vienna late and never took deep root. Viennese Secession as a style should really be considered as its countermovement. While the Secession association was not officially formed until 1897, elements of the movement's style had been present in the Viennese climate for some time before. The movement had its roots in the School for Arts and Crafts, annexed to the Oesterreichisches Museum für Kunst und Industrie. This institution had been established in 1864, when Vienna was the first city on the continent to respond to G. Semper's call for reform in art education. Its aim was to abolish the distinction between the fine and decorative arts and to establish studios in which these arts would be executed in a spirit of old *Bruderschaften,* brotherly cooperation between master and pupil—all ideas of the Nazarenes. It is most likely that Kupka, who had warm memories of similar teaching in Jaromer, would recognize the parallel concepts emanating from the Viennese school. Furthermore, Kupka himself, prior to leaving Vienna, made an effort to organize some sort of artists' association *(Künstlerbund)* on the lines of the Secession, but failed.[43]

43 Noted in letter to Roessler, October 10, 1910.

44 Though the book was not published until 1923, the notes were written between 1910 and 1914.

45 There are several hundred gouaches, watercolors, drawings and prints from his pre-abstract period in the Národní Galerie, Prague and nearly five hundred preparatory studies for his abstract paintings at The Museum of Modern Art, New York. I am indebted to Alfred H. Barr, Jr., himself deeply interested in Kupka, for allowing me to work for several years on these studies and thereby discover the origins of almost all of Kupka's abstract painting.

Road to the New Reality

Kupka's artistic development is a long, tortuous groping towards abstraction, with only a few, brief deviations with which he quickly grew disillusioned. His concept of non-objective art is clearly evident from several sources: notes for his book and the book itself *Tvoření v umění Výtvarném,*[44] his correspondence with friends and his preparatory studies for paintings and illustrations.[45] The book tells us about his philosophical ideas and his letters further reveal his commitment to spiritism and Theosophy. The studies for his paintings document his method of working and his creative process. Clearly, his early non-abstract work already contains the germs of his future abstractions. Kupka's particular interests and inclinations— folk art, spiritism, Theosophy, Nazarenism, Secession—evolve from one another; they are links in the chain of Kupka's evolution, which is continuous and logical.

Czech Folk Art and his knowledge of ornament awakened his interest in Greek vases of the sixth and fifth centuries B.C. which he studied in the Louvre. They confirmed his thinking that "ornament was not invented to fill empty spaces, but to complete the event the figures are describing."[46] Similarly, it awakened his interest in Celtic ornament, which enchanted him and which he studied during numerous trips to Brittany.[47] In referring to Celtic art, Kupka was justifying his decision to abandon reality.[48] His involvement with ornament led him finally to Islamic art. Its symbolic, ecstatic, rhythmic and decorative quality provided him with a source of constant delight and instruction. The pure form of Islamic ornament, conceived exclusively in aesthetic terms, without any reference to nature, merely a statement of formal relations, found similarities with his own aim in his final realizations. It was "the logic of purified concepts, Platonic form, beautiful in itself."[49] By final realizations, I mean not only the works from the period of 1930-1935 but also the final versions of all the series that he continued to rework throughout his life in a relentless process of simplification.

Islamic art, it seems, led Kupka back to Czech folk art. When the Musée des Arts Décoratifs in Paris exhibited Czech folk art in 1926 he valued this art above the contemporary efforts of some Czech artists to imitate western "high art."[50] Soon thereafter he decorated his home with Czech folk ornaments which he used on posters and other propaganda material during the war. In 1929 he redecorated his dining room with ornaments used for illustrations of the *Song of Songs* which were reminiscent of Czech and Islamic ornament.

Kupka's inclination to ornament was an "atavism" of which he was aware. "Following the art of any nation or time, we can clearly observe the typicality of tendency, taste or unusual attributes that it expresses. This is particularly observable in the outline of artificially created forms, as for example, in ornament," wrote Kupka.[51]

> *Spiritism* was responsible for Kupka's lifelong involvement with the occult and metapsychology, which had fundamental consequences for his general outlook and philosophy of art. His ability to function as a medium made him believe that he was capable of insight into reality inaccessible to most. He believed himself endowed with exceptional intuition and perception and ability for self-observation and self-analysis, which he considered vital for the discovery of the "essence of reality." He believed not only in transfer of thought but also in transfer of energy and strength. This belief was sustained by Mrs. Kupka who would complain that when her husband exerted himself with vigorous work he sapped not his but her strength.

Kupka never ceased to practice spiritism, except, probably, during long periods of illness and in very old age.[52] In the first years in Paris he was compensating with spiritist seances the strongly felt external reality which overwhelmed him while he tried to adapt to it. "Unfortunately—or may it even be good luck—I came again in contact with the Spiritists . . . Yesterday I experienced a split consciousness where it seemed I was observing

figs. 9a, 9b
Kupka, Preparatory sketches for *The Song of Songs*, c. 1909, Národní Galerie, Prague.

46 *Tvoření v umění výtvarném*, p. 32.

47 Noted in letters to Waldes, 1925.

48 Notes for *Tvoření v umění výtvarném*.

49 Interview with Kupka, *Koh-i-Noor*, Prague, no. 41, 1933.

50 Letter to Waldes, October 20, 1921.

51 *Tvoření v umění výtvarném*, p. 22.

52 This fact has been repeatedly confirmed to me by two men: the Symbolist poet and astrologer Louis Arnould-Grémilly, who was one of Kupka's closest friends from 1919-57, and Jacques Villon's brother-in-law, Jacques Bon, a fervent spiritist who was Kupka's neighbor from 1906.

the earth from outside. I was in great empty space and saw the planets rolling quietly. After that it was difficult to come back to the trivia of every day life . . . and so in my thoughts I seek refuge in you,"[53] wrote Kupka to Roessler in 1897. In 1902 in a short autobiographical letter he described the "discussions" he used to have with his idol Mánes and added: "By the way, I do believe until today that Mánes' ego still appears from time to time in complete consciousness."[54] Flashes of colored spots and lines which he described to his Theosophist friend in Vienna in 1895 obsessed him and he tried to capture them. As late as 1924 he wrote to his Czech friend: "I can now render what before was moving in my spirit like mysterious distant visions which I was unable to master and even not fully to perceive."[55] He ascribed this ability to express his visions to his "physical and spiritual exercise."[56]

During a colloquium about Kupka in Prague in 1968, René de Solier discussed Kupka's unusually intense and vivid colors which had struck color technicians at the time of Kupka's first abstract paintings and have since then been remarked upon by many. He suggested that they may have originated in his youthful spiritistic experiences from 1887 to 1891. De Solier was not aware that Kupka's spiritistic practices continued well through his Vienna and Paris years.

Theosophy as revived in the United States and Europe in the last quarter of the nineteenth century had strong occult tendencies and it is easy to understand why the spiritist Kupka was attracted to its doctrines. From what is known of Kupka's thinking, it is difficult to conclude that he embraced all the tenets of modern Theosophy. His philosophical outlook was a conglomerate of various influences rather than a closely knit, unalterable doctrine. Like the Theosophists he believed that life is a force of consciousness which is the essence of all things, that nature manifests itself rhythmically in geometric structures, which, being a thing of beauty can be discovered by an artist endowed with intuition. Thus, there was in Kupka a strong echo of the Bergsonian truth-finding role of art. Bergson's influence was remarkable in other respects, which, however, exceed the scope of this article. The contemporary theory of the subconscious also left its traces in Kupka's epistemology. He believed in the absorptive capacity of the subconscious and its ability to greatly enrich man by releasing into consciousness that which it has absorbed. In his ontology, Kupka consistently uses Platonic ideas. For Kupka the painter, the search for "ideas" of forms and color became an important goal on his road to a new reality.

Nazarenism, in particular, had a lasting influence not only on Kupka's theory of art but also on his method of creation. In his book Kupka distinguishes between two types of art: the first is realistic and profane and tends to represent exterior life; the second is based on speculative thought and is manifested through a combination of plastic elements. "The latter art wants to penetrate the substance with a supersensitive insight into the unknown as it is manifested in poetry or religious art."[57]

53 Letter, February 7, 1897.
54 To Machar, January 2, 1902.
55 Letter to Waldes, August 16, 1924.
56 Ibid.
57 *Tvoření v umění výtvarném,* p. 63.

Kupka believed that he was atavistically destined for the second category which, in his youth, was the art of the Nazarenes. His painting and the philosophy at which he arrived between 1910 and 1912 are the logical consequence of this realization. He recognized the problem of the relationship between form and content in a work of art. Mánes felt the incompatibility between the poetic content and the realistic rendering of his figures, which he therefore enveloped with ornament. Aleš felt this incompatability even more strongly and integrated his figures into ornamental space. Kupka, in his solution, transformed the figure itself into an ornamental form.

Kupka, like his teachers, believed that while people as a rule see nature globally, an artist sees it analytically: "We cannot perceive quickly and at the same time deeply . . ."[58] An artist observes life around him and adds to each impression images from his memory. He associates so much that he is unable to see reality clearly; moreover, "he is not bound to see things as they really are . . ."[59] Kupka's thinking had a logical consequence: "If the artist wants to be true to his model he has to betray his vision and if he wants to adhere to his vision he has to distort his model."[60] This finally resulted in his abandoning the object as we see it and in recreating it through his painter's vision, which would become, by his own definition, his "New Reality," governed only by rhythms and harmony. His visions did not come necessarily from nature; we can even say that they rarely came from nature. Like all the Classicists, Kupka did not see anything wrong with taking inspiration from his old paintings or from others which he liked. "Impressions from a work of art are normally stronger than those from nature. In art the last word is never pronounced. A work of art is in fact created only to inspire another work of art."[61] For Kupka, as for all the Nazarenes, art always had an ethical aim—a mission. He refused to accept art for art's sake. In Prague, when he was working under the influence of Mánes and Aleš and the Academy, it was to achieve and to communicate beauty and promote patriotic ideals. In Vienna, under the influence of Eastern philosophy, it was to contemplate and communicate the truth. To fight against the social order, to instruct people about man's evolution was the goal of his illustrations in Paris. Again in 1910 he decided to communicate beauty by way of his "New Reality." His constant preoccupation with the expression of the ethics of painting led to a continuous process of clarification and simplification. He believed that the future of art is in clarity.[62] Another consequence was his condemnation of a purely formalistic criticism: "To the history of art should be added a long chapter about psychology. It would be interesting to find out in the symbolic and religious art of Egypt and Mesopotamia how much of his own the artist contributed to works that were suggested, prescribed, or freely inspired."[63]

Typically Nazarene was also Kupka's desire to create a painting whose linear harmony and color scheme would produce effects similar to those of music. He had great examples in Mánes and Aleš, who succeeded admirably in uniting melody with form. Not without reason is Mánes' art often analyzed in Czechoslovakia in connection with the music of Bedrich Smetana. Kupka believed, just as Apollinaire did, that the Slavs have an

58 Ibid., p. 67.

59 Ibid., p. 68.

60 Kupka, preface, *Quatre histoires de blanc et noir*, Paris, 1926.

61 *Tvoření v umění výtvarném*, pp. 158, 173.

62 Kupka, "Créer," *Vie des Lettres*, Paris, July 1921, p. 569.

63 *Tvoření v umění výtvarném*, p. 13.

fig. 10
Late Corinthian Amphora, *Tydeus Killing Ismene,* c. 560-550 B.C. Musée du Louvre.

64 This theory was developed by Louis Arnould-Grémilly in the chapter "Orphisme et les Slaves," of his book *Frank Kupka,* Paris, 1922, p. 38.

65 Richard Weiner, "Návštěvou u nového Františka Kupky" [Visit to the New Kupka], *Samostatnost,* Prague, no. 218, August 1912. Reprinted in *Výtvarné Umění,* vol. XV, no. 8, Prague, 1968, pp. 367-371.

66 W. Warshawsky, "Orpheism, Latest of Painting Cults," *The New York Times,* New York, October 19, 1913, p. 4.

67 [Kupka in Prague: interview], *Svetozor,* September 1, 1936, p. 19. Kupka did not like his work, which did not originate in Cubism, to be confused with the Orphism of the painting described by Apollinaire; for him Orphism had a broader meaning.

68 *La Géométrie secrète des peintres,* Paris, 1963, p. 32.

69 February 2, 1913.

atavistic characteristic which permits them to hear as intensely as they see.[64] He wished to communicate the stirring of the spirit he experienced upon hearing music. "Kupka wants painting to sound like music," wrote the Czech poet Richard Weiner after visiting the artist in Paris in 1912.[65] "I am still groping in the dark, but I believe I can find something between sight and hearing and I can produce a fugue in colors as Bach has done in music," Kupka repeated in 1913, one year after exhibiting his *Amorpha, Fugue* in the *Salon d'Automne.*[66]

Greek art again—classical this time—confirmed the Nazarenes' theory about the role of art and the analogy between painting and music. It was Kupka's guide in Paris when he decided to abandon completely what he saw and paint again only what he felt. He remembered later: "It was in 1911, I created my own uniquely 'abstract' way of painting, Orphism, disregarding all other cultural systems except that of Greece."[67] "The perfect example of a melodic composition is the frieze of the Panathenaea in the Parthenon. There plastic art approaches music the closest," writes Charles Bouleau,[68] accompanying his photographs with a line of musical notes to show that the procession of a frieze creates a movement which develops in time as well as in space. Kupka spent many years contemplating Greek friezes in stone and on vases, in museums and in photographs. As late as 1913 he wrote to Roessler: "They did not paint the countryside or the trees, and even the human body was for them an 'ensemble' of beautiful lines and forms. Their reliefs are Sundays they left to us."[69]

Kupka was intensely interested in stained glass. His lasting interest in color penetrated by light led him to install a stained glass window in a corner of his studio soon after moving to his own house in 1906. It remained there until his death. A Czech critic, after discussing Orphism with Kupka, stated that the two stained glass windows in Notre Dame were the probable inspiration for Kupka's first Orphic experiments in 1911.[70] Kupka himself described the "vertiginous musicality of color"[71] of the Saint Germain-L'Auxerrois and Notre Dame windows in his book. He often visited Chartres with his students, where, as they remembered, they would spend the entire day, borrow a ladder and study the colored windows on the basis of Kupka's notes.[72] Because of his master-class work on cartoons for Bohemian churches, Kupka already was familiar with the mosaic-like process of assembling stained glass compositions out of geometric elements, a process which encouraged an abstract, ornamental style and tended to resist any attempt to render a three-dimensional effect. Kupka loved the mystical, continuous light of stained glass and used to show his students the uselessness of the details added in black on the glass surface. His desire to capture the "vertiginous musicality" and spirituality of stained glass led him to create *The Cathedral* of 1913.

Greek art and cathedrals also confirmed Kupka in his belief in the applicability of mathematical calculation to art. He had a complete knowledge of Golden Section measurement,[73] which was part of the Nazarene teaching and which was abandoned by the Realists, and, of course, by the Impressionists who were guided by the "eye."

> *The builders of Gothic cathedrals were men of feeling only to a certain degree, but they were above all mathematicians . . . look at the Doric temples, even the Ionic, and your blood circulation steps up rhythmically, putting you in a Sunday mood. . . . If the Egyptians thought, the Greeks measured . . .*[74]
>
> *We must start completely anew. . . . When we draw a line, a dot, it should sit so correctly in space that one has the impression that it is an event, that something has happened. The same for color. The whole immobility of a work, not the dynamics of the futurists, who are lyrically inclined and try to track down nature by experimenting with a style of action.*[75]

For Kupka art gives pleasure by satisfying an instinct for harmony, which derives from line, form and color; its principle is proportion and its chief aim is the communication of beauty.

Kupka's method of painting was also Nazarene. "I start to paint only when I can clearly visualize my product,"[76] he wrote in 1901. "Creation in art starts with a vision,"[77] he reaffirmed after spending thirty more years in the French capital. When Kupka's vision was clearly defined in his mind, he made a small schematic drawing. Then he made dozens of studies from nature or other works of art. Even during his most abstract period he used these studies, but they were only his "dictionary," never his inspiration. He used a microscope to see the unknown, a kaleidoscope to see the unusual, a fan, accordion shapes, and later, even perhaps a camera to capture movement. As he used to cut and add arms to a figure to find a more ideal form in his book illustrations, he would later cut a figure into strips to give it a feeling of progression and use translucent paper to multiply the same shape many times to suggest a melody. "One has to work on a problem for years in order to be able to produce a sketch, a viable study,"[78] he wrote to his friend in 1913.

70 B.S. Urban, "Kupkův Orphismus," *Cesta,* January 28, 1928.

71 *Tvoření v umění výtvarném,* p. 110.

72 Information furnished by Kupka's Parisian students Miloš Holý, Vaclav Fiala, Richard Wiesner and Jan Mehl in conversations with the author, Prague, Summer 1967.

73 The question of whether Kupka participated in the *Salon de la Section d'Or* has been raised (see this catalogue, pp. 310-11, fn. 6). However to this author's knowledge, no one has so far investigated to what extent Kupka influenced his Puteaux neighbors to use the Golden Section. Jacques Villon has been credited with its introduction. But, as Charles Bouleau has pointed out, in *La Géométrie secrète des Peintres,* Paris, 1963, p. 96, the idea of the Golden Section penetrated to France from Germany and Prague. It seems likely, therefore, that Kupka with his long academic training in Vienna and Prague, would have taken an active part in the discussions of the Puteaux group. During the opening of Kupka's retrospective at the Musée National d'Art Moderne in Paris in 1958, the aged and visibly moved Villon admired the paintings of his now dead friend. He said several times to me "Kupka était un grand peintre, c'était mon maître, j'ai beaucoup appris de lui." (Kupka was a great painter, he was my teacher, I learned a great deal from him.)

74 Letter to Roessler, February 18, 1913.

75 Letter to Roessler, February 2, 1913.

76 Letter to Machar, March 22, 1901.

77 Letter to Waldes, February 9, 1930.

78 Letter to Roessler, February 18, 1913.

Like all the Nazarenes, Kupka always verified his visions in front of a model and corrected them to achieve the right proportions.[79] He believed that "in order to make the outer expression of an idea, a feeling or an experience intelligible, it is necessary to give it the structure of objective nature."[80] "Great art consists of . . . a selection from the subjective world . . . we captivate the viewer only when the organism he is presented with is coherent."[81] Sometimes he would work directly with the already conceptualized forms. "Each work brings an experience. . . . The balance of proportions becomes a habit . . . and the artist becomes a happy master of the spatial structure. . . ."[82] The best example of this stylization from his own old pictures, without corrections from nature, is his series *Quatre histoires de blanc et noir,* woodcuts and many gouaches done at the same time to "prove the possibility of real creation without transforming nature."[83] They are also the best examples of a work in which Kupka suddenly used his great command of ornamentation and arabesque surface—like Dvořák, who composed his Slavonic dances inspired by folk melodies, as if for his own pleasure after completing work on a symphony.

When Kupka completed the final study for a painting, he covered the canvas with carefully calculated geometric lines which indicated the most important points of the painting's structure. Kupka's statements in his book indicate clearly that in the course of such procedures—in enlarging or reducing a figurative study—in his pre-abstract period, he realized that figures were unnecessary to express his vision, that it was the geometric structure, the "skeleton," as he called it, which fascinated him, because it contained the principle of beauty, the harmony and melody of the painting. From that point on, it was merely a question of time until he could faithfully execute his paintings according to his vision.

Czech and Viennese Secession marked Kupka's thinking and style for his entire life. One constantly used argument that Kupka could not have been influenced by the Viennese Secession is that Klimt's *Philosophy* was exhibited at Vienna University only in 1900, when Kupka was already in Paris. However, we know that he saw the painting that same year, exhibited in Paris much more prominently than it had been in Vienna. At the Paris World's Fair *Philosophy* received a prize of honor. Kupka often visited the exhibition where his compatriots were amply represented. His friend Alphons Mucha (1860-1939) decorated the section of Bosnia Herzegovina. Aleš, with other Czech Secessionists, decorated the interior of the Czech section, and Kupka himself exhibited his painting *Bibliomane* and, like Klimt, received a prize of honor. Both the Czech and the Viennese section were decorated by architects and painters in a spirit of *Gesamtkunstwerk* (collective art). Their collaboration was the logical consequence of the original Nazarenes' need to decorate great surfaces. There was also an awareness that "there exists a particular sympathy between ornament and structure, each enhancing the value of the other."[84] Kupka could again compare the structural and symbolic ornamentation of Aleš and the Czech Secessionists, who were in turn strongly influenced by folk art, with the simple exterior decorations of the new Viennese ornament. The Viennese

79 Kupka did not hesitate to use a model in a bathtub installed in his garden when he wanted to correct the play of light and lines on moving water. He even studied preserves cooking in order to imagine or correct his vision of matter or thoughts ascending. There are many errors of interpretation of these incidents as related by Mme. Kupka, such as the statement "from as ordinary a sight as a collection of jam jars Kupka drew a grandiose composition which evokes Indian architecture," (Fédit, op. cit., p. 73) or that "a moving curtain became *Ordonnance sur verticales*" (Ludmila Vachtová, *Kupka: Pioneer of Abstract Art,* New York, 1968, p. 104.)

80 *Tvoření v umění výtvarném,* p. 63.

81 Ibid., p. 196.

82 Ibid., p. 147.

83 Letter to Waldes, August 16, 1924.

84 Louis Sullivan, *Kindergarten Chats and Other Writings,* New York, 1947, p. 189.

fig. 11
Hoffmann, Architectural relief executed
for *14. Austellung Secession,* Vienna,
1902, Bildarchiv der Nationalbibliothek,
Vienna

architects also revealed something new which seems to have influenced
Kupka profoundly. The Viennese room, decorated by Josef Hoffmann
(1870-1956) in strictly geometrical, simple lines, was a sensation in Paris,
which was still full of the undulating lines of French Art Nouveau. It was
called the most modern expression of that time.[85] Comparison of the vertical
planes of Kupka's abstract period with photographs of Hoffmann's interior
and exterior architectural plans, which were reproduced in every German
and Czech art review, makes strong similarities obvious; Kupka's debt to
Secessionist architecture in his later years in Paris becomes irrefutable.
Structure as a complete artistic expression in itself, without ornament, an
architecture which drew its expressive forms from the subjective world enchanted Kupka. He compared it to music. "They both have the same great
advantage in comparison to painting—and even to poetry he writes, "they
draw their expressive forms from excitement and thoughts which they develop in abstraction. The architect doesn't copy natural sounds . . . both
architecture and music are superior because they are able to express the
inexpressible, to which we are sensitive."[86] Kupka ascribes the excitement
and emotions we feel contemplating beautiful architecture to perfect proportions, rightly evaluated and to the calculated divisions of all planes. He
created his first abstractions under the inspiration of both these arts—
architecture and music. He wanted to create as they do, and for the same
reason, "to give us joy, a sense of beauty."[87]

Kupka's departure from Vienna should not be interpreted as a separa-
tion from the Austrian scene. Not only did he maintain contact with Vienna
through German and Austrian art reviews, but he was kept informed by
Arthur Roessler, by his other close friend living in Vienna, the Czech poet
Josef Machar (1864-1942) and especially by his constant companion in
Paris, K. E. Schmidt, Austrian and German correspondent for *Ver Sacrum,*

85 *Ver Sacrum 1900; Deutsche Kunst
   und Dekoration,* 1900, p. 460.

86 *Tvoření v umění výtvarném,* pp.
   197-198.

87 Letter to Waldes, December 21,
   1920.

Deutsche Kunst und Dekoration, Meister der Farbe, among others. In 1901 Kupka was back in Vienna visiting his friends, at a time when the Secessionist movement was flourishing and very much in evidence in Vienna. He exhibited with the Secessionists in Vienna in 1900, 1901, 1903, and again in 1908.[88] Except for Koloman Moser, one of the principal members of the Secessionist group, it is not known which artists of the Viennese Secession he knew personally.

In 1913, he was still thinking a great deal about the Secession philosophy: "Your article about Secession came just in time. I am thinking about several problems underlined by you."[89]

For many years Kupka's thoughts, his opinions about art, his longings, seemed to race ahead of their incarnation in his works. In certain periods his paintings, drawings and illustrations appeared to be a retrogression from his line of evolution. Soon after his arrival in Paris he prophesied on his encounter with French Realism: "Realism is overpowering here; people in the streets are very colorful . . . but even if I sometimes struggle with realism, I know that I will remain a fantasist."[90] However, he temporarily lost some ground in his struggle, especially from 1905 to 1909 when he settled into a bourgeois life with Nini, and when symbol more and more gave way to reality. He painted portraits, some still lifes, flowers and even landscapes. He considered none of it worth including in the album of reproductions published by K. E. Schmidt in Bohemia in 1905, nor in any of his many exhibitions there.[90a]

His book illustrations often reveal a tendency toward compromise with current taste. He sometimes places three dimensional, realistic figures in the midst of abstract, flat ornament producing a striking impression of incongruity. And yet, at the same time, in his studio, almost clandestinely, he was already working on a different concept of art. He said in a letter to Machar: "It seems unnecessary to paint trees when people see more beautiful ones on the way to the exhibition. I paint, but only concepts . . . syntheses, chords . . . but this I do only for myself. I am not anxious to show it. . . ."[91]

88 See *Ver Sacrum,* no. 12, 1900; *Volné Směry,* Prague, 1901, p. 48; *Zeit,* Vienna, June 3, 1908.

89 Letter to Roessler, February 18, 1913.

90 Letter to Roessler, August 14, 1896.

90a *Album Frant. Kupka,* Čáslav, 1905.

91 Letter to Machar, April 24, 1905.

tes chevreaux près des tentes des bergers.
 A la jument attelée au char de Pharaon,
je te compare, Bien-Aimée.
 Que tes joues sont belles dans les perles,
ton cou dans les colliers !
 Nous te ferons des colliers d'or, pointillés
d'argent.
 Tandis que le Roi était sur son divan,
mon nard a répandu son parfum.
 Un sachet de myrrhe posé entre mes
seins, tel est pour moi mon Bien-Aimé.
 Une grappe de cypre des vignes d'En
Guedi, tel est pour moi mon Bien-Aimé.

fig. 13
Kupka, page from *The Song of Songs*,
1928, prepared 1905-09, Národní
Galerie, Prague.

The year 1909 seems to have been the time of breaking away from compromise if not yet the time of breakthrough. His illustrations for *Prometheus* show a complete renunciation of three-dimensionality. It was a trying year and he complained: "Life is full of difficulties; I am uprooted, and in spite of my already long sojourn here, I am still a stranger."[92] But only a year later he wrote to the same friend in Austria:

Even here, for years I had been a hungry soul, a soldier in the large army of great and small artists, until at last—but better late than never—I have gained consciousness and now I stand hale and hearty before myself. The moment has come for me to write, draw and paint my credo. In the last month I have destroyed much of my work. . . . looked at carefully, they were mostly tumors remaining from my bad times. I know them well and the sterner I am with myself the more easily I overcome everything that could hold me back, for I am boiling inside and although artistically I am gladly once again a youth, as we were—do you remember? . . . both excited by a concert . . . was not our excitement then a thing of beauty?[93]

To express the emotion provoked by beauty will now become the aim upon which he will concentrate his effort. And because he believed that music and architecture were the two arts capable of expressing those emotions autonomously, he will try to follow their example in creating his new art. His preoccupation with symbolically expressing his ideas changed into a preoccupation with symbolically expressing the perception of the form itself. "Formerly I was seeking to give form to an idea, now I am seeking the idea which corresponds to the form."[94] He realized that "the viewer doesn't remember the idea expressed in an art work. The action of plastic elements

92 Letter to Roessler, February 2, 1909.

93 Letter to Roessler, October 6, 1910.

94 Notes for *Tvoření v umění
   výtvarném.*

fig. 14
Kupka, *Prometheus*, prepared 1909-10.

95 Ibid.

96 For example, the Viennese theme of the movement of the human spirit toward light expressed in *Hymn to the Universe*, 1895, and *Toward Luminous Heights*, 1895, is continued in such work as *The Cathedral*, 1913, *Blue Scaffolding*, 1919, *Hindu Motif*, 1921-25, *Rising*, 1923. Again, the Viennese theme of *Quam ad Causum Sumus*, 1894, representing the creation of the world according to the Theosophic concepts of the evolution of life from vegetable to animal to human, is taken up in *Creation*, and *Cosmic Spring*, both 1911-20. The visions of immortality which absorbed him in Vienna are also reflected in *The Living Oval* (also called *Egg*), 1911-20, *Lines, Planes, Depths* (also called *Black Uterus* by Kupka in 1946), 1920-22, and the *Moving Blues* series of 1923-31. The more humorous view of human life as a market place is represented in *The Fair*, 1920-21.

97 Letter to Roessler, February 2, 1913.

which act upon the viewer and put him in a particular mood contribute to the development of the idea itself."[95] He believed that in finding the true substance of the form he would understand the substance of life itself. He would create a "new reality" which would be governed entirely by harmony and beauty. The artist's heightened consciousness is transferred through the work of art to the viewer and ignites his own consciousness. The new reality, created by the artist, is destined to enrich and elevate man. Yet, a great number of Kupka's paintings belie the concept of a mere search for beauty and harmony, not that they show an absence of painstaking effort to find form and color, but because they bear a deep imprint of their meditative origin.[96] Throughout his abstract period, Kupka's work shows the dualism of the meditative and the classicist-aesthetic concepts. This dualism may be followed in the appendices to the present text.

The years between 1910 and 1913, though they were not free of anxieties, doubts and even moments of despair, were Kupka's heroic years in which he drew and painted his credo and wrote his book. Early in 1913, he wrote a cheerful, self-confident letter to Roessler, despite the unfavorable reception of his work in Paris. "Paintings I exhibited recently are called *Planes by Colors, Amorpha, Fugue in Two Colors, Warm Chromatics,* etc. All in all what I am seeking now are symphonies. Do you remember the 'color symphonist.' You can't imagine the derision I have to put up with . . ." Kupka was amused by the puzzled viewer's questions: "What does it represent?" "What is it supposed to be?" and answered himself with a sarcastic rhetorical question: "Must then a work of art represent something?"[97] Questions and answers repeated thousand of times since. . . .

37

1a

1a

Mánes, *Calendar Plate*. 1865-66. Oil.
Muzeum Města, Prague.
A decorative, monumental figure of
a girl walking gracefully, represents
Balance. The circle which encloses
the girl echoes and emphasizes the
figure's motion and is thus an essential part of the composition.

2a

Kupka, *Girl with a Hoop*. c. 1903-05.
Pencil and watercolor. Bibliothèque
Nationale, Paris.

This is one of a series of compositions in which Kupka used a circle
and flowing robes to emphasize
fluidity of movement.

3a

Kupka, Study for *Amorpha, Fugue in
Two Colors*. 1912. Gouache. The
Museum of Modern Art, New York.

The dancer is schematized into an
entirely abstract pattern representing
pure rhythmic movement. Here the
circle is fully integrated with the
composition.

2a

3a

4a

Kupka, *Amorpha, Fugue in Two Colors*. 1912. Oil. Národní Galerie, Prague.

This is the final and strongly defined result of the studies. Kupka has attained what he calls the "new reality."

5a

Kupka, Study for *Amorpha, Fugue in Two Colors*. 1912. Pencil. The Museum of Modern Art, New York.

The same form is stylized into uninterrupted flowing lines.

6a

Kupka, Study for *Amorpha, Fugue in Two Colors*. After 1912. Gouache. The Museum of Modern Art, New York.

Kupka further stylizes this motif by eliminating lines not essential to the basic rhythm.

7a

Kupka, *Composition*. 1947-50. Oil. Collection P.P., Paris.

Years later Kupka used elements of these two series to create a new form which now no longer suggests either music or dance.

7a

6a

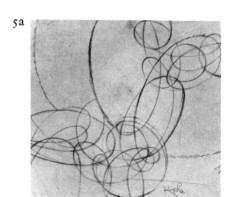

4a

5a

Continued

1b, 2b, 3b

Kupka, Studies for *Lines, Planes, Spaces*. c. 1912. Pencil. The Museum of Modern Art, New York.

Another series depicting schematized dancing motion. In the second, the elements are disconnected, depriving the figure of its cohesiveness. In the third, the intersecting curves, which form the visual center of gravity in the final painting, are established.

4b

Kupka, Study for *Lines, Planes, Spaces*. c. 1912. Woodcut. Národní Galerie, Prague.

1b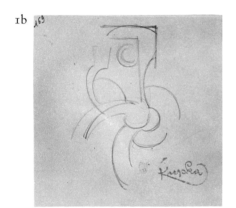

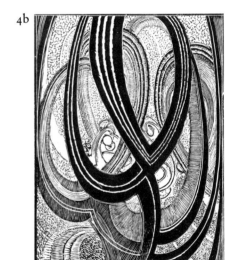
4b

2b

3b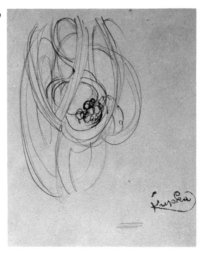

7b

5b

Kupka, *Lines, Planes, Spaces.* 1913-22. Oil. Private Collection.

Both are part of a series which occupied Kupka intensely. In it he attempted to express the progression of music in time through the use of melodious, multicolored lines projected in space, echoed by smaller background lines. The center of gravity was determined according to the rule of the Golden Section.

6b

Kupka, Study for *Lines, Planes, Spaces III.* c. 1913-23. The Museum of Modern Art, New York

7b

Kupka, *Lines, Planes, Spaces III.* c. 1923 [reworked 1934]. Oil. Musée National d'Art Moderne, Paris.

This is a simplification of the same theme, dated ten years later than Study for *Lines, Planes, Spaces* and *Lines, Planes, Spaces.*

5b

6b

This is one of many of Kupka's series of the Viennese period concerning metaphysical questions.
Quam ad Causum Sumus? (What is our purpose?)

1a
1b

Hádanka života.

2a

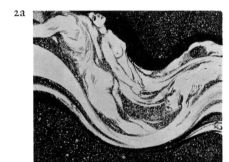

3a

1a

Enigma of Life. Vienna, 1894. Charcoal.

This allegory depicts the circle of life with figures swept by a current of water and two figures of women, one of which probably represents Minerva with the masks of science and wisdom, the other life and death. The scene is dominated by a mysterious sphinx.

2a

Rhythm of History. Paris, c. 1905. Charcoal and india ink over print. Národní Galerie, Prague.

Here Kupka focuses upon one of the elements of the *Enigma*—the figures carried by water—and elaborates the curves of the waves and the bodies of a man and woman swept by the current.

3a

Moving Blues II. 1922-36. Oil. Národní Galerie, Prague.

The painter retains the abstracted bodies of a man and a woman in an erotic pose, apparently in water, and repeats the curves of breaking waves. The rising oval shape suggests the idea of creation.

4a

2b

1b

Enigma of Life. Vienna, 1894.

2b

Meditation. Paris, 1899. Charcoal on paperboard. Galerie Ostrava.

A kneeling man—representing Kupka himself—faces a snow covered, sun-lit mountain with a dark barrier in front of it, both of which are reflected in water.

3b

Black Idol or *Defiance.* Paris, 1900. Colored aquatint. Národní Galerie, Prague.

Here Kupka symbolizes man's meta-physical fear with three figures: a gigantic, dark, horrifying deity which seems to grow out of the mountain seen in the previous picture; a petrified, probably human form; a diminutive, helpless man—a barely

discernible light vertical—again iso-lated by dark currents of water. The painting represents Kupka's evolution in this series, sometimes called *Land of Dreams,* away from the use of mythological allegory to express emotion. Ultimately, Kupka will also reject figurative symbolism as a means of expressing his metaphysical anxieties.

4b

Study for *Quam ad Causum Sumus.* 1900-03. Color etching and aquatint. Národní Galerie, Prague.

The impassable water of *Meditation* and *Defiance* is replaced here by an endless road flanked by Sphinxes asking the unanswerable questions.

3b

4b

4a

Moving Blues. c. 1925-27. Oil. Col-lection P.P., Paris.

The same figures are depicted, abstracted even further, almost to the point of ornamentation.

Continued

1c

Histoire Contemporaine. c. 1905.
Charcoal with india ink. Národní
Galerie, Prague. Study for Elisée
Reclus, *L'Homme et la terre.*

This academic representation of a
family looking toward the bright
horizon of the Promised Land symbolizes the future of humanity. The
composition's rhythmic forms
already suggest a geometric simplification of planes.

2c and 3c

Studies for *Organization of Graphic*
Motifs. 1910-13. Pencil. The Museum
of Modern Art, New York.

Here the figures represented in
Histoire contemporaine are freed of
inessential elements and integrated
into a new rhythmic form.

2c

3c

1c

4c

Study for *Organization of Graphic Motifs*. 1910-13. Pencil. The Museum of Modern Art, New York.

The same "new reality" revealed in the preceding drawings in integrated into a plastic space which is defined entirely by the intensity of lines and planes.

5c

Organization of Graphic Motifs I. 1912-13. Oil. Collection Royal S. Marks Gallery, New York.

6c

Study, *Organization of Graphic Motifs*. c. 1913. Pastel, Private Collection.

A totem-like figure derived from the family group in *Histoire contemporaine* perhaps symbolizes mankind. This figure is placed in a space similar in structure to the space which surrounds men contemplating their metaphysical dilemmas in *Meditation* and Study for *Quam ad Causum Sumus*.

4c

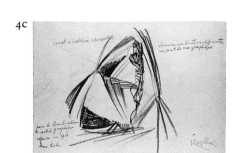

5c

6c

FRANTIŠEK KUPKA:
A METAPHYSICS OF ABSTRACTION

Margit Rowell

Kupka witnessed the birth of Cubism in Paris, but he never identified himself with it or any other movement. On February 2, 1913, the artist wrote to Arthur Roessler of his dissatisfaction at being labeled one of the Cubists and having his work exhibited with them: "In the last Salon d'Automne I had a beautiful place of honor, unfortunately in the room with the Cubists with whom I am almost on a parallel. It is with me as it was with Degas, who was classified as an Impressionist." In a continuation of the same letter, dated February 5, he wrote, obviously referring to Cubist-type painting: "[one] arrives at deformers: neoarchaics and neo-primitivists. You may have seen them in German exhibitions of Picasso's followers who cherish not only rigidity of line but rigidity of vision; who hate the color of the sun-loving Impressionists because ten years ago Picasso developed a new palette . . . I know the Parisian followers of Picasso, the Cubists, personally. I do not encourage their visits and I do not visit them either. I live like a hermit . . . woods and meadows around me, and I see many things in a tiny patch of grass, much more than in any exhibition."[1]

This rejection of Cubism is significant, for France was Kupka's country of choice and Cubism was France's dominant art form at the time Kupka's own expression began to mature, from about 1909-13. From 1900, one of Kupka's closest Parisian friends was Jacques Villon. Other friends and acquaintances included Duchamp-Villon, Duchamp, Picabia, Gleizes, Metzinger, Léger, Apollinaire. If any generation referred to Cubism for the formulation of its vision, it was this one.

It must be remembered that Kupka was much older than they and came from a radically different cultural background. As he wrote to Roessler in 1897, one year after his arrival in Paris:

1 Letter to Roessler, February 2, 1913, Collection Wiener Stadtbibliothek, Vienna. The author is indebted to Meda Mladek for bringing these letters to her attention.

Here in Paris I have lost the capacity to think; what remains are my sense perceptions. I would like to stop thinking altogether . . . so that I needn't adapt myself to endless metaphysics for no good reason. Even though I still have an impression of alienation from this world, and I still have visions which seem very real, I am working with all my strength to get out of the transcendental labyrinth, and to limit myself to my sense organs. . . . I am mentally intoxicated by the Parisian air which forces one to be very pragmatic and leads one away from introspection. . . .[2]

Vienna was like a sickness of a man who is not physically fit. . . . I became an emotionally sick man. Viennese air is not good for a painter. . . . It was decadent. Here I am once again enjoying the light and warmth of life. I am healed of these diseases. . . . I want to go back to learning from nature.[3]

These letters reveal the disparity between the context of experience of Kupka's past and the context of the present he is discovering. The shock of discovery is discernible in all his correspondence of the period. Yet equally perceptible is the imprint of his Central European heritage, a vision and philosophy which will remain with him throughout his lifetime.

Kupka's aesthetic was indeed foreign to French positivist thinking. For Kupka, art was the projection of the highest form of human spirituality through evocative but autonomous forms and colors. The artist does not reproduce nature; but nature is his model for understanding the universal cosmic order. The natural processes of growth, expansion, rotation, dilation, constriction are visible inferences of rhythms which man, as a part of the cosmic order, contains within his innermost being. These rhythms provide the structure of the artist's vision.

Whereas the artist's vision is "subjective"—a term which Kupka understood to mean a personal interpretation of cosmic forces—his formal means must be objective; he must invent a repertory of forms and colors which evoke universally legible concepts, instincts and rhythms. Technical perfection is of prime importance in order to project one's vision in unequivocal terms. Like Kandinsky, Kupka analyzed the configuration, function and significance of a spot, a point, a line, a plane and every color. Vehicles of universal values, emotions and ideas, each one was to be used according to its specific function.

Kupka's aesthetic can be traced to two dominant influences in his early life. The first is his involvement with occult sciences and mystical experiences, continuous since his early exposure to spiritism as a child in Bohemia. Later he became interested in astrology, Theosophy and Eastern religions. He probably remained a medium all his life. These disciplines made him receptive to visionary experiences and taught him that a world beyond the perceptual realm exists, a world ruled by dynamic causality and change, colored by imaginary not perceived hues, infinite in its dimensions. Nothing is still, everything moves in a vital flux. Man can only intuit its rhythms.

The second abiding influence in Kupka's life was the specific kind of academic training he received, first in Jaroměř in Bohemia and later in Prague and Vienna. His professor Studnička may have been the most important element in this schooling, as he instructed him in the associative powers of colors and the emotional implications of dynamic line. This teaching was based on the study of folklore motifs as universal archetypal configura-

2 Ibid., February 7, 1897.
3 Ibid., March 10, 1897.

tions.[4] Kupka's Nazarene professors were a lesser influence. Nonetheless, their Symbolist aesthetics contributed to his turning away from descriptive, narrative painting and to his understanding of art as embodying spiritual significance.

With these dimensions of Kupka's past experience in mind, it is understandable that Paris appeared to him as another, entirely foreign world. It is also understandable that he found the conceptual basis of Cubism incompatible with the abstract concepts which he understood as the real content of art. Formally it was inappropriate as well. Cubism was static, monochromatic, flat and spatially restricted, a distortion of perceptual reality based on a sum of rational or pictorially logical choices. However Kupka's vision was one of constant change, which implied dynamic rhythms, arbitrary color, undetermined space.

Abstraction would be Kupka's alternative to Cubism: a translation of his vision into pure rhythmic forms and colors. Understanding the cosmic order as a kaleidoscope of changing light, color forms and space, Kupka was keenly aware of the difficulties involved in capturing its sense and structure:

> *Alas, Nature is ever-changing, rapid are its metamorphoses. The laws of physiology are beginning to be disseminated; Daguerre, the moving picture, reproduce more exactly what the most faithful realist painters attempted to give the world. The most skillful artist is absolutely incapable of capturing the life of nature with traditional means. Poetry is creation. The artist must be able to create, like musicians, constructors of machines, architects.[5]*

Paradoxically, Kupka's aesthetic was determined and clarified by his exposure to positivist philosophical modes, advanced scientific discoveries and a diversity of artistic models and theories in France. Through his discovery of the moving picture in its preliminary forms and extensions—from the physiological experiment to the art form—he learned to endow the two-dimensional image with implications of motion and, by thus extending the subject into its surrounding space, he arrived at the pure visual expression of universal rhythms. Although he had been versed in color theory since his early training in Jaroměř, the example of Neo-Impressionist practice and theories enlarged his understanding of the potential of free color-form. And new discoveries in the natural sciences, as well as Kupka's increased attention to the objects of his perception helped him discern microcosmic indices in the cosmic order in nature.

Kupka came from Central Europe with a vision developed through the exercise of metaphysics. His exposure to positivism taught him to perceive the physical equivalents of this vision and distill them into abstract equivalents. His vision, his new perceptual experiences and their formal technical implementation would interact, producing a unique personal form of expression.

Kupka and the Depiction of Movement

At first glance, rhythmic organic activity and the evenly measured sequences of the film strip appear as diametrically opposed concepts of the displacement of matter in time and space. However the history of scientific investigation in these domains proves this to be untrue. The forefathers of the

4 The author is indebted to Mladek for bringing Studnička to her attention and helping her understand his significance, as well as that of the Nazarenes in the context of Kupka's development.

5 Undated manuscript; courtesy Andrée Martinel-Kupka.

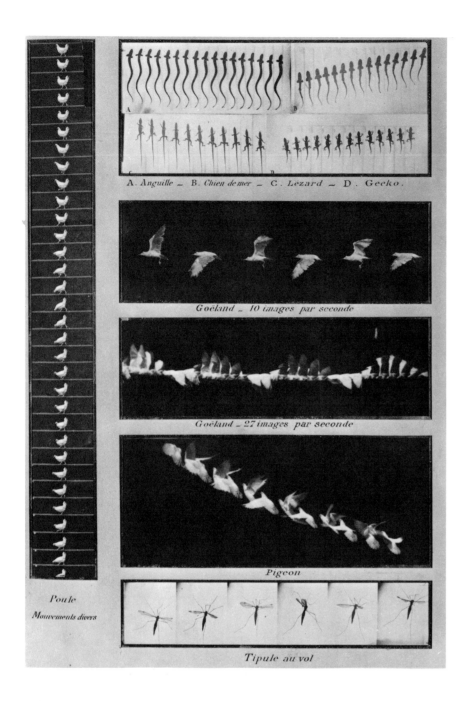

A. Anguille _ B. Chien de mer _ C. Lézard _ D. Gecko.

Goéland _ 10 images par seconde

Goéland _ 27 images par seconde

Pigeon

Poule
Mouvements divers

Tipule au vol

fig. 1.
Marey, *Diverse Examples of Animal Locomotion.* Musée Marey, Beaune, France.

cinematographic technique were physiologists, men of science who were exploring the dynamic natural processes of the universe.

For example, Etienne-Jules Marey is best known for his late nineteenth-century photographs of animal and human locomotion. (see figs. 1 and 2). In fact, his area of investigation extended far beyond this achievement. First with his chronographic process, then with his chronophotographs, Marey recorded images of the muscular, respiratory and circulatory activity of the human body; the minute patterns of insects in flight (see fig. 3); the movement of water and air currents (see fig. 4). Other contemporaneous physiologists photographed and graphed the accumulation and disintegration of cloud formations, the effects of lightning, eclipses of the sun, positions of the moon. Still others studied the kinetic variations in currents of electricity.

fig. 2.
Marey, *Man Walking*, c. 1882.
Cinémathèque française, Paris.

6 Muybridge's photographs were first published in France in the periodical *La Nature*, December 14, 1878. Marey's first book on animal locomotion, *La Machine animale*, appeared in 1873. See Aaron Scharf, *Art and Photography*, London, c. 1968, chapter 9, for extensive discussion of these events and their influences.

And by 1895, with the inventions of microphotography and X-ray photography, it was possible to trace the changing phases of biological growth.

Photography was a tool which these men developed into an exact science. Essentially they were measuring the space and time of common occurrences. To this end, they devised systems of evenly spaced visual intervals which, measured by periods of seconds and minutes, allowed an understanding of displacement in time. Paradoxically, these scientific experiments provided the bases for cinematography as an art form, as it emerged in the last decades of the nineteenth century.

The impact on artists of these scientific discoveries and the more popular forms which derived from them was immeasurable. Some artists reacted positively to them; others considered all forms of photography a threat to their art. However, all artists of the period recognized that photography added a dimension to visual experience, in its revelation to the transitory aspects of natural phenomena which are invisible to the naked eye.

By the 1890's it would have been virtually impossible for an artist living in Paris to remain ignorant of the photographic revolution. Moreover, whereas up to the 1870's artists were concerned with the applications of still photography, after the publications of Marey's and Muybridge's experiments,[6] attention turned to the kinetic or moving image (see figs. 1-13). Scientific and popular journals were filled with photography's breakthroughs. Albums of photographs were published in profusion. One could attend public lectures and demonstrations all over Paris. And as early as the 1880's, cameras, photographs and film strips were exhibited at the Conservatoire des Arts et Métiers.

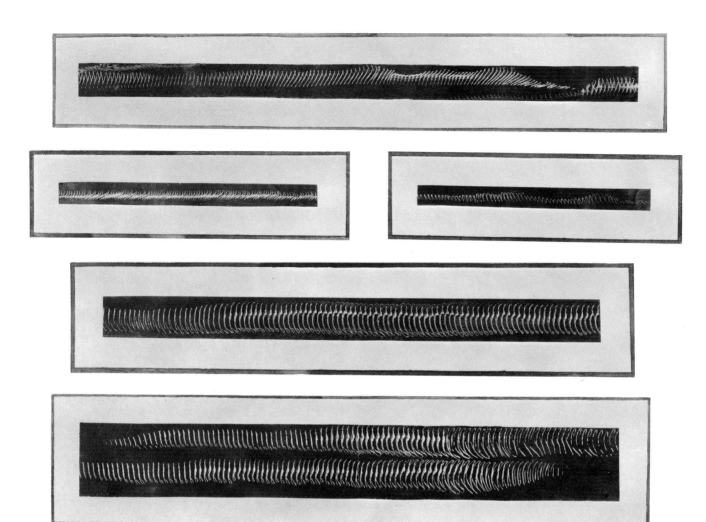

It was therefore not only logical but inevitable that, during the first two decades of the twentieth-century, artists came to question the traditional definition of painting as an immobilized image, a static configuration of a single immutable moment in time and space. Kupka, living in France by this time, was no exception. In fact, although his experiments tend to be overlooked, he may have made the first attempts to capture the kinetic dimension in painting.

Kupka arrived in Paris in the spring of 1896, at a time when cinematographic activity was at its height. Emile Reynaud had been showing his Optical Theater at the Musée Grévin since 1892. Edison's Kinetoscope of 1891 had been available to the general public since 1894, the year a Kinetoscope Parlor was opened at 20, boulevard Poissonnière. The Lumière brothers' Cinematograph had been unveiled in December 1895 and, since then, projected films daily at the Grand Café, 14, boulevard des Capucines. By 1896, the Lumière brothers could show footage backwards and Georges Méliès was projecting fast-motion films. In the year 1896 alone, 129 patents were registered in France relating to moving picture filming and projection.[7] All over Paris, music halls, theaters and cabarets presented kinetic light and image shows, from primitive magic lantern productions to the most technically sophisticated projections.

fig. 3.
Marey, *Partial Traces of Insect's Flight,* before 1885. Musée Marey, Beaune, France.

7 Georges Sadoul, *Histoire générale du cinéma,* vol. 1, Paris, 1973, p. 200.

MOUVEMENTS DE L'AIR
à la rencontre de Corps de diverses formes

fig. 4.
Marey, *Air Movements*. Musée Marey,
Beaune, France.

8 Denise Fédit of Paris, in preparing
the Kupka inventory catalogue for
the Musée National d'Art Moderne
(1966), found a prospectus for
Reynaud's séances of 1896 or 1897
among Kupka's personal papers. The
author is indebted to her for her
assistance and information (both
published and unpublished material)
concerning this particular aspect of
Kupka's development.

The cinematographic industry was concentrated on the right bank in
Paris, in Montmartre and on the *grands boulevards*. Kupka's studio was in
this neighborhood, as were the newspapers and cabarets which assured his
precarious livelihood as an illustrator. To Kupka, coming from a tradition
steeped in allegory, mysticism and metaphysics, Parisian life was a continuous revelation: a world of vivid sense perceptions opening up before him.
He may therefore have been more vulnerable to the visual seduction and
implications of cinematography than his French colleagues and contemporaries.

A prospectus found among Kupka's possessions indicates that he discovered the moving picture in the form of Reynaud's Praxinoscope or his
Optical Theater as early as 1896 or 1897[8] (see fig., p. 92). Reynaud showed
his Optical Theater at the Musée Grévin almost daily between 1892 and

1900. The Praxinoscope and the Optical Theater were constructed on an identical principle of two nested cylinders. The outer one was lined with panels on its inner face, each one depicting a different and consecutive phase of a figure in motion. The center drum was sheathed with mirrors. As the outer cylinder revolved around the stationary inner drum, the mirrors registered the turning images, reconstituting them into one consecutive movement. Reynaud's first bands were drawn by hand. In August 1896, he began making bands based on photographs, inspired by Marey's chronophotographs. Yet since Reynaud colored and retouched even the photographs by hand, his projections retained a hand-made quality.

Around 1900-02, Kupka executed a drawing, *The Horsemen* (cat. no. 9), inspired by the Praxinoscope principle. It is a precocious but isolated experiment at this point in Kupka's career. A revolutionary depiction of movement, the early date of this drawing is often questioned.[9] However in view of the fact that Reynaud's presentations at the Musée Grévin were discontinued in 1900 and that around that time moving picture production entered a more sophisticated phase—based on documentary footage (Lumière) and theatrical mises-en-scènes (Méliès)—the dates 1900-02 appear more plausible than a later date. Furthermore, Kupka's style in this drawing is close to the rapid brush and ink manner he developed for *L'Assiette au beurre, Le Rire* and the other satirical journals for which he started working around the turn of the century.

The representation of movement in *The Horsemen* is primitive. The surface is divided into rhythmic vertical bands. The vertical seams which scan the drawing's surface reproduce the effect of the Praxinoscope's mirror panels which ripple at each juncture. In the left foreground Kupka presents a positive image whose shadow is multiplied and reflected across the mirror panels. On the far right, the horseman's shadow is shown turning to the rear, indicating that Kupka was inspired by a convex image, or, more exactly, an image on a circular drum.

Although the technique for recording movement is based essentially on Reynaud's invention (in fact Reynaud did bands of moving horses), Kupka could as well have been referring to Muybridge's and Marey's studies (see figs. 5, 12, 13). These photographs were known all over Paris and some of them were exhibited at the 1900 World's Fair.

The 1900 World's Fair dominated the life of the French capital throughout that year. Kupka exhibited at the Fair and visited a number of the pavilions. In a letter to Machar, he mentioned a vertiginous ascent in a balloon which can only refer to the Cinéorama which was conceived specially for the Fair and duplicated a balloon voyage in all its details.[10] His already evident interest in photography and the cinema suggests that he must have visited the large photography pavilion exhibition organized by Marey.

Marey's exhibition was divided into two parts, both of which would have been of immediate or long-range interest to Kupka. The first section, "Instruments and Images Related to the History of Chronophotography," included the following displays: photographs showing the analysis of animal locomotion according to the Muybridge method (photographs of horses) (see fig. 5); chronophotographs by Marey, showing a fencer (fig. 6)

9 Mladek prefers a 1909-10 date; Virginia Spate dates the drawing 1906-08 in her forthcoming book *Orphism* (Oxford University Press); Jindřich Chalupecký dates it 1909-12 ("Nothing but an Artist," *Studio International*, vol. 189, January-February 1975, p. 32). On the other hand, Fédit dates it 1900-02, as does Vachtová.

10 Invented by Raoul Grimoin-Sanson, a disciple of Marey and friend of Méliès, Reynaud and Albert Londe, the Cinéorama was built for the Fair at the foot of the Eiffel Tower. It consisted of a circular drum in which the audience sat as though in the nacelle of an airship. This was surmounted by a balloon. A moving picture depicting a voyage over Europe and North Africa was projected on the circular screen. For further information on this invention, see Grimoin-Sanson's autobiography, *Le Film de ma vie,* Paris, 1926, pp. 88-127.

fig. 5.
Muybridge, *Daisy Jumping a Hurdle*,
1883-87. The Museum of Modern Art,
New York, Gift of the Philadelphia
Commercial Museum.

fig. 6.
Marey, *Fencer,* 1882. Cinémathèque française, Paris.

and a walking man (fig. 2); three-dimensional sculptures based on chrono-photographs; a multiple-lens camera invented by Albert Londe, accompanied by photographs of a horseman; multiple images, including the schematization of a running man (fig. 7); double-action chronophotographs; chronophotographic projectors; Edison's Kinetoscope; the Lumière brothers' Cinematograph.

The second part of Marey's exhibition demonstrated the "Scientific Applications of Chronophotography." In the catalogue accompanying the exhibition, Marey explained how the chronophotographic process can capture the consecutive positions of a moving object and create a visual (virtual) volume or a compound image consisting of elements invisible to the naked eye. The examples given, and exhibited, included photographs of a single thread or band of paper rotating around a central axis, forming a sphere or a skein-like configuration; photographs of water and air currents; patterns of animal locomotion on land (horses), in water (eels, other fish), in the air (birds, insects), etc.[11]

By 1900, Marey's and Muybridge's experiments were widely known. Not only cinematographers and artists but poets and writers on aesthetics had immediately seized upon their implications. Paul Valéry's *Introduction à la*

11 [Marey], *Musée centennal de la classe 12 (Photographie) à l'Exposition Universelle Internationale de 1900 à Paris,* exhibition catalogue, St. Cloud, n.d.

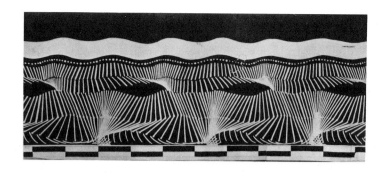

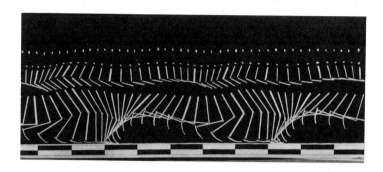

fig. 7.
Marey, *Chronophotographic Study of Human Locomotion,* 1887-88. Musée National des Techniques, Paris.

méthode de Léonardo da Vinci, first published in 1894, contains a passage on motion which engenders form which probably could not have been written without knowledge of Marey's discoveries.[12] More directly relevant to our subject, in 1889 and in 1893, Paul Souriau referred to Marey and Muybridge in his books of art theory, *L'Esthétique du mouvement* and *La Suggestion dans l'art.* The second book remained in Kupka's library until his death. It is unfortunately impossible to determine when he acquired it. However, certain passages of this 1893 publication discuss the translation of movement onto a two-dimensional support in a way which explicitly forecasts Kupka's somewhat later approach to the problem.

In the chapter entitled "The Representation of Movement," Souriau gives the following indications:

> *The most exact and the most expressive pose can only show us one phase of represented movement; mobility consists of a sequence of these phases. How can one project an idea of that sequence? By depicting several figures which enact approximately the same movement, each one depicting a different phase. Thus one produces an illusion like that of the zootrope: the diverse images which succeed one another on our retina give the impression of a jerky movement at high speed. . . . Each part of the total image presents a figure which the next figure modifies and the total impression of movement is extraordinary.*[13]

12 Reprinted in Paul Valéry, *Variété,* Paris, 1924, pp. 213-268; the passage referred to is on pp. 232-233.

13 Paul Souriau, *La Suggestion dans l'art,* Paris, 1893, p. 126.

This particular passage evokes Marey's multiple exposure images more than Muybridge's separately framed photographs (see figs. 8-11). Although often grouped together, the two photographers had very different approaches to their subject of human or animal locomotion. Muybridge's photographs of consecutive phases of motion were made by a battery of cameras placed around or along a moving subject's path. Thus the photographer virtually moved around or with the figure, capturing its progression from slightly different points of view. Marey, who was interested in patterns of motion, not in the specific characteristics of each arrested phase, captured the consecutive imprints of a moving subject on a single stationary lens. The subject moved before the camera; the camera did not move. The resulting chronophotograph showed a compound image of separate but overlapping silhouettes of a single figure moving through space and time. The trajectory of displacement and the minute oscillation patterns, both invisible as such to the naked eye, were rendered as a sequence of superimposed forms in which trace images and impressions assumed as much presence and substance as the figure itself which was conversely dematerialized in its kinetic progression. Thus, as Marey liked to point out,[14] the process neutralized all positions of the subject to the status of a virtual presence.

14 [Marey], op. cit., p. 26.

In 1908, the influence of high-speed photography appeared in the work of the sculptor Raymond Duchamp-Villon. Prior to 1898, Duchamp-Villon had studied medicine and completed his internship at the Salpétrière hospital in Paris where he came in contact with Dr. Albert Londe, who was then Director of the Photographic and Radiographic Division.[15] Londe, a disciple of Marey, was interested in the decomposition and analysis of physiological activity. Inspired by Muybridge's experiments, by 1883 Londe had developed a single camera with multiple lenses activated by a metronome with which he could photograph nine or twelve consecutive movements in space. Thus it is safe to assume that Duchamp-Villon was familiar with high-speed photography and the physiological analysis of movement before he left the medical profession to become a sculptor.

The small sculpture *Song*, of which the first plaster version dates from 1908, shows Duchamp-Villon's first explicit reference to high-speed photography. William Agee has argued that a sequence of Muybridge photographs of a "seated figure slightly turning with arm raised" helped the sculptor arrive at the formulation of this sculpture.[16] Agee points out that Duchamp-Villon turned to Muybridge "to confirm his own observation." His earlier attempts to capture motion had not completely satisfied him and he realized that a true understanding of muscular activity depended on these recent developments in photography.

The Kupka/Duchamp-Villon family friendship dated from at least as early as 1900, the year Kupka moved in next to Jacques Villon on the rue de Caulaincourt in Montmartre. In 1906 both Villon and Kupka moved to adjoining houses at 7, rue Lemaître in Puteaux, a Parisian suburb. They were to be joined in 1907 by Raymond Duchamp-Villon who took a house which shared the same garden. Marcel Duchamp, who was living in nearby Neuilly by that time, was a frequent visitor to Puteaux.

15 The author is indebted to Michel Frizot of Dijon for bringing this contact to her attention.

16 George Heard Hamilton and William C. Agee, *Raymond Duchamp-Villon, 1876-1918,* New York, 1967, discussion and reproduction, pp. 40-41.

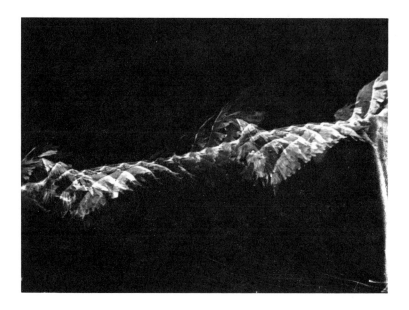

fig. 10.
Marey, *Bird in Flight.* Cinémathèque française, Paris.

fig. 11.
Muybridge, *Bird in Flight,* 1883-87. The Museum of Modern Art, New York, Gift of the Philadelphia Commercial Museum.

In 1908, the same year it appeared in Duchamp-Villon's sculpture, evidence of interest in high-speed photography began to emerge in Kupka's work. Yet Kupka, who was less interested in pinpointing anatomical changes than in motion as a time-space progression, turned toward Marey and chronophotography for his models. His initial subject was his wife's daughter Andrée playing in the garden with a ball (cat. no. 31). Frustrated by the impossibility of capturing the kinetic dimension of both the ball in the air and the child at play, he began doing diagrams of the child with the ball. The schematic sketches of the child's curving gestures combined with an analysis of color derived from the colored ball rotating through the spectrum led to the series of 1911-12, *Disks of Newton* (cat. nos. 72-75) and finally to the *Amorpha, Fugue in Two Colors* (cat. no. 92) of 1912. However simultaneous studies of the child's silhouette as it turned upon itself established the basis for another, parallel series of works of 1909-11, *Woman Picking Flowers,* which depicts overlapping consecutive phases of motion. These works, less abstract, and therefore less spectacular than the studies leading to the *Fugue,* are visually closer to chronophotography. They are also closer to and may in fact adumbrate Marcel Duchamp's paintings of 1911[17] and Villon's paintings of 1912-13 (for example, *Soldiers on the March*). It is therefore important to examine them here in order to understand Kupka's position in relation to other artists of his time.

The theme of a woman picking flowers culminates in 1909-10 in a large series of vibrant pastels (see cat. nos. 46-51).[18] In the two earliest studies shown here, the subject—a woman rising from a seated position and leaning forward to pick a flower—is decomposed into several evenly spaced and flattened overlapping silhouettes strung out across a vertical grid. A pronounced blur of even hatching suggests the trajectory from one position to another. Kupka was to write a few years later: "In order to give the impression of movement through the use of static agents . . . one must evoke a sequence of presences; to do so in the visual arts, one must indicate different intensities of impressions, from the least to the most easily perceptible. . . .

17 For discussion of Duchamp's 1911 paintings, see this author's "Kupka, Duchamp and Marey," *Studio International,* vol. 189, January-February, 1975, pp. 49-50.

18 Visitors to Kupka's studio in the fifties (Lilli Lonngren, Meda Mladek) remember seeing perhaps as many as fifteen pastels on this theme. Unfortunately the whereabouts of the others are unknown today.

19 At the time of writing this text, the author had had access to four undated manuscripts (in French), all of which showed some stage of preparation for Kupka's book *Tvoření v Umění Výtvarném,* finished in 1913 and published in 1923. These manuscripts have been classified as follows, and will be referred to accordingly throughout this catalogue. Manuscript I: Notebook, 1910-11 (?) Preliminary notes. Courtesy Andrée Martinel-Kupka; Manuscript II:

Thus one can render an effect of displacement, especially if the contours of the forms—moving—are cinematically unfolded, multiplied, moving from degree to degree, plane to plane."[19]

In later versions of the same subject (cat. nos. 49-50),[20] this evenly cadenced pattern of motion is loosened and dissolved into a cluster of ever more fluid arabesques. Whereas the earlier images were based on a fairly literal analysis of sense perceptions, dependent on the chronophotographic process, the later group shows a more personal interpretation. Here Kupka translates the moving subject into the abstract concept of motion itself, seen in the rhythmic articulation of ethereal shadows fanning out from a central upright axis.

In the last version shown here (cat. no. 51), although the grid structure is once more visible, the figure is shattered and integrated into the surrounding space. Here Kupka achieves a unified all-over pattern in which focal image, trace or memory imprints and ambient space are fragmented, flattened and enmeshed in a single plane. Kupka wrote in his notebook of approximately the same time (1910-11): "When we try to remember a dream . . . often we only retain a skeleton of the dream images . . . a vague grid through which fragmented forms emerge and disappear as quickly as they came."[21] However, more relevant to the artist's specific pictorial concerns is the passage in the same notes where he states: "The projection of a form on the surface of the canvas is in fact merely the limiting of one surface in relationship to the surrounding surfaces. The better painter one is, the better one binds the two." Contour, shading, light, he continues, are means to articulate the surface and, used in a particular manner, to destroy the traditional priority of closed focalized forms.[22] Obviously Kupka is attempting to slide his forms into a less differentiated spatial pattern.

Handwritten version of Chapter V. courtesy Karl Flinker; Manuscript III: Miscellaneous notes. Courtesy Denise Fédit; Manuscript IV: Complete manuscript of book (preliminary form); Courtesy Denise Fédit. Since Kupka's French is often not only repetitious but syntactically incorrect, for brevity and clarity's sake, all texts have been translated by the author into English. The above quote is from Manuscript II, p. 66. Manuscripts II-IV may be dated 1912-13.

20 It is impossible to determine the exact order in which these pastels were executed. But it does seem that cat. nos. 49 and 50, more fluid and synthetic, could not have been done unless they were preceded by the analytical approach seen in the first two described here.

21 Kupka, Manuscript I, p. 5.

22 Ibid., p. 29.

fig. 12.
Marey, *Horseman*, Cinémathèque française, Paris.

There is reason to believe (but unfortunately there is no proof) that the original inspiration for these drawings was a photograph of Madame Kupka in the garden in Puteaux. Kupka was only an amateur photographer. However at approximately the same time (c. 1908), he devised a camera with which to take photographs of himself running naked in his garden. The resulting shots were rather crude multiple-exposure photographs for which Marey unquestionably provided the inspiration.[23]

A second series of works executed between 1909 and 1911 depicts a woman with one arm raised, the other on her hip. Whereas the final oil version *Planes by Colors* (cat. no. 59) appears as a static composition flattened across a vertical grid, two preparatory pastels (cat. nos. 56, 57) reveal an implicit kinetic content. The studies show the head and arms in several consecutive positions simultaneously. And as the upper limbs shift positions, the torso, hips and thighs seem to rotate from a three-quarter to a frontal position. Thus once again we have a composite image of a perceived subject enhanced by memory impressions. And, in a manner similar to Marey's process, as the subject extends its image to encompass the temporal dimension, its substance is diluted in space to that of a virtual presence.

23 Once again the source of this information is Fédit who has reported (in conversation with the author) that she saw the photographs of Kupka in the garden (photographs which are now lost?). Fédit has also said she cannot believe that these pastels were not based on a photograph. Kupka's stepdaughter, Andrée Martinel-Kupka, says that she believes the series was "inspired by my mother in the garden at Puteaux." (Correspondence with the author, Spring 1975.)

fig. 13.
Marey, *Walking Horse*. Cinémathèque
française, Paris.

The theme of *Planes by Colors* is rotational motion. It depicts a figure moving toward and away from the viewer around a central axis. Interestingly, this is a subject which Souriau discussed in some detail, saying that a figure supposedly moving from one side of the canvas to the other never transmits a successful illusion of movement because the object must be captured at a single arrested point of its path. However, in real life a figure moving toward the viewer does not perceptibly move in his field of vision, and therefore its painted version does not present a discrepancy to the viewer. Souriau suggests that the most effective image is ". . . the oblique movement which presents figures in three-quarter view. The impression may be less strong but the aesthetic effect is . . . more satisfying than an abrupt foreshortening."[24]

The imagery of this figure rotating in space engenders the notion of a virtual volume situated in shallow depth behind the surface plane. However the illusion of volume and its implications of depth perspective were antithetical to Kupka's pictorial aims. Acutely conscious of the two-dimensional specificity of the painter's art, Kupka rejected modeling and shading, relegating them to the sculptor. He rejected perspective as well, which he de-

24 Souriau, op. cit., p. 127.

fined as a staggering of planes in depth through "the differentiation of dimensions, hues and tones."[25] As an alternative to these conventions, Kupka proposed the juxtaposition of colors according to their progression on the spectrum.[26]

These ideas were already visible in the *Woman Picking Flowers* series, as was Kupka's rejection of the anthropomorphic centrally focussed image: "If I employ forms of different dimensions, composed according to rhythmic concerns, I will achieve a 'symmorphy,' which, like a symphony, will develop in space. That way I will achieve an effect of printed material [*morceau d'étoffe à motifs*]. There will be no specific center of attraction. We are too accustomed to letting our eyes be drawn to the human figure, its details, etc."[27]

These passages from Kupka's writings help to explain his pictorial options of this period. The painting *Planes by Colors* is their consummate illustration. In order to suppress not only the pictorial conventions he rejected but also the push-pull effects of the vibrant color contrasts found in the pastel studies, Kupka took each fluid silhouette and compressed it into a flat rectilinear plane. Coloring the planes according to a chromatic progression of prismatic color, he laid them laterally in an even grid arrangement across the surface of the canvas. Thus he dissolved his subject into ambient space and light and destroyed conventional perspective, the illusion of volume and the traditional spatial distinction between a focalized figure and a neutral ground.

Despite its ultimate flatness, the picture summons an idea of simultaneous gesture in time and space. Here simultaneous gesture denotes an indistinct shifting of perceived or remembered forms within a single figure. The transition from sequential to simultaneous gesture as it is seen in this painting, executed in 1911 and exhibited in March 1912, shows an approach to the concept of motion which is quite different from both that of the Italian Futurists and the late 1911 paintings of Duchamp.

Simultaneity was a popular concept in the years 1912 to 1914, so generalized in fact that it was hopelessly imprecise. A number of individual artists felt they had invented the term but it was appropriated by poets, writers and musicians. Canudo applied it to Stravinsky; Apollinaire and Blaise Cendrars applied it to themselves; Henri Martin Barzun wrote a *Manifeste sur le simultanéisme poétique* in 1913; Delaunay and the Futurists disputed it among themselves. In reality, the term was a catch-all for many things: associations, impressions, images, motion, colors in complementarity, modernism.

Although the Futurists spoke of simultaneity, they more often depicted movement as a sequential unfolding of a single action or image of a state of mind *(stato d'animo)*. Futurist painting has been described as "a mode of analytical Cubism, the examination of moving parts in disarticulation, Cubism in motion."[28] Marcel Duchamp reportedly said, "My interest . . . was closer to the Cubists' interest in decomposing forms than to the Futurists' interest in suggesting movement, or even to Delaunay's Simultaneist suggestions of it. My aim was a static representation of movement . . ."[29]

25 Kupka, Manuscript I, p. 18.

26 Ibid., p. 11.

27 Ibid., p. 10.

28 Arthur A. Cohen, *Sonia Delaunay*, New York, 1975, p. 30 and discussion of simultaneity, pp. 29-30.

29 Arturo Schwarz, *The Complete Works of Marcel Duchamp*, New York, 1969, p. 18.

fig. 14.
Kupka, *Untitled Sketch,* c. 1910. Collection Karl Flinker.

Delaunay understood simultaneity as a juxtaposition on the one hand of complementary colors (inspired by Chevreul's "simultaneous contrasts") and on the other as an integration of scenes, objects, forms which could never be reconciled in nature. As Roger Allard suggested in June 1911, Delaunay's paintings were conceived as an assemblage of different points of view.[30] This is what characterizes the Cubists and Delaunay and what separates them from Kupka. Like Muybridge, the Cubists moved around the object, capturing several points of view. Metzinger said about Picasso in 1910: "... he lays out a free mobile perspective...."[31] Whereas Kupka, emulating Marey, forced the object to move before his "stationary lens" or eyes.

Curiously Kupka never used the term simultaneity in reference to his own ambitions. Yet one could say he was the most simultaneist of them all. In fact, without using the term, Kupka defined it in an interview with a young Czech journalist in July 1912 who recorded their conversation in the following terms: "Although he used to be puzzled by the Futurist 'simultaneity of sequences,' all his effort today is directed toward solving the problem of *shifting.* He is stubborn. When I argue with him and say that it is impossible *to convey with one view what in reality is perceived through a continuous succession of views,* he gets excited and says, 'Maybe I'll believe that tomorrow; today I swear by this.' "[32]

Kupka's transition from sequential to simultaneous imagery may be situated sometime during the years 1910-11. A small annotated sketch from that period may mark the turning point in the artist's thinking. This drawing (fig. 14) shows indistinctly overlapping silhouettes of a female figure turning

30 Roger Allard in *Les Marches du Sud-Ouest,* no. 2, Paris, June 1911, p. 69.

31 Jean Metzinger, "Note sur la peinture," *Pan,* Paris, October-November 1910, pp. 649-651. English translation from Edward F. Fry, *Cubism,* New York-Toronto, (1966?), p. 60.

32 Richard Weiner, "Návštěvou u nového Františka Kupky," *Samostatnost,* August 8, 1912. Reprinted and presented by Jindřich Chalupecký, *Výtvarné umění* XV, c. 8, 1968, pp. 367-371. Translation by Suzanna Simor. Italics mine.

and bowing slightly to the right. It may be placed c. 1910, between the two series studied above. In the upper right corner, Kupka has written: "Three-dimensional displacement takes place in space, whereas four dimensional displacement [takes place] through an exchange of atoms. But to capture [fix, arrest] a gesture, a movement on the space of the canvas . . . capture several consecutive movements." Under the inscription, four stick figures walking from left to right illustrate the idea of consecutive displacement.

The second sentence is clearly inspired by Marey's definition of movement in which discontinuity is a major element: "By passing a series of analytical images before the spectator's eyes, one reconstitutes the appearance of movement itself."[33] Kupka confirms his adherence to this notion in further notes of 1912-13: "Movement is no more than a series of different positions in space."[34]

However, the first sentence of the inscription is more enigmatic. Although the fourth dimension was a common subject of conversation in artists' circles as early as 1910, Kupka's terminology suggests a direct reference to an explicit text. Throughout the year 1908, Gaston de Pawlowski, the editor of *Comoedia*, published a series of articles in his newspaper in which he evoked the experience of the fourth dimension. These preliminary essays were in fact sketches for a series of articles he published more regularly in 1911-12, and of which at least the 1912 series would finally appear in book form in late 1912 as *Voyage au pays de la quatrième dimension*.[35]

Compare this passage by Pawlowski to Kupka's notes above:

Whereas in three-dimensional displacement the atoms constituting a body are pushed aside and replaced by other atoms forming another body . . . displacement in the country of the fourth dimension is enacted by what one used to call a transmutation. The world of the fourth dimension being continuous, no movement in the ordinary sense of the word can be produced as in the mobile world of three dimensions. Therefore, a displacement is made through an exchange of qualities between neighboring atoms. . . . When one enters the country of the fourth dimension, movement such as we know it, no longer exists; there are only qualitative changes and we remain immobile, in the common sense of the word.[36]

Pawlowski's central ideas are pinpointed in Kupka's lapidary phrases and illustrated by the two juxtaposed drawings. The qualitative changes seen in Kupka's rendering of simultaneous gesture are produced by a shifting of energies sliding into one another and thereby cohere to Pawlowski's text. However, Kupka will not completely discard the notion of linear consecutive motion as enacted in the three-dimensional world. Both concepts of displacement will accompany the artist in his progressive distillation of perceptual experience into abstract terms.

Unquestionably Kupka had developed his own theoretical premises concerning the depiction of motion well before the first Futurist paintings reached Paris in February 1912. And just as certainly, they developed in relation to sources within his Parisian context. The same sources, and perhaps even Kupka's example, inspired Marcel Duchamp when he began his own studies of moving figures. Duchamp's response to the 1912 Futurist exhibition corresponds to the Kupka/Marey concept of motion based on analytical discontinuity rather than the synthetic continuity to which the Futurists at least theoretically aspired: "It was quite exciting for me to see the painting

33 [Marey], op. cit., p. 9.

34 Manuscript II, p. 32.

35 See Jean Clair, *Marcel Duchamp ou le grand fictif*, Paris, 1975, pp. 31-32.

36 Gaston de Pawlowski, *Voyage au pays de la quatrième dimension*, Paris, 1971, pp. 79-80 (first published in 1912).

Dog on a Leash by Balla, showing also the successive static positions of the dog's legs and leash."[37]

Nonetheless it must be recognized that despite an autonomous development and the fact that artists in Paris *could not have seen* any Futurist painting prior to February 1912, Futurist ideas were in the air, transmitted by the Futurist manifestoes. Marinetti's *First Futurist Manifesto* appeared in *Le Figaro* on February 20, 1909. The *Technical Manifesto of Futurist Painting* was published in *Comoedia* on May 18, 1910, accompanied by cartoons by André Warnod. There are ideas in the *Technical Manifesto* which are so close to those circulating in the Puteaux milieu that it is far from clear who actually initiated them. It can only be said that many of the shared notions derived from a European community of ideas. Common to both groups was the influence of Neo-Impressionism, an interest in Bergson, a knowledge of Marey, and diverse and multiple extensions of pictorial, philosophical and scientific contexts of thought. Combined, these made up a total context of modernism, a context to which Kupka belonged. His personal contributions to this context are only beginning to emerge today.

Kupka and Color

During the first decades of this century, the introduction of the kinetic dimension was capital to the redefinition of the function of painting. As capital was the shift of emphasis from color subjected to form and content to color which dictates its own laws. This shift was anticipated in the late nineteenth century by Symbolist and Impressionist painters. Not only their examples but the theories to which they referred were meaningful to the generation active around 1910-12, particularly in France and Italy. Indeed, nineteenth-century color theory was as important a factor in the emancipation of color as was moving-picture photography for the emancipation of form.

Whereas the emerging moving-picture industry was a revelation to Kupka upon his arrival in Paris, his knowledge of color theory was well advanced, and the theories he encountered in Paris could not have surprised him. He had learned color theory from his professor Studnička who, as early as the 1880's in Bohemia, had analyzed prismatic color and invented color scales for its study.[38] Yet the application of these principles in the art of Seurat, van Gogh, Gauguin, Redon, Whistler was light-years away from the way in which color was used in the Central European Academies where Kupka had received his training.

By 1896, the year Kupka arrived in Paris, the Neo-Impressionists were exhibiting regularly. Kupka made a brief excursion into divisionism (see cat. nos. 1, 8) but quickly retreated from all forms of pointillism, declaring them a dishonest approach to color and light. He looked at Redon (see cat. no. 4) and Toulouse-Lautrec (see cat. no. 12), but may have found their softly colored light-filled compositions too dependent on symbolic or psychological associations. It was not until after c. 1906 that color for its own sake began to assert itself in his work.

Some of the 1906 paintings are distinctly Northern in feeling, in the full sensuous volumes, rich gestural brushstroke and the dissonances of juxta-

37 Marcel Duchamp, quoted in Anne D'Harnoncourt and Kynaston McShine, eds., *Marcel Duchamp*, New York, 1973, p. 258. There is some problem about this reference since, according to most historians (John Golding, Marianne Martin for example) Balla did not exhibit in the 1912 Futurist exhibition.

38 According to Mladek, Studnička's color teaching derived from Bezold. If this is true then Kupka may have learned the distinction between color-light and color-pigment at this time.

posed colors (see cat. no. 17). Others, slightly later, have the controlled brushwork and delicately keyed hues of the French Fauves (cat. no. 27). Impulsive or carefully controlled, these works show an artist exploring the function of color and concomitantly seeking a personal style.

The Yellow Scale (cat. no. 29) is Kupka's first attempt to come to terms with color theory in which the result is both personal and successful. In this enigmatic portrait of 1907-08, Kupka's debt to Neo-Impressionism and even Symbolism is obvious. The dominant yellow hues evoke Gauguin and van Gogh, painters Kupka admired at that time. Furthermore the loosely rendered features of the sitter indicate that he was not aiming for a resemblance, but attempting a symbolic evocative image. Like Mallarmé, to whom Kupka often made allusions, he was seeking harmonies and chords.[39] But beyond its symbolic associations, both the painting's title and the restricted palette—confined to the constituents of the chromatic scale of yellow—suggest an allusion to color theory and probably to Chevreul.

Chevreul's best-known work, *De la loi du contraste simultané des couleurs* of 1839, was a bible for the Neo-Impressionist and Nabi painters who diffused his teachings in both theoretical discussions and practice. Particularly popular was his famous law of simultaneous contrast,[40] first defined in this publication and elaborated in many others. Most of Chevreul's major works (his bibliography is extensive) were accompanied by lithographic plates of chromatic circles *(cercles chromatiques)* and chromatic scales *(gammes chromatiques)*. Conceived not only for the primaries but for mixed colors, the high quality of the plates captured all the nuances of each chromatic progression. Kupka's painting *The Yellow Scale (La Gamme jaune)* shows all the variations of orange and yellow in Chevreul's "Yellow-Orange Chromatic Scale" *(Gamme chromatique orangé-jaune)*.

Aside from a general allusion to color theory, in his depiction of green hair, Kupka may be referring to an obscure volume of 1875, *L'Enseignement devant l'étude de la vision* by Chevreul. Here the author presents an anecdote in support of his theory of simultaneous contrasts, in which he explains that gray or blond hair may appear greenish or bluish when seen in a favorable light. He explains that an optical effect of this sort is produced by a juxtaposition with golden, pinkish or orange skin. We have no proof that Kupka knew this book; yet his painting illustrates Chevreul's unusual example of simultaneous contrast.

Kupka's allusions to color theory were usually more empirical than systematic. Yet he did adhere to a number of basic laws which he referred to constantly in the major body of his writings between 1910-13. He made a firm distinction between prismatic and pigmentary color, based on his belief that light is a coefficient of color and that color does not exist without light. His most frequent references were to the facts that red advances, blue recedes in space; black and white are determinants of color intensity; the interaction of juxtaposed colors depends on their position on the spectrum; a spinning color wheel either dilutes the intensity of the original hues or turns them to gray or white; large areas have a different impact and emotional value than small.

39 See p. 309.

40 The law of simultaneous contrast most simply stated, concerns the reciprocal modification in hue, tone, intensity between two juxtaposed colors viewed in simultaneity.

In his writings he referred to the theories of Newton and Herschel, Helmholz and Ogden Rood and Charles Blanc indiscriminately. He was also familiar with Signac's *D'Eugène Delacroix au néo-impressionnisme*, first published in 1899, the second (1911) edition of which remained in his library until his death.

Between 1906 and 1910, Kupka experimented widely. As suggested earlier, his personal style of expression began to emerge around 1908. Yet obviously Kupka was dissatisfied with *The Yellow Scale*'s inchoate or amorphous composition. He subsequently began to articulate his surfaces more visibly with strips or pastilles of color. Not surprisingly, his first experiments in this direction are congruent with his first studies of motion. In fact, evidence of his researches in both color and motion are contained in the *Woman Picking Flowers* series (cat. nos. 46-51).

The function of color, as Kupka began to conceive of it, was to structure space. He devised a system of large colored planes which cannot be mixed by the eye, which are not equivalent to shading or modeling and which dictate the rhythmic structure of the composition (see cat. no. 42). Kupka admittedly derived this solution from the Neo-Impressionist example. He even referred to the planes as an enlarged pointillism. Since the first examples of this technique are seen in his work around 1908 (see cat. no. 35), perhaps he was inspired by H. E. Cross' or Signac's latest work, exhibited in Paris in 1907.[41]

All of Kupka's written notes, starting 1910-11, express a consistent attempt to define painting as a specifically two-dimensional non-illusionistic activity. In this context, a plane of color can be subordinated to nothing else. It functions as area, hue, coefficient of light; it is a given term in a relationship to white, to related values or contrasting hues. In and of itself it determines the rhythmic structure of the perceptual field.

The 1910 oil *Family Portrait* (cat. no. 44) presents a summation of Kupka's chromatic experiments over the preceding years. A sumptuous composition, built on color alone, it encompasses two different, almost contradictory notions of how color as plane may function. Divided virtually on the diagonal, the brilliant luminosity, broad masses and clarity of contour of the lower left triangle contrast sharply with the busy mosaic of dark graded colors, applied in short even square strokes, which animate the remaining area.

The highly saturated planes of the woman's dress achieve a flatness unprecedented in Kupka's work. This is due not only to the absence of modeling but to the choice and disposition of colors. As noted above, Kupka believed that red and warm colors advance, whereas blue and cool colors recede in space. Here he has reversed these axioms and the colors' usual roles. The areas of blue appear as broad sunstruck planes whereas the jagged red stripes elicit shadows, describing the folds and creases of the woman's garment as they underscore her arms, her spine, her buttocks and thighs. The paradox is intensified as the red becomes warmer, the blue colder through their juxtaposition. Finally the orange line which inscribes the woman's silhouette is similarly contradictory in its function. The warm-

41 *Exposition H. E. Cross,* Galerie Bernheim Jeune, Paris, April 22-May 8, 1907; *Paul Signac,* Galerie Bernheim Jeune, Paris, January 21-February 2, 1907.

est color on the canvas, it has been assigned a role as shadow. Lying contiguous to areas of red, it pushes the latter hue back toward violet or blue. As a result of this complex color play, all the volumes in this area level out into a broad flat pattern of jagged shapes.

In contrast to these broad brilliant masses, the remaining portion of the canvas is articulated as a dull non-reflecting mosaic pattern. The short tessera-like strokes are in mixed and dulled secondary, even tertiary colors, from deep blue to green to yellow, brown and violet. Since the local color is no longer white but black, most light is absorbed rather than reflected.

Thus *Family Portrait* illustrates two entirely different ways of articulating a flat surface: the first through luminous vibration, the second through pattern. Both were legacies of Neo-Impressionism, although Kupka adapted the Neo-Impressionist example to different ends.[42] Although Kupka will continue to use the modularized brushstroke to animate a surface through 1911, his real understanding of color was prismatic: color as a quantity and quality of light; planes of color generating their own optical vibration. This will be the basis of all his subsequent experiments. It will be an important factor in his dissolution of the image and evolution toward abstraction.

Despite the pictorial tensions inherent in *Family Portrait,* it is essentially a static composition. An interpretation of space as a flattened perceptual field, it is structurally articulated by broad or tightly knit planes, reflection and refraction, contrasts and passages.

Whereas the concurrent series *Woman Picking Flowers* shows the analysis and synthesis of a temporal progression, *Large Nude* and *Family Portrait* helped Kupka define his chromatic vocabulary and spatial syntax. The translation of a subject seen in a sequence of positions into an abstract idea of simultaneity and finally to abstract rhythms alone was as dependent on the dissolution of the object through color-light as on its temporal decomposition. The interpenetration of figure and space, the fusion of present and remembered perceptual images could only be achieved through a coincidence of spatial and temporal dimensions.

Kupka's development toward this objective was characteristically long and painstaking. Between 1908 and 1910, the artist executed a series of pencil and colored pencil studies of movement, inspired by his stepdaughter Andrée playing with a ball in the garden (cat. nos. 32, 45, 61, 62). One of these drawings (cat. no. 45) contains a dissection into planes and leads into the *Woman Picking Flowers* series. The others are based on circular motion and show a diagraming of corporal gestures into predominantly circular rhythms and an attempt to encompass figure and space in one integrated pattern. In a first stage, Kupka schematized the child's body according to its essential contours and silhouettes (cat. no.32a). Next he superimposed circles on the body extending its muscular rhythms into the ambient space (cat. no. 32b). Occasionally at the intersections of circles and limbs (or circles and circles), he shaded the enclosed area emphasizing its identity as a quadrant or plane.

Obviously the interpenetration of figure and ground was the crucial concept in these drawings. However Kupka did not find these diagrams convincing. In the right margin of one he noted: "Here, only the surfaces are

42 The Neo-Impressionists achieved luminous vibration through the divisionist technique in which pure hues, applied in juxtaposed dots, produce an optical mixture and an optical flicker. Although this technique inspired Kupka, he did not adopt it.

dissected; the concept of atmospheric copenetration is still to be found. As long as there is a difference between the ground colors and the flesh, I will fall once again into photographic post card imagery." (cat. no. 32b).

The idea of "atmospheric copenetration," or fusion of figure and ground through the dissection of a figure into flat open planes, was to be an analytical Cubist and Futurist concern. The French group would concentrate on a cohesive spatial scaffolding resulting in static and monochromatic imagery. The Italians, oriented toward the depiction of continuous motion, would tend to underplay formal spatial arrangements, resulting in disarticulated images. Kupka sought to develop an organic network of color planes which would act as both spatial and temporal referents and generate dynamic visual rhythms.

In slightly later sketches, the visual and conceptual boundaries between the figure as physical entity and the gesture as virtual entity, between closed colored planes and open-ended motion are progressively undermined. *The Oval Mirror* of 1910 (cat. no. 53) shows an early attempt to resolve these contradictions on canvas. However, despite the multiplication of contours, the circular rhythms and the suggestion of atmospheric copenetration seen in this monochromatic image of reflected and actual forms, the picture remains essentially static. Finally, in *Study for Amorpha, Fugue*, 1910-11 (cat. no. 63), Kupka comes close to a solution in which the temporal dimension is engendered by the manipulation of color planes.

The subject is a revolving anthropomorphic figure which, as it turns, assimilates aspects (light, color, space) of its environment into its own ambiguous silhouette. An analysis of this image reveals a composite silhouette drawn from all the studies inspired by the *Girl with a Ball* and even from the *Woman Picking Flowers* series. The central vertical structure is common to them all. The kinetic dimension of the image is produced by the planes of color which advance or recede, become denser, dissolve or change in key, each transformation signifying a modified position in space and time. The colored rhythms in the lower area are the slowest and most compact; they connote legs, ambiguously clothed but partially visible, which shift from a frontal to a profile view, nonetheless remaining within the restricted keys of red and blue.[43] In contrast, the bright intersecting arabesques in the upper portion of the canvas, which weave in and out, forward and backward, elicit a compound image of swift curving gestures. These variegated loops composed of splintered color and light follow a chromatic progression which maintains their structural and temporal continuity. The dominant oval on the left moves rapidly through the spectrum from green to yellow to orange. It signifies pure gesture, a visual imprint infused with light. Conversely, the smaller red and blue loop on the right, despite its flickering divided color, evokes a more stable presence, echoing the lower denser portion of the silhouette.

The preliminary sketches described earlier reveal the morphology of this complex dynamic image. Yet the artist seemed to realize that this painting did not make his premises totally clear. His interest in cinematography and his study of color theory had taught him that motion is a sequence of equal consecutive phases whereas color is a juxtaposition of even consecutive

43 Compare the legs here to those seen in the *Woman Picking Flowers* series.

hues and tones. Moved by a desire to make the temporal and spatial dimensions coincide in an image intelligible as color and rhythm alone, he decided to try a more systematic approach. He would calibrate gestures and colors simultaneously on a grid.

His decision was not arbitrary. Kupka believed that the perceptual field appears to us as a grid structure composed of planes and accents enmeshed in an all-over rhythm. The last version of the *Woman Picking Flowers* series shows this eloquently. In his notes of the same years in which this series was executed, he described the recollection of a dream as a kind of skeletal grid pattern.[44] Elsewhere he notes: "The screen of squares one lays over a sketch which one intends to enlarge gives it a rhythm. This is probably due to the fact that it thus acquires a unity, a dominant element."[45]

In contrast to the elliptical imagery of *Study for Amorpha, Fugue, Planes by Colors* of the same year (cat. no. 59) is a gridded or screened image of the same subject, a figure pivoting in space. The central axis of the radiating motion is blue; it denotes the densest and purest color and the most compacted action. As the arms pivot around this core, they dissolve in motion, mix with light and slide through the spectrum from shades of green to yellow-greens to oranges and yellows. In contrast to the densely woven concentrated image of the trunk of the figure, the gestures retain little presence. The transparent prisms imply gestures which have been, are or will be. Redefined as equal intervals in space, equal intervals in time, equal intervals on the color spectrum, the figure's limbs have the presence or non-presence of after-images; they are trace imprints in light, space and time.

Kupka's support was two-dimensional. Yet any image of rotational movement carries connotations of virtual volume or depth. In order to dispel this illusion, once again Kupka reversed the color-values' usual roles, placing the most luminous tints or light-reflecting values in the background and the darker cooler tones in the frontal plane. The result of this reverse chiaroscuro is a unified surface plane.

Planes by Colors inspires two chromatic readings. For both interpretations, one must imagine a view of the figure from the top in which the torso acts as a central blue core or axis. The first reading likens the configuration to a traditional color wheel in which each consecutive gesture, attached to the center, corresponds to a different chromatic segment leading out from the nucleus. The second reading again takes the torso as a core, this time circumscribed by continuous bands or haloes of color, from a red-green around the central axis to ever lighter shades of orange and green and finally to a yellow-white at the outer rim. Both interpretations are based on the notion of an even progression of color, either around a circle in juxtaposed wedges, or rippling out in circumscribed bands.[46]

Now that Kupka had developed a new pictorial syntax based on even and consecutive time-space intervals, he returned to the more ambiguously dynamic *Study for Amorpha, Fugue* and recast its essential imagery. In *Red and Blue Disks* (cat. no. 71), he reduced the gesturing figure shifting on the grass to a red-blue core. Taking each gesture of the original image, he translated it into a chain of axially-connected, overlapping disks rippling outward from the center. Each evenly cadenced chain of disks—like transparent

44 For exact quotation, see p. 61.

45 Kupka, Manuscript I, p. 26 (incorrectly numbered 22).

46 Of course, a third reading (see pp. 63-64 above) is that of vertical planes lined up in spectral progression across the two-dimensional surface of the canvas.

circular blades of color whirling out from the center—is limited virtually to a single key. The upper left segment is predominantly yellow. Consecutively, and counter-clockwise, color progresses to green, then to blue in the lower right area and up through a deep orange to light oranges and reds. Although this sequence of chromatic zones follows loosely the order of the spectrum, as well as the chromatic order in the original painting, the complex interlacing of orders in time and layers in space destroys any literal reading. The ripples of swiveling color and light are as ephemeral as a gesture. Yet they transcend the notion of bodily movement to suggest cosmic motion in time and space.

Since Kupka conceived of man as a microcosm of a greater order, whose being reflects those grander rhythms, his passage from the human to the cosmic dimension was pictorially logical and consistent with his beliefs. 1911 is the year of passage from figuration to abstraction, from the particular to the universal, from the phenomenal world to the noumenal idea. The next series, the *Disks of Newton* of 1911-12, are pure studies of color. All allusions to earthly experience, that is, allusions to human time and space have been discarded. References to human displacement, modeling, shading, perspective are irrelevant. The imagery is situated in a cosmic void.

The first *Disks of Newton* (cat. no. 73) comprises three series of disks set off against a black or dark blue background. The largest disk configuration consists of concentric bands of color laid out according to Herschel and Young's color table. This table was published in Ogden Rood's *Modern Chromatics* of 1879.[47] Kupka copied it and referred to it frequently, preferring it to Newton's theories which he found outdated. The Herschel-Young table calculated the relative length, density and velocity of the wave lengths of color, from red (shortest waves, lowest number per square inch, lowest number per second) to purple (longest waves, highest number per square inch, highest number per second). This analysis of color became fundamental to Kupka's thinking. He even devised a theory of the shapes of color which he illustrated in a series of paintings after World War I. (see cat. no. 168)

Kupka knew that a spinning disk alters if it does not annihilate its own color. The pure clearly differentiated hues of the upper disk imply that it is static. By contrast, the two remaining disks have no secure identity; they draw their tenuous substance and hues—like those of a rainbow—from the dominant image behind them. The spiraling circle in the right foreground, as it cuts through the bands of pure color behind it, generates three circumscribed bands of prismatic mixtures. As the disk in the lower left shifts forward in three consecutive phases, it is transmuted from a compartmented arc in the key of blue, to a continuous band in its complementary orange, then yellow, to a spinning disk of pure white light.

Situated between the *Planes by Color* and *Amorpha, Fugue* (cat. no. 92), one would be tempted to call this painting "Theme and Variations on Color." The parts or voices are distinctly separate yet entirely interdependent and clearly derived from one and the same theme. The organic structure and rhythmic counterpoint make this painting a fitting prelude to the *Fugue*.

47 Ogden N. Rood, *Modern Chromatics with Applications to Art and Industry,* London, 1879, p. 26 (French translation *Théorie scientifique des couleurs,* Paris, 1881, p. 16.)

The second *Disks of Newton* (cat. no. 75) is more densely woven, more ambiguous, more dynamic. Although it evolves directly from the *Red and Blue Disks,* the composition is completely severed from its original anthropomorphic inspiration and severed from the bottom edge of the canvas; the disks swirl and revolve freely in space.

In the *Red and Blue Disks,* each cluster of colored disks fanned out along a radial axis in a tonal progression from the center of the composition to the frame. Each of these zones of graded color was juxtaposed laterally to its contiguous color zone on the color wheel so that a sense of consecutive movement around a center was achieved. In the *Disks of Newton,* Kupka abandons these methodical sequences. Although the zones of light and color echo the original composition as the transparent disks radiate out from the center, and although broad areas of the painting are still defined by a dominant hue, the distribution of color is less systematic. Interspersed accents of complementaries and random mixtures with white or black heighten the intensity of the composition through contrast.

The transparent webbing of the colored disks destroys any illusion of volume or depth. Although the red center advances toward the viewer and anchors the image at some point in space, the spinning haloes massed around it are spatially undetermined. Thus Kupka arrives at a more immediate and intuitive dynamic image based on the tensions generated by form and color alone, finally freed from subject matter, illusionistic devices and theoretical premises.

Kupka's *Disks of Newton* are often compared to the solar disks of Robert Delaunay. The comparison is apt, although the relationship between the two artists is not clear. Kupka and Delaunay had many friends in common, artists and writers who visited back and forth between Paris and Puteaux. Delaunay himself visited Puteaux upon occasion. Although Kupka was a member of the Puteaux group starting in 1911, his participation in their activities was sporadic. Older than most of the participating artists, according to some eyewitnesses he was upset because they did not consider him a mentor.[48] He also felt they leaned too far toward Cubism. Furthermore, he was known to complain bitterly that when he showed them his work, they picked up his ideas. By 1913, according to his correspondence with Roessler[49] and other first-hand accounts, he had retired into relative seclusion.[50]

Clearly, Kupka was never a Cubist. He passed directly from a form of Fauvism to a post-Cubist idiom, in which spatial structure derived from units of color and motion, two pictorial components which were outside the sphere of pure Cubist theory and practice. Still more peculiar to Kupka's personal style was his identification of consecutive color with consecutive motion, or a sequential unfolding of measures of color. Ultimately, as we have seen, through his interpenetration of space and time, he arrived at the dissolution of the object and sublimated it into an abstract image of the kinetic dimension. Thus he bypassed Futurism as well.

Delaunay, on the other hand, was more closely involved with the Cubist and Neo-Impressionist traditions, as expressed through fragmentation, contrast and complementarity of forms, light and color. His 1909-11 *Eiffel*

48 Interviews (1974) with Gabrielle Buffet-Picabia, who attended the Puteaux meetings and Juliette Gleizes. Although Mme. Gleizes was not present at the meetings, she reported her husband's impressions.

49 See p. 47 above.

50 Again, Gabrielle Buffet-Picabia reported that the Puteaux artists complained that Kupka refused to participate in their discussions, even though he lived next door to Villon's house, where weekly meetings were held.

Towers, for example, are disjointed and twisted in a writhing spatial continuum. Rising among tortured cityscapes, shards of light and burgeoning or brittle cloud formations, they are beautiful and broken images whose intensity is enhanced by sharply defined color contrasts. As Apollinaire said about Delaunay's paintings of this period, they showed "forms fractured by light."

Only his most nuanced works, the 1912 *Windows* series, show a subtle unification of plane, color and light. The diffuse flicker which skims the surface of these paintings is punctuated by passages and contrasts much in the manner of Cézanne. Here color generates a web of structure; the laws of complementarity are ignored.

Delaunay's *Disks,* or *Sun and Moon* pictures, begun in 1913, on the contrary show a more contrasted palette. The segments of flat pure pigment suggest a more systematic approach to color. In these paintings, Delaunay sought to portray motion through color interaction. At first glance, many of his *Disks* appear more lively than Kupka's evenly scaled progressions. However a closer look reveals that the former are singularly non-dynamic. Just as a spinning color wheel loses its intensity—dissolving into tonal values or becoming gray or white—the brightly contrasted intervals of Delaunay's *Disks* arrest them peremptorily in space.

Although at least one of Delaunay's *Disks* is dated 1912, no works of this series were exhibited in his January 1913 one-man exhibition in Berlin. He sent three paintings to the New York Armory Show in March 1913, but no *Disks* were among them. His first references to them are in his letters of April to June 1913. In particular, in a letter to Macke of June 1913, he expresses his excitement about these new works based on the structure of color. He first exhibited his *Disks* late in 1913, at the Berlin *Herbstsalon.* They were not shown in France until after World War I.[51]

Without drawing any conclusions about the nature of Delaunay's relationship to Kupka, the priority of Kupka's circular color forms can be securely argued. Furthermore, Kupka's interest in rotational form went far beyond the theorizing about motion, color and light then in fashion. The study of these phenomena were merely dimensions of Kupka's concept of the function of painting, which was to capture the rhythmic unity and diversity of the cosmos. As we have seen, Kupka's development followed a single unswerving path: from the microcosm of human experience to the intuited rhythms of the Final Cause.

Kupka and the Cosmic Order

The Final Cause was in fact Kupka's primary cause. It is evident that a teleological vision was the subliminal source of Kupka's aesthetic. His early mystical experiences, his clairvoyant sensibility, his exposure to German Romantic philosophy, Theosophy and occult disciplines shaped an approach to the work of art, even in formal terms, which set him apart from his French contemporaries. Despite his attempts to rid himself of the influences of his Central European background, the imprint of his original intellectual and spiritual milieu would leave an indelible mark. What Kupka

51 The author is grateful to Virginia Spate for clarifying the dates and facts relating to Delaunay's *Disks.*

learned in Paris, concerning motion, color and the function of painting itself, was a vocabulary and syntax with which to express his inner vision. But his vision would remain peculiarly his own.

For Kupka, the mission of the artist was a cosmic one, and this point of view, as well as the style and content of his thinking as seen in his 1910-11 notes, show a definite debt to Goethe. Kupka obviously read Goethe in Prague or Vienna; Goethe was one of the most pervasive cultural influences of the time. Even earlier, Studnička may have referred to Goethe's color theory. However any early knowledge was surely revitalized by Kupka's reading of Rudolf Steiner who, starting in 1883, edited and annotated Goethe's writings on art and published his own essays on Goethe's aesthetics. Through Steiner, many aspects of Goethe's artistic philosophy filtered into the basic ideology of the Munich Theosophical group.

Kupka's most fundamental premises—that nature has a spiritual reality determined by final causes, that the hidden laws of this reality are present in all of nature's manifestations including man and that the artist's function is to make visible these laws, not by copying nature but by creating a parallel order—spring from Goethe's aesthetic. More specifically, Kupka's terminology echoes Steiner's formulation of Goethe's thought. For example, Steiner discusses Goethe's discovery that "the Beautiful is not . . . an Idea in the form of a sensory phenomenon, but *a sensory phenomenon in the form of an Idea*."[52] Parallel to this, Kupka noted on the first page of his 1910-11 notebook, "Formerly I was seeking to give form to an idea; now I am seeking the idea which corresponds to the form."[53]

In this context, Kupka's philosophy of art presents striking analogies with that of Kandinsky. This was apparent even during Kupka's lifetime, since he always argued defensively that he discovered Kandinsky's *Uber das Geistige in der Kunst* in 1913, when his ideas and his abstraction were already fully formulated. The most obvious similarities in the two artists' thought are in the concept of a hidden necessity or hidden laws in nature; the idea that art does not copy nature but is subjected to the same cosmic order; and the notion that whereas the artist's vision or interpretation of the universal order may be subjective, the means of transmission—the medium—must be objective.[54] Since both Kupka and Kandinsky were indebted to Goethe's aesthetic and to Steiner's interpretation of it[55], it seems apparent that neither artist influenced the other but both were drawing on the same source.

Kupka's study of the natural sciences was consistent with his ideology. Through a better understanding of natural causes, rhythms, structures and progressions, he hoped to develop a parallel vision, order and language. His interest in physiology, biology and astronomy therefore had their roots in mystical thought. By extension, he paid acute attention to his own sense impressions and evoked coenesthesis as a form of access to higher knowledge. Through a close observation of his own body's rhythms, reactions to stimuli, sense perceptions, emotional responses, he attempted to develop a sixth sense, an extrasensory receptivity which he believed led to a state of superconsciousness, a term Kupka appropriated from H. P. Blavatsky.

52 See discussion in Sixten Ringbom, "Art in 'The Epoch of the Great Spiritual,'" *Journal of the Warburg and Courtauld Institutes,* London, XXIX, 1966, pp. 390-391.

53 Kupka, Manuscript I, p. 1.

54 See p. 48 above.

55 See Ringbom, op. cit., for discussion of Kandinsky in this context.

The Theosophical concept of superconsciousness is equivalent to that of clairvoyant vision or a hypnotized trance. In this experience the perceiver's relationship to matter and space is altogether different from that of conscious perception. The objects perceived exist as disconnected fragments; they have no defined spatial position, no volume, no gravity. They have no utilitarian function, no relation to the laws of lived or conceptualized reality. They are seen only in terms of intensity of existence, profundity of significance and relations within their immediate pattern.[56] Space itself, free from the constraints of conceptual thought, is determined by neither depth nor relationships; it does not exist as an organic whole. Colors have the intensity of preternatural and non-verbalized experience. Superconsciousness allows one to see worlds in a plot of grass, as Kupka said to Roessler in 1913.[57]

Through his experience as a medium and his life-long receptivity to visions, Kupka was predisposed to superconsciousness and conversant with the kind of perceptions it made accessible. In an early letter from Paris to Roessler, Kupka describes a clairvoyant vision which is revealing of the extra-worldly dimension of his experience—the insights and images which he accepted as quite normal: "Yesterday I had a mood of split consciousness where it seemed that I was observing the globe from the outside. I was in great empty space and saw the planets rolling quietly. After that it was difficult to come back to the trivia of everyday life."[58]

Since Kupka believed that the artist was a visionary, his clairvoyant perceptions were eminently meaningful to him as reflections of a superconscious state. They provided the structure of much of his imagery. In 1912-13, he described the artist's relationship to inner visions in the following terms:

In our inner visions, the different fragments which float in our heads are incoherently situated in space. Even in remembered so-called representative images of organic complexes, they are so strangely situated that the painter . . . who would wish to project them would have to go even beyond the fourth dimension. Some parts penetrate each other; others seem completely detached, disconnected from the organism to which they are supposed to belong. The same is true of purely subjective visions where often only fragments, plexuses of forms, or colors are given. Before we can seize them and set them down, we must draw lines between them and establish a structural coherence. But often they will never form a coherent, logical or intelligible whole.[59]

Thus the artist organizes his imaginary or mental images and tries to project them in concrete form. A Theosophical text about clairvoyant images, Annie Besant's and C. W. Leadbeater's *Thought-Forms,* formulates the same visualizing process: ". . . the painter who forms a conception of the future picture builds it up out of the matter of his mental body, and then projects it into space in front of him, keeps it before his mind's eye, and copies it."[60] Although this particular passage refers to figurative images derived from material objects, another passage evokes images (or "thought-forms") which express pure feeling or thought. Apparently the Nabis and the Cubists knew this text, and Kandinsky referred to it frequently.[61]

56 Many of the terms used here are borrowed from Aldous Huxley's descriptions of the mescalin experience, in *The Doors of Perception* and *Heaven and Hell*, New York, 1963, particularly p. 20. The drug-induced trance is comparable to the experience of clairvoyance or hypnosis.

57 See p. 47 above.

58 Letter to Roessler, February 7, 1897.

59 Kupka, Manuscript II, p. 28.

60 Annie Besant and C. W. Leadbeater, *Thought-Forms,* Wheaton, Illinois, 1971, p. 27. First published in English in 1901, French translation 1905, German translation, 1908. The author is grateful to Yvonne Hagen for bringing this book to her attention.

61 See Ringbom, op. cit., pp. 397-398 and his fn. 73.

Kupka's visionary sensibility and his cosmic philosophy united to form a peculiar notion of higher reality. In turn, this notion of a higher reality influenced his concept of space. His mystical background helps us to understand the fundamental spatial contradictions in his art. Although Kupka spoke frequently, sometimes obsessively, of the two-dimensional specificity of the painter's art, at other times he as easily evoked the fourth or fifth dimension. This theoretical inconsistency is reflected equally strongly in his paintings. Only occasional works can be defined as strictly two-dimensional. More often, there is an ambiguous allusion to spatial depth, a fourth dimension which, as defined by Apollinaire, "represents the immensity of space eternalizing itself in all directions at any given moment. It is space itself, the dimension of the infinite . . . ."[62]

In fact, it would be valid to say that Kupka's theories were not only inconsistent, they were incompatible with his vision. His vision, based on forms in nature elevated to the status of an idea, dictated his images and their spatial context. Many components of his vision are recognizable. They derive from crystals of frost on a window, the organic structure of a flower, stalactite and stalagmite concretions, the concentric ripples of water, prehistoric Celtic stone formations, banks of clouds, photographs or models of the moon and planets. Kupka selected these phenomena as manifestations of major natural laws. Disembodied as they passed through the filter of his superconsciousness, the incarnate laws were translated into abstract pictorial ideas.

Romantic naturalism.

Kupka's concept of cosmic rhythms and cosmic space is most literally depicted in the body of work inspired by reproductions of the moon. The artist may have seen the large-scale model of the moon displayed at Uccle where he visited Onésime Reclus in 1909.[63] He devoured journals on astronomy and was an assiduous visitor to the Observatoire, the Palais de la Découverte and the Musée des Arts et Métiers, where photographs of the moon and planets were displayed.

Kupka appropriated the image of the moon and the space surrounding it first almost literally, then as a basic spatial framework for many studies of the period 1909-14. In the latter case he created an infinite undetermined space of cosmic implications within which can be seen a reminiscence of the moon's surface (cat. nos. 77-78). This lunar impression remains at an undefined distance from the surface plane. Sometimes it suggests concavity, a tunnelling through space to boundless depths; at other times the background appears as a bulge, which nonetheless never disrupts the frontal plane.

A series of paintings started in 1911 effectively and explicitly captures this infinite yet ambiguous recessive depth (cat. nos. 80, 81). Pulsating organic matter and free-floating clouds swell forward, in sharp contrast to a dramatic thrust into luminous and infinite depth in the central area. The circular rhythms which inform the whole composition project a sense of dynamic biomorphic growth and cosmic gravitation. Some more reductive studies which continue to explore this kind of space show a silhouette of revolving intertwined bands in the left foreground, set off against a luminous zone of

62 Apollinaire, *Les Peintres cubistes*, 1913, Chapter 3. English translation from Edward F. Fry, op. cit., p. 116. (see fn. 31).

63 This hypothesis was first suggested by Fédit in her preface to exhibition catalogue, *Kupka avant 1914*, Paris, Galerie Karl Flinker, 1966, n.p.

infinitely receding color, bounded on the right by an arc of light. Again a nebulous sense of perspective is created.

The cosmic theme could assimilate and reinforce other pictorial preoccupations such as rotational dynamics and the theatrical use of colored light. Arbitrary spatial articulation was also justified by it. For inasmuch as cosmic gravitation implies attraction to a pole which may be anywhere in space, Kupka was freed from the necessity of dealing with gravity or perspective in conventional terms.

Kupka's emancipation from traditional spatial conventions was essential to his vision and is illustrated in a broad variety of themes initiated during the period 1911-14. These themes provided the formal and conceptual framework of his oeuvre for approximately the next fifteen years. Throughout their development, his forms shifted back and forth between biomorphic and geometric schemata, softly graded tonal compositions and brittle brightly contrasted patterns. But the artist's preoccupations remained consistent: the rhythms of growth or expansion, consecutive or cyclical motion, the dynamic interplay of color and light.

The painting *Around a Point* (cat. no. 160) is the consummate expression of Kupka's vision. The clear syncopated rhythms of dissected circles spinning around telescoping axes, the chromatic juxtapositions which recall the highlights and tonal shading of floral and faunal nature, intermittently broken or fused by zones of hot white light and, finally, the monumental scale of the image which swells to bursting beyond the frame, evoke a supreme cosmic vision.

Most histories of twentieth-century art identify Kupka as an Orphic painter. Orphism, or Orphic Cubism, as defined by Apollinaire "is the art of painting new structures with elements which have not been borrowed from the visual sphere, but have been created entirely by the artist himself, and been endowed by him with fullness of reality. The works of the orphic artist must simultaneously give a pure aesthetic pleasure; a structure which is self-evident; and a sublime meaning, that is, a subject. This is pure art."[64] Apollinaire's examples included Picasso, Delaunay, Léger, Picabia and Duchamp. Kupka's name is not mentioned.

Apollinaire coined his definition in the autumn of 1912, apparently at the *Section d'Or* exhibition. Eyewitnesses writing several decades later reported that Apollinaire invented the term in front of Kupka's paintings, calling attention to their self-generating dynamics (*"cette peinture puisant son dynamisme en elle-même"*) and comparing them to music.[65] There is still some question as to whether this event actually took place.[66] In any case, Kupka was never satisfied with the Orphic designation. He expressed his displeasure on many occasions, explaining that a comparison of his work with music was an extreme simplification, and solely based on the inclusion of musical terms in his titles.

Apollinaire's understanding of Kupka's art as representative of Orphic Cubism is not only a simplification but inexact. Kupka's reference to music

64 Apollinaire, op. cit., Chapter 7. English translation from Fry, op. cit., p. 117.

65 See Nicolas Bauduin, "Les Temps héroiques, à propos du Salon de la Section d'Or," *Masques et Visages,* no. 39, June 1956, p. 7.

66 See pp. 310-11, fn. 6.

or poetry was of no more significance than that of Seurat or Signac or any of the other artists who evoked the notion of correspondences between the arts. In Kupka's case, the musical terms were intended to discourage the viewer from looking for literal subject matter and stimulate him to consider chromatic and structural rhythms alone. Although Kupka's art may be superficially related to Cubism in his rejection of volume and perspective, his aesthetic may as plausibly be associated with that of many other artists. It echoes Seurat in the combination of the metaphysical and the scientific; it is parallel to Futurism in the artist's understanding of motion and light as the only two forces which can penetrate and dissolve matter; it shows analogies with Mondrian and Kandinsky in its reference to a cosmic order.

On a more fundamental level, Apollinaire's terminology is inappropriate in that it reflects the emphasis, common among writers of the period 1910-13, upon the priority of the conceptual over the perceptual experience. For the Cubist painter, the conceptual reality of an object was superior to its perceived reality. He therefore complemented what he saw with what he knew, moving around the object to capture all facets of its outer appearance and presenting them in simultaneity.

Apollinaire notwithstanding, Kupka *did* borrow from the visual sphere, as did all the artists the poet named in this context. Kupka's subject *was* perceptual reality. His aesthetic did not allow him to discard the forms of nature and, like the Cubists and even Kandinsky and Mondrian, distill his lived experience into abstract schemas and ciphers. For Kupka, the spiritual reality or cosmic order which governs nature *is present* in natural forms. The phenomenon is not a symbol; it is an order incarnate. And without the particular configuration of each manifestation in the phenomenal world, the order, idea or noumen would be invisible and inaccessible to human understanding.

For Kupka, the artist's role is to decipher the idea inherent in the phenomena of perceptual experience, and to present concrete forms where the idea is clearly visible. Thus Kupka aspired to an imagery in which a richness of sensuous presence, a clarity of structure, and rhythmic implications of dynamic change would simultaneously express the true nature of experience in both physical and metaphysical terms.

CATALOGUE OF THE EXHIBITION

by Margit Rowell

The chronology and dating of the individual works are the author's. It must be remembered that Kupka rarely dated works at the time of their execution. Most of his dates were given retrospectively at the time of his 1946 Prague exhibition. The dates of the present catalogue are based on exhibition histories, the artist's notes and letters, and stylistic considerations.

Citations of Fédit and Vachtová refer to Denise Fédit, *L'Oeuvre de Kupka,* Paris, 1966 and Ludmila Vachtová, *Frank Kupka, Pioneer of Abstract Art,* New York and Toronto, 1968.

Complete information is cited here only for exhibitions which do not recur and in which only one or two works appear. Full information for all other exhibitions is given in the selected exhibitions list, pp. 318 to 322. * denotes one-man show. Names of exhibitions are given only for Salons; the names of galleries are included but museum names are listed only when necessary to distinguish between two or more exhibitions taking place in the same city in one year. In cases of traveling exhibitions with a single catalogue, only the year in which the show originated is given. However in circulating exhibitions where each institution produced its own catalogue, or where the painting was not shown at all participating museums, separate dates are listed.

MNAM is Musée National d'Art Moderne, Paris
MOMA, The Museum of Modern Art, New York
NG, Národní Galerie, Prague
SRGM, The Solomon R. Guggenheim Museum, New York

†denotes not in exhibition

†1 *Money (L'Argent).* 1899

Oil on canvas, 31⅞ x 31⅞″
(81 x 81 cm.)
Signed lr "Kupka"
Vachtová, no. 16, repr. p. 44
Collection Národní Galerie, Prague
(O 2191)

PROVENANCE:

the artist
Jindřich Waldes
to present owner, 1940

EXHIBITIONS:

*Písek—České Budějovice, 1961,
    no. 1
Dobruška, 1962
*Prague, 1968, no. 11, repr.

One of Kupka's more obviously Symbolist paintings, *Money* shows the influence of Segantini (in the fine pin-striping of the woman's body) and of Ensor (in the row of demonic figures in the right background and in the palette). Segantini was well known in Eastern and Western Europe at the turn of the century and exhibited in Vienna in 1896 and 1898 in shows Kupka probably saw. He also exhibited in Paris in 1898 and his work was widely reproduced. As for Ensor, the gallery La Plume held a retrospective of his work in 1898, and the magazine of the same name devoted a special issue to him. Kupka himself exhibited prints at the gallery in 1899, and the Ensor issue of *La Plume* remained in his library until his death.

A pastel drawing of the same subject is signed and dated 1899 (NG, Prague). A dedication to Machar was added later. The theme of the lurid fascination of money would be taken up again in Kupka's 1902 illustrations for *L'Assiette au beurre*. The woman depicted is Kupka's friend Gabrielle.

†2 *The Way of Silence (La Voie du Silence).* 1900?

Pastel on paper, 22⅞ x 25⅝"
(58.1 x 65 cm.)

Signed and inscribed lr "Kupka quam
ad causam sumus"

Collection Národní Galerie, Prague

PROVENANCE:

the artist
Jindřich Waldes
to present owner, 1940

Although drawn in Paris, the subject of sphinxes and the philosophical query
"Quam ad causum sumus" ("Why are we here?") are carry-overs from the artist's
Viennese years. When Kupka arrived in Paris, he tried to escape from what he
considered decadent metaphysical inquiry and find his sources of inspiration in
the perceptual world. Nonetheless, until c. 1902-03, themes of this sort persist.
The central figure is the artist's self-portrait.

3   *Black Idol or Defiance (L'Idole*
    noire or La Résistance, La Révolte,
    L'Entêtement). 1900

Colored aquatint, 17⅝ x 15″
(44.8 x 38.2 cm.)

Signed lr "Kupka"

Fédit, no. 1, repr.
Vachtová, addenda cat. no. 1

Collection The Solomon R.
Guggenheim Museum, New York,
Gift of Andrée Martinel-Kupka, 1975

PROVENANCE:

the artist
Andrée Martinel-Kupka
to present owner, gift

Among the several titles of this aquatint, the Prague version is called *La Résistance,* the Paris version *L'Entêtement,* and photographs which remained in Kupka's possession were marked on the back *La Révolte.* All seemed to mean essentially the same thing to Kupka, best translated in English as *Defiance,* and all were probably added somewhat later. The aquatint is an illustration for Poe's "Dreamland," in which the first stanza reads:

> *By a route obscure and lonely,*
> *Haunted by ill angels only,*
> *Where an Eidolon, named NIGHT,*
> *On a black throne reigns upright,*
> *I have reached these lands but newly,*
> *From an ultimate dim Thule—*
> *From a wild weird clime that lieth, sublime,*
> *Out of SPACE—out of TIME.*

Kupka did many variations on this theme (mostly pencil drawings) in which the idol is seen facing different directions. It is interesting to compare Kupka's image to a drawing by Fernand Fau, reproduced in *La Plume,* no. 234, of January 15, 1899,[1] representing *Le Destin* (Fate) as a monumental and menacing single statue-like figure seated amidst the ripples of a whirlpool.

According to Fédit (p. 29), there was a painting on this theme (present where-abouts unknown).

1 Slatkine reprints, Geneva, 1968, p. 49.

4 *The Beginning of Life* or *Water Lilies (Les Nénuphars).* 1900

Colored aquatint, 13⅝ x 13⅝″
(34.5 x 34.5 cm.)

Signed ll "Kupka"

Fédit, no. 2, repr.

Musée National d'Art Moderne,
Paris (AM 10 889-Gr.)

PROVENANCE:

the artist
Eugénie Kupka
to present owner, gift, 1963

Known both as *Water Lilies* and *The Beginning of Life,* the first title is surely incorrect. Since this is probably the illustration of a Theosophical idea, the flowers are certainly lotus. This identification of the flowers is supported by the watercolor, *The Soul of the Lotus* (1898) in which exactly the same blossoms are found. The Theosophical subject is described by Madame Blavatsky in *Isis Unveiled* (first published in 1877): "Man is a little world—a microcosm inside the great universe. Like a foetus, he is suspended by all his three spirits, in the matrix of the macrocosmos; and while his terrestrial body is in sympathy with its parent earth, his astral soul lives in unison with the sidereal *anima mundi....*"[1] The depiction of the fetus is quite naturalistic, reflecting Kupka's interest in the natural sciences. The coloring and atmosphere of Kupka's aquatints of this period evoke Redon, an artist he knew and admired not only for his use of color but for his mystical insights.

1 Quoted from Robert Welsh, in *Piet Mondrian, 1872-1944: Centennial Exhibition,* New York, The Solomon R. Guggenheim Museum, 1971, p. 46.

5   *The Witches (Les Sorcières).*
1900-01

Pastel on paper, 10¼ x 10¼″
(26 x 26 cm.)
Unsigned
Collection Nancy Schwartz

PROVENANCE:
the artist
Estate of the artist
Karl Flinker
to present owner

This pastel may be inspired by Kupka's interest in Edgar Allen Poe, and may even allude to Poe's "The Black Cat," a story which illustrates the superstitious belief that a black cat is a witch in disguise. This pastel relates to a group of drawings of c. 1898-1900 in which Kupka depicted women identified as witches in mysterious, sometimes supernatural, settings. Some of these drawings reveal a debt to Félicien Rops, another artist published by *La Plume,* whom Kupka admired. The most prominent woman, with blond hair, probably represented Maria Bruhn. Gabrielle is seated behind her on the right. The rocks in the foreground resemble those found on the seacoast at Trégastel where Kupka spent the summer of 1900. They are found in many works of 1900-02.

†6   Illustration for Sova's *Ballad*.
1901-02

Ink on paper, 11¾ x 8″
(30 x 20.2 cm.)

Signed ll "Kupka"

Collection Národní Galerie, Prague
(K 12.397)

PROVENANCE:

the artist
to present owner, 1949

This is a preliminary drawing for the illustrations of *Balada o jednom člověku a jeho radostech [Ballad of a Man and his Joys],* by the Czech poet Antonin Sova (1864-1928), published in 1903. The Národní Galerie, Prague, owns at least two of these drawings which show Kupka's typical illustrational style of the period. The two women in this drawing, here mounted on men's shoulders, are the same as those on horseback in *Ballad-Joys* (cat. no. 8). This motif, together with the similar title, suggests that the literary work may have been a catalyst for the painting.

†7   Study for *Ballad-Joys*. 1901-02

Colored crayons on white paper,
17⅜ x 11⅛″ (44.1 x 28.3 cm.)

Unsigned

Collection Národní Galerie, Prague
(K 4986)

PROVENANCE:

the artist
Jindřich Waldes
to present owner, 1940

In sharp contrast to the many academic studies Kupka did for *Ballad-Joys,* this drawing shows a completely dematerialized silhouette seemingly composed of auras of colored light. The supernatural impression produced suggests an astral rather than a physical portrait of Kupka's friend Gabrielle.

†8 *Ballad-Joys (Epona-ballade)*.
1901-02

Oil on wood, 32⅞ x 49⅞"
(83.5 x 126.5 cm.)

Signed and dated lr "Kupka//1901"

Vachtová, no. 17, repr. p. 51; color
pl. 1

Collection Národní Galerie, Prague
(O 1822)

PROVENANCE:

the artist
K. E. Schmidt, 1902
George Barbier, Paris
Jindřich Waldes, May 1932
to present owner, 1940

EXHIBITIONS:

Paris, 1902, no. 663, repr.
St. Louis, 1904, no. 165 (as *Joy*)
*Prague, 1906, no. 56
*Paris, 1936, Jeu de Paume, no. 2
  (dated 1902)
*Prague, 1946, Mánes, no. 3 (dated
  1901)
*Písek—České Budějovice, 1961,
  no. 2
Hluboké—Brno, 1966, no. 221
*Prague, 1968, no. 12, repr.
*Belgrade, 1969, no. 1, repr.

When Kupka painted this canvas, he was deeply immersed in the study of pagan antiquity and symbolism. The painting is sometimes called *Epona-ballade,* a title found on a label on the reverse, which refers to the Roman goddess Epona, protectress of horses, mules and donkeys. Perhaps of Celtic origin, she was particularly honored in Gaul, Germania and the valley of the Danube.

However Kupka's personal symbolism may be more complex. In letters to Machar of around the same period, he wrote that he felt as vigorous as a colt and was doing many studies of horses. The two women depicted have been identified as his past and present loves, Maria Bruhn and Gabrielle. Since the Sova illustration (cat. no. 6) shows the same two women on human male mounts, the horses here may be symbolic of male partners, or even of Kupka himself.

That Kupka's ambitions were more general or allegorical is indicated in a letter to Machar of 1902: "Using subtle, quite simple means I want to express something of what I felt when I used to sit alone on the seashore . . . . The seashore and the clouds are humming with some unknown joy. In the air thousands of elves seem to dance about joyfully . . . . All of us have a desire for joy, for some pure immaterial feeling of well-being. I want everyone who sees the picture to experience such feelings . . . ." (quoted in Vachtová, p. 45)

The seascape which also appears in many gouaches of the period is inspired by the beaches at Trégastel in Brittany. The fine pastel pin-striping threaded with white in the sky once again shows Kupka's divisionist style (see cat. no. 1), seen here probably for the last time. When *Ballad* was exhibited at the 1902 *Salon National des Beaux-Arts,* the landscape included high rock formations in the right background. At this time, the painting belonged to Kupka's friend the German art historian K. E. Schmidt. A gouache dedicated to Schmidt depicting the same formations is in The Museum of Modern Art, New York (*Window on the Beach,* probably 1901, The Joan and Lester Avnet Collection). By 1903, when the painting was reproduced in the Czech magazine *Volné Směry,* the background rocks had been painted out. This canvas was obviously important to Kupka, as he showed it frequently in the years after it was painted. *Ballad-Joys* is probably his last symbolic painting.

9   *Horsemen (Les Cavaliers).*
1901-02

India ink on paper, 16 x 21¼″
(40.5 x 54 cm.)
Signed lr "Kupka"
Musée National d'Art Moderne,
Paris (AM 2771—D)

PROVENANCE:

the artist
Eugénie Kupka
to present owner, gift, 1963

Emile Reynaud, Praxinoscope, invented
1876, patented 1877.

At least three small pencil sketches on the same theme exist: The Museum of
Modern Art, New York, Study Collection; Collection Karl Flinker, Paris; Národní
Galerie drawings collection, Prague. However none of them contribute to a more
secure dating.

For a discussion of this drawing, see p. 54.

10 *The Sleeper (La Dormeuse).* 1902

Etching, 7⅛ x 4⅞" (18 x 12.5 cm.)
Signed ll in plate "Kupka"
Vachtová, repr. p. 112 (dated 1907)
Collection Karl Flinker

PROVENANCE:

the artist
Eugénie Kupka
to present owner

Once again Kupka draws his inspiration from Edgar Allen Poe whose poem "The Sleeper" was translated into French as *"La Dormeuse"* at least as early as 1862.[1] The second stanza describes a pale woman with long hair sleeping in a canopied bed around which wild breezes move the curtains and create fantastic and sometimes terrifying shadows. In earlier more literal versions of the same theme, Kupka shows monstrous forms, similar to those found in *Money,* watching over the bed. The vertical format, rich linear quality and taut arabesque motifs recall Alphonse Mucha's exemplary Art Nouveau style. The contrasts created by shading and crosshatching are comparabe to master etchers Kupka admired such as Rops and Whistler.

Kupka did a large number of variations on this theme, some of which are highly contrasted and fully rendered in a more popular illustrational style. Some show a dying rather than a sleeping woman. Kupka's subject may be drawn in part from Maria Bruhn's death in Vienna in 1898, which he witnessed. Whatever the inspiration, this final etching appears to be the most subtle distillation of the theme. Vachtová (p. 70) has suggested that this etching was conceived as an illustration for Mallarmé's "Hérodiade." However, the title, subject and inscriptions on preliminary versions reveal that Kupka was illustrating Poe's poem.

1 in *Contes inédits d'Edgar Poe,* translated from the English by William L. Hughes, Paris, Collection Hetzel, E. Jung-Treuttel, 1862, pp. 303-306.

11a-b   Two special issues of *L'Assiette au beurre*
   a.   *L'Argent (Money)*. 1902

         12⅝ x 9¾″ (32.1 x 24.8 cm.)
         Private Collection, New York

   b.   *Religions (Religions)*. 1904

         12½ x 9¾″ (31.8 x 24.8 cm.)
         Private Collection, New York

Between 1901 and 1904, Kupka did many satirical illustrations for the anarchist magazine *L'Assiette au beurre*. He was also commissioned for three special issues exclusively illustrated by him on the themes of *Money* (January 11, 1902); *Religion* (May 7, 1904) and *Peace* (August 20, 1904).

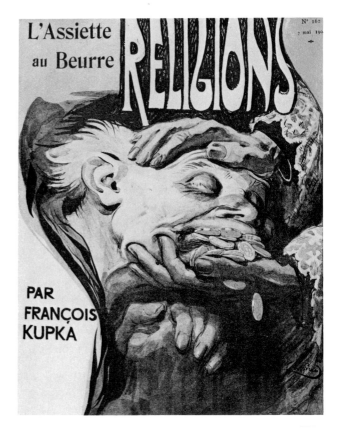

12 *Nude in Black Stockings (Nu aux bas noirs).* c. 1904

Oil on paperboard, 28⅜ x 15″
(72 x 38 cm.)

Signed lr "Kupka"

Collection Dr. Altmayer, Paris

PROVENANCE:

the artist
Andrée Martinel-Kupka
to present owner

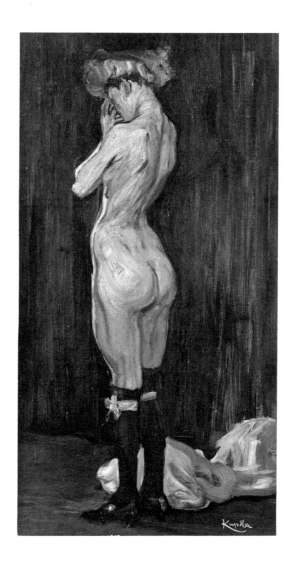

Rops, *Les Exercices de dévotion de Monsieur Henri Roche,* color etching, Courtesy Lucien Goldschmidt, Inc., New York.

1 *Félicien Rops,* catalogue raisonné by Maurice Exsteens, 1928, vol. II, no. 362.

2 One thinks for example of Toulouse-Lautrec's *La Modiste (The Hatmaker)* of 1900, Musée d'Albi, France

Kupka did at least two earlier paintings on this theme (NG, Prague), as well as one known pastel (Spencer A. Samuels and Company, Ltd., 1968, cat. no. 4). The other oil versions dating from 1902-03 are more conventional in color and form and place more importance on the setting (furnishings of a dressing-room, mirrors, draperies, etc.). The most obvious and probable source of this theme is an etching by Félicien Rops called *Les Exercices de dévotion de Monsieur Henri Roche (The Devotional Exercises of Monsieur Henri Roche)*[1] showing a young girl in black stockings standing before her dressing table (fig.). Yet Kupka's style as it has developed here reveals a debt to Toulouse-Lautrec. Since Kupka made posters for night clubs in Montmartre and lived almost directly over Aristide Bruant's cabaret, he was certainly acquainted with the French artist's work. The influence of Toulouse-Lautrec is seen in the fluidity of color, the lush yet muted tonal combinations and the intimate glow of the composition, as well as in the psychologically astute depiction of the figure's solitude.[2] Most importantly, this c. 1904 painting shows an early attempt to deal with the autonomous expressive powers of color.

†13 *Dancers.* 1904-05

Sanguine and charcoal on paper,
17⅝ x 21⅛″ (44.7 x 53.8 cm.)

Signed lr "Kupka"

Collection Národní Galerie, Prague
(K 12751)

PROVENANCE:

the artist
to present owner, 1906

14 *Portrait of Madame Kupka I (Portrait de Madame Kupka I)*. 1905

Oil on mattress ticking, 24¾ x 24¾″
(63 x 63 cm.)

Signed and dated ur "Kupka//1905;"
inscribed ll "JANVIER//1905"

Fédit, no. 13, repr.

Vachtová, no. 32, repr. p. 294

Musée National d'Art Moderne,
Paris (AM 3560–P)

PROVENANCE:

the artist
Eugénie Kupka
to present owner, 1957

EXHIBITIONS:

*Paris, 1936, Jeu de Paume (hors
   catalogue, information from installation photograph)
*Prague, 1946, Mánes, no. 8
*Paris, 1958, MNAM, no. 1

Painted from a photograph of Madame Kupka which shows her in an almost identical position (see Fédit, cat. no. 13, p. 33), this portrait reveals Kupka's conventional painterly style and is one of the earliest known examples of Kupka working from a photograph. The date is probably correct as it does not seem to have been added later as is so often the case. In 1919 Kupka did a replica of this portrait at his patron Waldes' request (now in NG, Prague).

15 *The Song of Songs (Le Cantique
   des Cantiques).* 1905

15½ x 11½″ (39.4 x 29.3 cm.)
Private Collection, New York

Kupka made three illustrated editions of *The Song of Songs,* published in 1905,
1928 and 1931. The illustrations for all three, executed before 1909, reveal the full
range of Kupka's decorative style at that time, a style which drew on Viennese
Secession motifs, decorative arts and folk art, and show thorough knowledge of
the art of book illustration.

15 *The Song of Songs (Le Cantique
   des Cantiques).* 1905

98

16 *Standing Woman, Study for Autumn Sun (Femme debout, étude pour Soleil d'automne).* 1905

Watercolor and pencil on paper,
21½ x 15⅜" (54.5 x 39 cm.)
Stamped lr "Kupka"
Collection Karl Flinker

PROVENANCE:

the artist
Eugénie Kupka
to present owner

17 *Autumn Sun (Soleil d'automne).*
1905-06

Oil on canvas, 40½ x 46⅛″
(103 x 117 cm.)

Signed lr "Kupka"

Vachtová, no. 54, incorrect repr. p. 60

Collection Národní Galerie, Prague
(O 3835)

PROVENANCE:

the artist
Eugénie Kupka
to present owner, 1946

EXHIBITIONS:

Paris, 1906, *Salon d'Automne,*
no. 896
Vienna, 1908, no. 12
*Paris, 1936, Jeu de Paume, no. 14
(dated 1906)
*Písek—České Budějovice, 1961 (hors
catalogue)
*Prague, 1968, no. 24, repr.

The subject of three women, usually allegorical, was a popular one at the turn of the century (Munch, Klimt and others treated this theme). It is therefore not surprising to find it in Kupka's work, even though the meaning remains ambiguous.

Many studies and at least two oil paintings[1] were executed in preparation for the canvas seen here in its final form. Work on the theme was probably started in St. Prix during the summer of 1905. The apple tree in the garden was used in illustrations for *The Song of Songs* and it occurs again here.

The thick impasto, tonal density and heavily massed forms reveal an exposure to Germanic art, if not a northern temperament. Apparently Kupka traveled to Munich often after the turn of the century, although this is not clearly documented.

More interesting however is the gradual emergence of colored shadows, modeling the figures in lavenders, greens, turquoises; planes of color which are seen again tentatively in the pastel for the *Girl with a Ball* of 1907-08 (cat. no. 30), and which adumbrate *Planes by Colors: Large Nude* of 1909-10 (cat. no. 42). The vertical planes of horizontal or diagonal brushstrokes in the background evoke a rhythmic play of light and shadow. They are seen for the first time here,[2] and they will appear in other works of 1906 (see cat. no. 19, for example).

An etching on this theme was exhibited at the 1910 *Salon d'Automne.* For further references and interpretations, see Fédit, cat. no. 16, p. 35.

1 MNAM, Paris, first version; NG, Prague, second version

2 After painting the final version, Kupka added similar vertical planes to the first of the two preparatory oil sketches.

18   Study after *Autumn Sun* (Etude d'après *Soleil d'automne*). 1906

Pencil on paper, 7⅞ x 6⅞"
(20 x 17.5 cm.)
Signed lr "Kupka"
Collection Karl Flinker

PROVENANCE:

the artist
Eugénie Kupka
to present owner

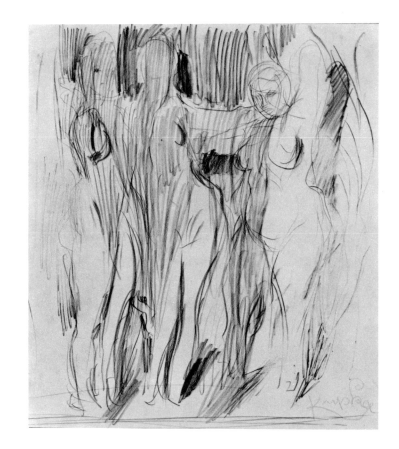

† 19   *Self-Portrait*. 1906

Oil on canvas, 25⅝ x 25⅝"
(65 x 65 cm.)
Signed and dated lr "Kupka 1905"
Vachtová, no. 30, repr. pp. 104-105
Collection Národní Galerie, Prague
(O 1807)

PROVENANCE:

the artist
Jindřich Waldes
to present owner, 1940

EXHIBITIONS:

*Prague, 1906, no. 133
Prague, 1939, no. 301
Prague, 1950
Gottwaldov, 1959
Liberec—Prague, 1959
Dobruška, 1962
Hluboké—Brno, 1966, no. 224
*Prague, 1968, no. 18, repr.
*Belgrade, 1969, no. 3, repr.

Although this *Self Portrait* is dated 1905, there is reason to believe it was painted in 1906. The most compelling evidence is provided by a photograph which undoubtedly served as a model for the painting and shows the artist in his Puteaux studio, where he moved in the early spring of 1906 (fig. larger repr. page 46). The photograph shows documents of Kupka's artistic activity which are of interest; some of the details also point to a 1906 dating.

Kupka in his studio, Puteaux, c. 1906.

On the far left are drawings for the book *Les Erinnyes,* which Kupka began working on in 1906. Two sketches are visible on Kupka's easel: directly under his hand is a drawing for *L'Homme et la terre,* on which he worked between 1904 and 1908. Under it one can see a study for *Autumn Sun* (see cat. no. 17). Tacked to the easel is a torn paper showing Egyptian figures in profile and Mycenaen motifs. Kupka began looking closely at the art of these cultures c. 1906, in preparation for *Les Erinnyes.*

On the wall behind Kupka's head is the painting *The Judgment of Paris* which he exhibited at the 1907 *Salon d'Automne* under the title *Project for a Mural Painting.* Below it hangs an antique scene of a man with two Percherons and women at a well, a painting signed and dated 1904, which shows the influence of Puvis de Chavannes. Finally, on the far right, one can see a large early version of Kupka's *Large Nude* (see cat. no. 42), a version which is documented nowhere else and which appears to have been lost.

In addition to the evidence offered by this photograph, the painting itself is more stylistically advanced than Kupka's 1905 work. Compared to the *Portrait of Madame Kupka* of 1905 (cat. no. 14), for example, here the clothing and background show a flatter more controlled brushwork. The vertical planes of light and shadow in the right-hand area were first seen in the late versions of *Autumn Sun,* also of 1906. Finally, examination reveals that the date was added sometime after the signature, a fact which makes the accuracy of the date questionable.

20 *Cabbage (Le Chou).* 1906

Oil on canvas, 28⅜ x 31½″
(72 x 80 cm.)

Signed lr "Kupka"

Fédit, no. 15, repr.
Vachtová, no. 46, repr. p. 99

Musée National d'Art Moderne,
Paris (AM 4163—P)

PROVENANCE:

the artist
Eugénie Kupka
to present owner, gift, 1963

EXHIBITIONS:

*Prague, 1946, Mánes, no. 10
*Cologne, 1967, no. 2, repr.; Munich,
1967, no. 2, repr.; Vienna 1967, no.
2; Amsterdam, 1968, no. 3, repr.;
Prague, 1968, no. 26, repr.

1 Manuscript 1, p. 18

The subject, probably drawn from Kupka's vegetable garden in Puteaux, illustrates his interest in the organic structural rhythms and textures found in nature. In Kupka's 1910-11 manuscript, he evokes the brilliant white borders formed by drops of rain on a spider web, and "the white velvet on the leaves of a cabbage" as natural phenomena full of artistic potential.[1] The loose spiraling organic structure around a central core will be found in much of Kupka's later abstract work. The painting's rich yet dark tonalities evoke a Northern painting tradition, as perpetuated in Ensor's still lifes, for example.

21 *Standing Woman, Rear View*
    (Femme debout, vue de dos). 1906

Etching, 9⅜ x 6¼″ (24 x 15.5 cm.)
Signed ll "Kupka" in unknown hand
Gallien Collection, Paris

PROVENANCE:

the artist
to present owner

1 According to Andrée Martinel-Kupka,
  in conversation with the author,
  January 23, 1975.

This etching was done from a gouache study now in the Musée National d'Art Moderne, Paris (Fédit, cat. no. 17, p. 35). Although Fédit identifies the gouache as a preliminary study for *Autumn Sun,* the similarity of pose to that in *Standing Bather* (cat. no. 22), the advanced coloristic treatment and the flat horizontal brush-strokes arranged in vertical planes on either side of the figure suggest that the gouache was painted after *Autumn Sun,* probably during the summer of 1906 at Théoule.

The etching is almost identical to the gouache; however the animation produced by color in the original gouache has been replaced by tight abstract arabesques which show Kupka's debt to Rembrandt's etching style.

The model is thought to be Kupka's wife Eugénie.[1]

22 *Standing Bather (Baigneuse debout).* 1906

Pastel on gray paper, 18⅞ x 11¾″ (48 x 29 cm.)

Signed lr "Kupka"

Musée National d'Art Moderne, Paris (AM 2762−D)

PROVENANCE:

the artist
Eugénie Kupka
to present owner, gift, 1963

23 *Bather (La Baigneuse).* 1906

Pastel on gray paper, 11½ x 15¾″ (29.1 x 40 cm.)

Signed lr "Kupka"

Collection The Museum of Modern Art, New York, Gift of the Saidenberg Gallery, 1965

PROVENANCE:

the artist
Eugénie Kupka
Galerie Karl Flinker, Paris
Saidenberg Gallery, New York
to present owner, gift

These two pastels, like the painting for which they are studies, were conceived if not finished during a summer vacation at Théoule in 1906. Both show the beginnings of Kupka's "archaic" style, influenced by his illustrations for *Les Erinnyes* begun that year (see fig. 5, p. 308), and subsequently developed into the *"Gigolettes"* series. The first pastel is an adaptation of cat. no. 21. The second, showing a bather in the water, was elaborated with the help of a photograph of Kupka's stepdaughter (then age five) playing in a bathtub in the garden (see upper left corner). Other pastel and watercolor sketches depict the two bathers facing each other on the same sheet. Since the paper for these two is the same quality and format, one can assume that they were done almost as pendants at the same time.

24 *Water; The Bather (L'Eau; La Baigneuse).* 1906-07

Oil on canvas, 24¾ x 31⅛"
(63 x 80 cm.)

Signed ll "Kupka"

Fédit, no. 19, repr.

Vachtová, no. 38, repr. p. 143

Musée National d'Art Moderne,
Paris (AM 4161—P)

PROVENANCE:

the artist
Eugénie Kupka
to present owner, gift, 1963

EXHIBITIONS:

São Paulo, 1957, no. 44
*Cologne, 1967, no. 5, repr.; Munich,
1967, no. 5, repr.; Vienna, 1967, no.
3, repr. p. 25; Amsterdam, 1968, no.
6, repr.; Prague, 1968, no. 25, repr.

1 *The Other Shore,* 1896, NG, Prague;
  The Pond, 1902, Collection Karl
  Flinker, Paris

2 Manuscript II, p. 47

Based on Madame Kupka bathing in Théoule, Kupka's fascination with the laws of nature is vividly illustrated here. Although he had done several paintings of reflection on water,[1] he had never shown forms immersed and disarticulated by water as seen here. Surely the idea of the human microcosm's absorption into the macrocosm of nature appealed to him almost as much as the purely formal innovations such a subject permitted. Moreover the pictorial idea is exemplary of the philosophical concept: the natural element of water dissolves what was once a discrete form into an uninterrupted pattern. As Kupka was to say in his manuscript of 1912-13, discussing the phenomenon of reflection: "What adorable tricks on the absolute limits of things."[2]

†25 Study for *In the Bois de Boulogne*.
1906-07

India ink on tracing paper, 8⅝ x 5½″
(22 x 14.1 cm.)
Unsigned
Vachtová, p. 54 (dated 1904)
Collection Národní Galerie, Prague
(K 5006)

PROVENANCE:

the artist
Jindřich Waldes
to present owner, 1940

†26 *In the Bois de Boulogne*. 1906-07

Oil on canvas, 25⅝ x 25⅝″
(65 x 65 cm.)
Signed and dated ll "Kupka//1907"
Vachtová, no. 49, repr. p. 55
Collection Národní Galerie, Prague
(O 1985)

PROVENANCE:

the artist
Jindřich Waldes, 1921
to present owner, 1940

EXHIBITIONS:

*Písek—České Budějovice, 1961, no.
3, repr.
*Prague, 1968, no. 27, repr.
*Belgrade, 1969, no. 5, repr.

Around 1906-07, Kupka's work took a turn which suggests that he was looking at French painting and moving away from the heavy Germanic and more baroque models of his past. At the same time, he began working on outdoor themes and drawing his inspiration from more spontaneous subjects or events in his everyday existence. Possibly this corresponded to his move to a house with a garden in Puteaux which was close to the Bois de Boulogne. *In the Bois de Boulogne* is a good example of this development.

Kupka did many drawings and a few oil sketches on this theme. A cul-de-lampe for Elisée Reclus' *L'Homme et la terre*[1] presents its point of departure. It depicts the proletariat picnicking and dancing in the Bois de Boulogne on a Sunday. The class of society shown here is intentionally different from that usually portrayed by the Impressionists: the women are hatless and in simple dress, the men are in shirt-sleeves and sport the red anarchist sash. The vertical divisions of the composition are not as innovative as they are often assumed to be. They are found in many Impressionist and Neo-Impressionist paintings: in Manet, Degas, Vuillard, Denis, Seurat, to cite a few obvious examples.

1 *L'Homme et la terre,* vol. I, book IV,
ch. II: "Répartition des hommes,"
published October 25, 1905.

27 *Portrait of a Lady.* 1906-07

Oil on canvas, 28¾ x 26″
(73 x 66 cm.)
Signed lr "Kupka"
Vachtová, no. 45, repr. p. 297
Collection Národní Galerie, Prague
(O 8540)

PROVENANCE:

the artist
Jaroslav Jindra, Prague
to present owner, 1961

EXHIBITION:

*Prague, 1968, no. 30, repr.

Probably of the same period as *In the Bois de Boulogne,* this portrait of a woman seated in Kupka's Puteaux garden seems to contain several references to French painting. The diagonal line in the background and the open brushwork on a white ground evoke Cézanne, whereas the close patterning effects suggest a knowledge of Bonnard or Vuillard. Finally the brilliant colors and shading recall Matisse's portraits of Madame Matisse of 1905. A painting on paperboard of a couple on the grass dated 1906 (*In the Garden,* NG, Prague) is even closer to Matisse's 1905 style, showing green planes modeled with lavender shadows on the woman's face.

The refined silhouette of the model—her small head, delicate profile, discreetly open neckline and layered sleeves—suggests that she may have been the model for the initial pastels in the *Woman Picking Flowers* series. Her chair is the same as that in the earliest pastel shown here (cat. no. 46). Since neither this painting nor the pastels can be dated with complete accuracy, they may be somewhat closer in time than is indicated here.

28 Study for *The Yellow Scale* (Etude pour *La Gamme jaune*). 1907

Charcoal on paper, 16⅞ x 14⅛″
(42.8 x 35.5 cm.)
Stamped lr "Kupka"
Private Collection

PROVENANCE:

the artist
Eugénie Kupka
Karl Flinker
Gimpel Fils Ltd., London, 1965
Spencer A. Samuels and Co., Ltd.,
1968
Mr. and Mrs. Warren Brandt
to present owner

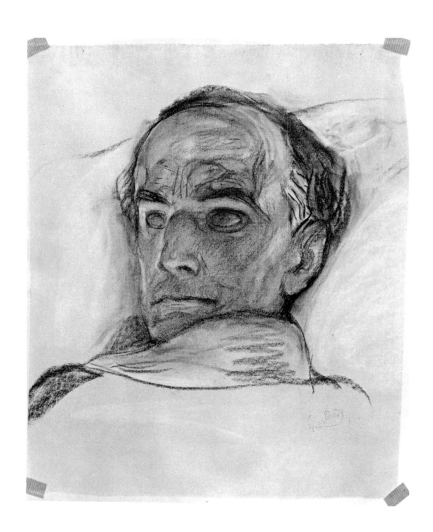

29 *The Yellow Scale (La Gamme jaune).* 1907-08

Oil on canvas, 31⅛ x 31⅛"
(79 x 79 cm.)

Signed and dated lr "Kupka//1907"

Fédit, no. 18, repr.

Vachtová, no. 61, repr. p. 63

Musée National d'Art Moderne,
Paris (AM 4165—P)

PROVENANCE:

the artist
Collection Reitz, Vienna
the artist
Eugénie Kupka
to present owner, gift, 1963

EXHIBITIONS:

Paris, 1910, *Salon d'Automne,*
no. 676

*Prague, 1946, Mánes, no. 14 (dated
1907-09)

Florence, 1964, no. 348, repr.

*Cologne, 1967, no. 4, repr.; Munich,
1967, no. 4, repr.; Vienna, 1967, no.
4; Amsterdam, 1968, no. 7, repr.;
Prague, 1968, no. 32, repr.

1 Ruskin, in *The Stones of Venice,*
quoted in Wylie Sypher, *Rococo to
Cubism in Art and Literature,*
New York, 1960, p. 145.

2 First published in *The World,* May 22,
1878; reprinted in *The Gentle Art of
Making Enemies,* first published, 1890.

3 Manuscript I, p. 17.

4 Manuscript II, p. 55; paraphrased here.

5 Vachtová, p. 69.

6 Bibliothèque Nationale, Paris. Reproduced in Van Deren Coke, *The Painter
and the Photograph,* Albuquerque,
1972, p. 46.

As the discussion on p. 68 proposes, *The Yellow Scale* may be understood as both a Symbolist portrait and an inquiry into the laws of color as disseminated through Chevreul. In support of the Symbolist hypothesis, one may refer to many writers and painters of the late nineteenth century. At random, consider Ruskin writing on van Gogh "He . . . learned the orchestration of pure tone by all the derivatives of this tone." Subject matter, said Ruskin in this reference, "was replaced by great harmonies of solid colors suggesting the total harmony of the picture. . . ."[1] Or consider Whistler, whose work Kupka knew, and who wrote in 1878: "It is for the artist to do something beyond this [imitation]: in portrait painting to put on canvas something more than the face the model wears for that one day; to paint the man, in short, as well as his features; in arrangement of colors to treat a flower as his key, not as his model."[2]

Kupka was to say in 1910-11: "It is the ensemble of forms in a human face which impresses us at first. It is only afterwards that we understand the importance of each feature."[3] In reference to unified color, he wrote in 1912-13: "the atmosphere of a work is more or less its spiritual factor. Atmosphere in a painting is achieved through bathing the canvas in a single scale of colors [*une seule gamme de teintes*]. Naturally this can be a scale of bright yellows, of brilliant reds, as long as there is a chromatic unity. This is arrived at through the elimination of complementaries, contrasts and even the diminution of light intensity. Thus one achieves an '*état d'âme,*' exteriorized in luminous form."[4]

Whether this is a symbolic portrait or an investigation of the function of color, the more precise individual features of the preparatory sketch suggest that Kupka may have started from a particular model. Vachtová states that it was merely "a friend."[5] Fédit, at Kupka's suggestion, refers to a painting by Gauguin, called *Poet in Yellow (Le Poète en jaune).*

Many of the individual features evoke photographs of Baudelaire, in particular Nadar's 1860 portrait:[6] the hollowed eyes, the irregular nose, the razor-sharp mouth, the receding hairline and graying temples. This and other photographs of the poet served as models for many artists. For example, Duchamp-Villon's 1911 portrait sculpture of Baudelaire was apparently done from a photograph. Although one cannot prove that Baudelaire was Kupka's model, one may suggest that a photograph of Baudelaire may have contributed its general morphology to what is probably an imaginary portrait of composite inspiration.

30 *Girl with a Ball (Petite fille au ballon)*. 1907-08

Pastel on paper, 24½ x 18¾″
(62.2 x 47.5 cm.)
Signed lr "Kupka"

Collection The Museum of Modern Art, New York, Gift of Mr. and Mrs. František Kupka, 1956 (567.56)

PROVENANCE:

the artist
to present owner, gift

31 *Girl with a Ball (Petite fille au ballon).* 1908

Oil on canvas, 44⅞ x 27½″
(114 x 70 cm.)

Signed and dated ll "Kupka//1908"

Fédit, no. 60, repr.
Vachtová, no. 69, repr. p. 77
Musée National d'Art Moderne,
Paris (AM 3464—P)

PROVENANCE:

the artist
to present owner, gift, 1956

EXHIBITION:

*Paris, 1958, MNAM, no. 2

A fairly conventional and unpretentious portrayal of Kupka's stepdaughter Andrée in the garden holding a ball, paradoxically, this painting contains the seeds for much of the artist's development toward abstraction during the period 1909-12. This evolution is discussed in detail on pp. 60-67, 70-74. The painting appears unfinished and may be so, due to Kupka's frustration at being unable to resolve problems of movement, color and perspective as they were beginning to crystallize in his mind.

32a-c   Three studies after *Girl with a Ball*
(mounted in a single mat).
1908-09

a. Pencil on paper, 8⅛ x 5¼″
(20.6 x 13.3 cm.)
Stamped ll "Kupka"

b. Pencil on paper, 10¾ x 7⅜″
(27.3 x 18.7 cm.)
Inscribed and signed r margin "ici il
n'y a que//la dissection//des sur-
faces//la conception//de la//con-
pénétration [sic]//atmosphérique//
est à trouver//tant qu'il y//aura la
différence//des couleurs//du fond
et//de la chair//je retomberai//dans
le [sic] photo//carte postale;" ll
"Kupka"

c. Colored crayons on paper,
8⅜ x 5½″ (21.2 x 14 cm.)
Signed and dated lr "Kupka//1907"

Collection The Museum of Modern
Art, New York, Gift of Mr. and Mrs.
František Kupka, 1956 (568.56.4-5-2)

PROVENANCE:

the artist
to present owner, gift

For the complete sequence of these
works, see cat. nos. 45, 61-62

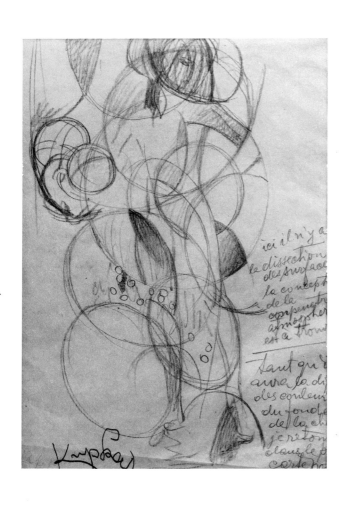

ici il n'y a
la dissection
des surface
la concept
de la
compenetr
atmospher
est à trouv

tant qu'i
aura la di
des couleur
du fond e
de la ch
je reston
dans le p
certain

1907

33   *The First Step (Le Premier pas).*
1909-13

Oil on canvas, 32¾ x 51″
(83.2 x 129.6 cm.)

Signed and dated lr "Kupka//1909"

Vachtová, no. 97, repr. p. 79

Collection The Museum of Modern
Art, New York, Hillman Periodicals
Fund, 1956 (562.56)

PROVENANCE:

the artist
to present owner, 1956

EXHIBITIONS:

New York, 1957; March-April 1958;
October 1958-October 1959, MOMA
*New York, 1961, Royal S. Marks,
   no. 3
Washington, D.C., 1963
New York, 1964-65; 1969; 1972;
December 1972-March 1973,
MOMA

The First Step is one of the most difficult paintings to situate in Kupka's oeuvre. It is hard to understand how and why the artist would have executed this painting in 1909, the date given it by Kupka. There is no other work of the period which even slightly resembles it. Yet there is no adequate justification for dating it later. Superficially, *The First Step* can be related to the *Disks of Newton* series of 1911-12. But a careful comparison of these paintings reveals few if any real similarities.

The First Step is painted on the reverse of a commercially primed canvas. The primed side had already been used for a *Gigolette* painting which, although unfinished, was nonetheless signed and dated 1909-10 (fig.). However, the tentative treatment and weak stylization argue for a dating of 1908 (see cat. no. 36). Subsequently, presumably between 1908 and 1909, Kupka unstretched the canvas and restretched it to use the other side.

The thin matte ground of *The First Step,* which is entirely uncharacteristic for Kupka, is explained by the fact that it is painted on the reverse of a primed canvas. This unprimed side seems to have been worked on in at least two if not three phases: the first c. 1909; the later reworkings c. 1911 and 1913.

A careful examination reveals that the first version consisted of two large central planets, surrounded by a ring of evenly spaced small disks on a stained black field, essentially the same composition as exists today. In this initial version, the largest

Kupka, Reverse of *The First Step*, Collection The Museum of Modern Art, New York, Hillman Periodicals Fund.

white disk was threaded with black veins on a white ground, depicting a lunar landscape. The second disk, behind it and to the left, may have been somewhat whiter than it is now. The small disks which revolve around these two focalized overlapping circles were originally white with slightly gray haloes.

Around 1911, when Kupka was doing studies for the *Fugue,* he reworked the painting. He repainted the dominant form a solid white, so that all that remains of the earlier veined surface is a barely visible network of gray lines. At intersecting points of this web, he studded the surface with blobs of white. The second large disk was repainted gray, its left edge high-lighted with white, creating a reverberation against the black ground. He also added a shadow to further separate the two. At the same time he encircled the smaller disks with loosely intertwined wreaths of dark green which virtually destroy the original even spacing and add a sense of spiraling rotation and dynamic continuity between them. Probably concurrently, he drew a sketchy single blood-red ring in the bare black field on the left. Finally, perhaps in a third version c. 1913, he articulated the satellites with blue and red splinters of color, encompassed them with gray-blue haloes and punctuated the green and red wreaths of color with brighter shades of the same hues. This partial accentuation of the green orbits makes them advance and recede in space. The cherry-red stippling on the deeper red ring is more evenly distributed than the green and anchors that circle in a single more recessive plane in space.

The knotted lines of color of the red and green wreaths are seen in some late studies for the *Amorpha Fugue* (MOMA Study Collection). Both the use of green and the linking of motifs in a continuous movement occur in *"Copenetrations"* of 1910-11, where an arabesque anticipating the *Fugue* is found (see cat. no. 68). The separate yet interpenetrating colored orbits on a black ground set in a relation to two over-lapping white disks suggest that this painting, at least in 1911, was conceived as a very tentative and unique study for the *Fugue,* particularly since in 1911, Kupka was beginning to work on obviously cosmic themes which added a dimension to his *Fugue* development. However the precise arrangement of splintered red and blue shards does not appear in Kupka's work until 1913. One can therefore safely suggest that they were added after the *Fugue* at the time of *The Cathedral* (cat. no. 99).

This discussion of formal characteristics does not tell us why Kupka chose to do such a subject as early as 1909. His long interest in astronomy is of course relevant, especially since he kept abreast of the most recent astronomical discoveries through scientific journals and the more general periodicals which were full of articles about them. Eclipses of the sun were seen in Europe in 1900 and 1905. They were photographed and widely reproduced as were many other astronomical discoveries concerning the sun, the moon and individual planets. Astronomical photographs were shown at the Observatory, the Palais de la Découverte, and the museum of the Conservatoire des Arts et Métiers, places Kupka visited frequently. More specifically, a large-scale model of the moon was exhibited at Uccle in Belgium in 1909, a year Kupka visited Onésime Reclus in that same town. One can only conjecture that this monumental relief model of the moon (now at the Palais de la Découverte, Paris) catalyzed Kupka's desire to formulate the image in *The First Step*.

Furthermore, in 1908-09, he was working on the orbital relationships of the girl with the ball theme. Sketches (cat. nos. 32a-c) show the girl as a focal image, or a double shifting center with the ball beginning to sweep in a fuller circle around her. On one of these drawings, Kupka wrote, expressing his frustration: "Here I am only dissecting surfaces. The atmospheric co-penetration is still to be found. As long as there is a distinction between ground and flesh color, I will fall back into the postcard photograph." (cat. no. 32b) It seems plausible to conjecture that in order to escape the constraints of figurative representation, and inspired by a vivid exposure to another rotational system at Uccle, Kupka moved to a new context of experience—from the microcosmic to the macrocosmic—to capture the sense of rotation which was his ultimate goal.

34   *Prometheus Blue and Red.*
      1908-09

Watercolor on paper, 12⅝ x 11½″
(32.1 x 29.3 cm.)

Signed ll "Kupka"

Vachtová, no. 67, repr. p. 299

Collection Národní Galerie, Prague
(K 11134)

PROVENANCE:

the artist
to present owner, 1946

35 *Portrait of Eugénie Kupka, from the Back (Portrait d'Eugénie Kupka, de dos).* c. 1908-09

Oil on paperboard, 15⅜ x 20⅛″
(39 x 51 cm.)
Signed and dated lr "Kupka//$\overline{05}$"
Private Collection

PROVENANCE:

the artist
Andrée Martinel-Kupka
Galerie Karl Flinker, Paris
to present owner, April 1966

EXHIBITION:

*Paris, 1966, Karl Flinker, no. 23, repr.

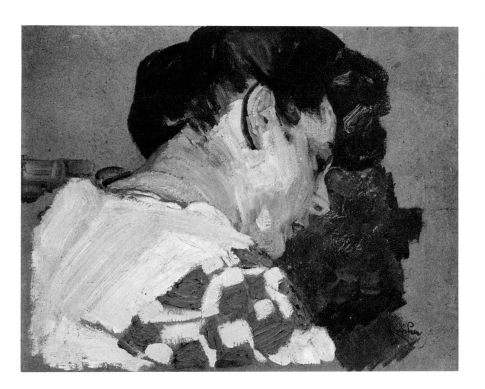

The subject of a woman from the back was one which intrigued Kupka over a period of many years (see cat. nos. 1, 12, 21 and 44 for example). This portrait of Eugénie, although dated 1905, appears on stylistic grounds to have been painted later. The bold swatches of primary and secondary colors and the almost planar modeling forecast *Family Portrait* of 1910. This style is not found in any of Kupka's work before c. 1908-09.

36 *"Gigolettes" and Marlou*
    (Gigolettes et Marlou). 1908-09

Oil on paperboard 29½ x 28⅜"
(75 x 72 cm.)

Signed ll "Kupka;" signed and dated
middle l "Kupka//o̅6̅"

Collection Karl Flinker

PROVENANCE:

the artist
Andrée Martinel-Kupka
to present owner

EXHIBITIONS:

*Paris, 1966, Karl Flinker, no. 29
  (dated 1906), repr.
*Cologne, 1967, no. 85, repr.;
  Munich, 1967, no. 85, repr.; Vienna,
  1967, no. 1; Amsterdam, 1968, no.
  5, repr.; Prague, 1968, no. 33, repr.

1 Although Fédit moves the beginning of
  the period back to 1906, all of the
  works known to the present author
  can be situated between 1908-10 and,
  except for this particular work, are
  dated accordingly. Since this work is
  signed twice, one can question the
  accuracy of the second signature and
  date.

2 MNAM, Paris; see Fédit, cat. no. 29,
  p. 45.

Like cat. no. 35, this oil sketch seems to have been incorrectly dated by Kupka. All
of the *Gigolette* series were done in the period 1908-10.[1] Although the dates may be
confused even within that period, one can distinguish between the earlier more tentative interpretations of the theme and others such as this one which show supreme
control of color, brushstroke, stylized forms and composition. What must be considered a first version of the same composition was painted on the reverse of *The
First Step* of 1909-13 (see fig., p. 119). Sketchy, unfinished, more literal in its depiction, Kupka nonetheless dated it 1909-10 which once again seems impossible in
view of the sure stylistic development of the theme through 1909 (see cat. no. 38
and other unexhibited works from the series in the MNAM, Paris). The male figure
"Marlou" is found again in a painting *Le Mec (The Pimp),* dated 1910 (once more
probably incorrectly dated).[2]

   "Gigolettes" and Marlou shows a consummate stylistic treatment of the *Gigolette* theme equal to that found in *Gallien's Girl* of 1909.

37 *Rolled-up Hair (Cheveux roulés).*
1909

Pastel on heavy beige paper or paper-
board, 18½ x 12⅝″ (47 x 32 cm.)
Signed dated lr "Kupka//1909"
Collection Karl Flinker

PROVENANCE:

the artist
Eugénie Kupka
to present owner

Obviously inspired by the art of Crete and Mycenae which Kupka had studied in
preparing the illustrations for *Les Erinnyes* (see fig. 5, p. 308), in this highly stylized
drawing he also attempted to capture the powdery texture and muted colors of
fresco painting.

38 *Gallien's Girl; Gallien's Taste;
The Cabaret Singer (La Mome à
Gallien; Au goût de Gallien; La
Chanteuse de Cabaret).* 1909

Oil on canvas, 42½ x 39⅜″
(108 x 100 cm.)

Signed lr "Kupka"

Vachtová, no. 73, color pl. II

Collection Národní Galerie, Prague
(O 3836)

PROVENANCE:

the artist
to present owner, 1946

EXHIBITIONS:

*Prague, 1946, Mánes, no. 24
Amsterdam, 1957, no. 58, repr.
*Paris, 1958, MNAM, no. 3, pl. II
Hluboké—Brno, 1966, no. 226, repr.
London, 1967, no. 74, repr.
Brussels—Rotterdam, 1967, no. 74,
repr.
*Prague, 1968, no. 39, repr.
*Belgrade, 1969, no. 7, repr.
Munich, 1970, no. 39; Paris, 1970,
no. 26, repr.
Stockholm—Göteborg, 1973, no. 87

Known today as *Gallien's Girl*, the original title of this painting was probably *The Cabaret Singer*. Kupka changed the title after meeting Gallien c. 1920. In 1946, he exhibited it as *Gallien's Taste (Gallienovo gusto)* and thereafter under this title or either of the other two interchangeably. As in the other works in the *Gigolette* series, this painting shows the influence of archaic Mediterranean art as well as that of Kees van Dongen, an artist widely exhibited in Paris at that time and whom Kupka admired for a short period. Although the painting appears somewhat unfinished, the large format, extreme stylization, brilliant yet economical palette and the controlled and contrasted composition imply that it was one of the last paintings of this series.

39 *Piano Keys—Lake (Les Touches
    du piano).* 1909

Oil on canvas, 31⅛ x 28⅜"
(79 x 72 cm.)

Signed ll "Kupka"

Vachtová, no. 74, color pl. VII

Collection Národní Galerie, Prague
(O 3790)

PROVENANCE:

the artist
to present owner, 1946

EXHIBITIONS:

*Prague, 1946, Mánes, no. 20

*Paris, 1958, MNAM, no. 4

Edinburgh—Leeds, 1959, no. 52,
pl. XVIII

*Písek—České Budějovice, 1961, no.
  5, repr.

Hluboké—Brno, 1966, no. 227, color
frontispiece

London, 1967, no. 75

Brussels—Rotterdam, 1967, no. 75

*Prague, 1968, no. 37, repr. black and
  white and color

Toronto, 1969, no. 292, repr.

Geneva, 1970, no. 67; Zurich, 1970,
no. 67

Stockholm—Göteborg, 1973, no. 86,
repr.

The substructural image of a lake, boat and a distant shore was obviously painted earlier than the short vertical bands of color of the surface plane. In the original image, the bright enameled colors, the rich impastoed brushstrokes and the general organization along a central vertical axis blossoming at the top in a bouquet of floral motifs is comparable to the composition of *Gallien's Girl.* The piano theme, applied over this descriptive image like an acoustical grid, may also relate to jazz or the cabaret.

Obviously Kupka was trying to destroy perspective and unify the composition through the use of a surface grid of neutral color slabs unrelated in all aspects to the original subject matter. Since to Kupka's mind, music was an arrangement of non-descriptive units, he evidently felt that this reference to notes and chords, which create harmony when superimposed, would telescope his image into a single plane. Thus he would arrive at an abstract visual pattern, parallel to musical composition. The textures, structures and visual impact of the two pictorial ideas are so different that a true unity is not achieved. Nonetheless a basic component of Kupka's future development is present in this dissonant composition.

40 Study for *Planes by Colors, Large Nude* (Etude pour *Plans par couleurs, Grand Nu*). 1906-07

Pastel on paper, 19¾ x 23¼"
(50 x 59 cm.)
Stamped lr "Kupka"
Collection Joseph H. Hazen

PROVENANCE:
the artist
Andrée Martinel-Kupka
Galerie Karl Flinker, Paris
to present owner

41 Study for *Planes by Colors, Large
    Nude* (Etude pour *Plans par
    couleurs, Grand Nu*). 1909

Pastel on paper, 18⅞ x 23⅝"
(48 x 60 cm.)

Signed lr "Kupka"

Fédit, no. 35, repr.

Musée National d'Art Moderne,
Paris (AM 2759-D)

PROVENANCE:

the artist
Eugénie Kupka
to present owner, gift, 1963

*Planes by Colors, Large Nude
(Plans par couleurs, Grand Nu).*
1909-10

Oil on canvas, 59⅛ x 71⅛"
(150.1 x 180.8 cm.)

Signed and dated lr "Kupka//1909"

Vachtová, no. 87, repr. p. 73

Collection The Solomon R.
Guggenheim Museum, New York,
Gift of Mrs. Andrew P. Fuller, 1968
(1860)

PROVENANCE:

the artist
Eugénie Kupka
Richard L. Feigen, Inc., New York,
1958
Mrs. Andrew P. Fuller, April 1961
to present owner, gift

EXHIBITIONS:

Paris, 1911, *Salon d'Automne,*
no. 811
*Paris, 1936, Jeu de Paume, no. 16
(dated 1910), repr. p. 21
*Prague, 1946, Mánes, no. 9 (dated
1910)
Paris, 1954, *Salon des Indépendants,*
no. 1630
São Paulo, 1957, no. 45
*Paris, 1958, MNAM, no. 5
New York, 1969, April-May;
September-October, SRGM
New York, 1970, SRGM, p. 254,
repr. color
New York, 1971, SRGM, p. 254,
repr. color
New York, 1972-73, SRGM
New York, 1973, SRGM

1 See the forthcoming catalogue of The
 Solomon R. Guggenheim Museum
 collection, *Paintings 1880-1945,* by
 Angelica Zander Rudenstine, where
 all the known studies will be
 reproduced.

2 Siblik, 1929; Turpin, 1931, for example.

3 Manuscript I, p. 49.

4 Manuscript II, p. 44.

Kupka worked on the theme of the *Large Nude* over a period of many years: at least from 1904 to 1909-10. Over twenty studies in pencil, charcoal and pastel are known today.[1] In comparison to the final interpretation seen here, the earliest versions are extremely academic (see cat. no. 40 and fig., p. 132). Through the years, the subject evolved from a reclining nude to a formal arrangement of color planes.

Writers of the twenties and thirties[2] spoke of this painting in terms of *"plans-souchettes"* (blunt or stub-like planes) and a *"sorte de pointillisme grossi"* (a magnified pointillism). Since these phrases are found consistently in Kupka's autobiographical notes, this was a terminology which he either created or adopted to describe his activity.

In his manuscript of 1910-11, Kupka wrote: "We who have the conquests of the Impressionists behind us, we enlarge their pointillism into planes by colors; we know very well that light is not in white and black but in color, in the more or less scientific theory of complementarity."[3] This text was written shortly after the final version of the painting had been completed. It is the first time that the term "planes by colors" appears in Kupka's writings.

In the artist's 1912-13 manuscript, he took up the subject of the "plane" in greater detail. One passage in particular provides an insight into what Kupka was striving to achieve in the *Large Nude:* "The principle of construction, the scaffolding of a work, is in the large planes of color."[4]

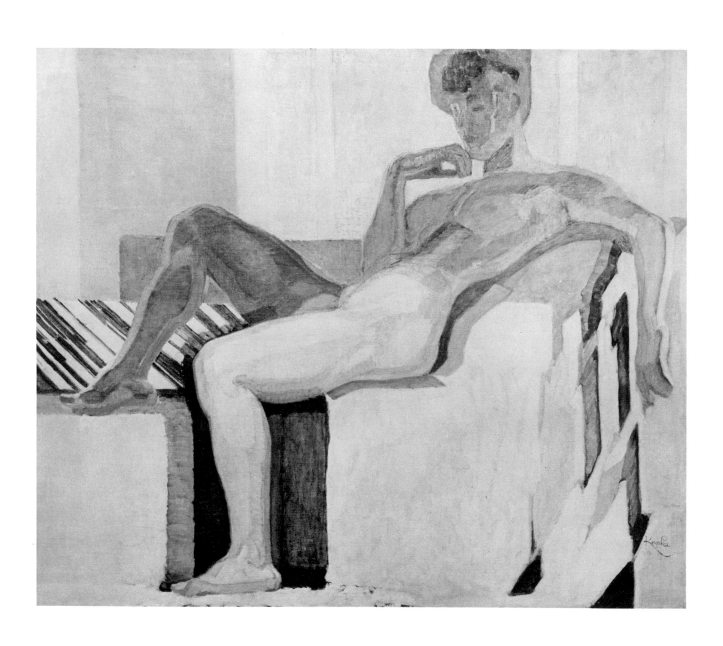

Obviously Kupka was trying to break away from the traditional practices of rendering illusionistic volume through shading and perspective. To Kupka, modeling and three-dimensional form belong to the sculptor's art. The painter, whose support is two-dimensional, determines his forms by color alone.

Planes by Colors: Large Nude, exhibited for the first time in 1911, attracted a wide critical response which was, needless to say, not always positive. The satirical magazine *Fantasio* devoted a long paragraph to the painting, in which a doctor was described standing before the canvas, crying out, "We must alert the Service of Hygiene. This unhappy woman is suffering from *pityriasis versicolore....* These skin infections may be contagious."[5] André Salmon, in *Paris-Journal,* described the painting as a decomposition inspired by Matisse.[6] Maurice Dekobra, in *La Revue des beaux-arts,* spoke of "the woman in a process of decomposition ... whose body is adorned with fluorescent greens, yellows, and reds.... It is the magic lantern of old men about to succumb to second childhood."[7] Only Gustave Kahn, in *Mercure de France,* expressed a more positive response: "On the borders of Impressionism, among those seeking a strict form of modeling through color, one finds Mr. Kupka whose nude astonishes by its polychromatics...."[8]

5 Signed Roland Catenoy, November 1, 1911, p. 231.

6 September 30, 1911, p. 5.

7 October 15, 1911, pp. 4-5.

8 October 16, 1911, p. 872.

Kupka, *Large Nude,* signed and dated 1904, oil, present whereabouts unknown.

43   Study for *Family Portrait* (Etude
      pour *Portrait de famille*). 1909

Pastel on paper, 18½ x 19½"
(47 x 49.5 cm.)
Signed ll "Kupka"
Private Collection

PROVENANCE:

the artist
to present owner

44   *Family Portrait (Portraits; Portrait de famille).* 1909-10

Oil on canvas, 40½ x 44⅛″
(103 x 112 cm.)

Signed and dated ll "Kupka//1910"

Vachtová, no. 82, color pl. III

Collection Národní Galerie, Prague
(O 3821)

PROVENANCE:

the artist
to present owner, 1946

EXHIBITIONS:

Paris, 1911, *Salon d'Automne,* no.
812 (as *Portraits*)
*Paris, 1936, Jeu de Paume, no. 17
(dated 1910)
*Prague, 1946, Mánes, no. 29, pl. II
*Paris, 1958, MNAM, no. 7
Edinburgh—Leeds, 1959, no. 51
*Písek—České Budějovice, 1961, no.
7, repr.
Hluboké—Brno, 1966, no. 228, repr.
*Cologne, 1967, no. 68, repr.;
Munich, 1967, no. 68, repr.; Vienna,
1967, no. 12; Amsterdam, 1968, no.
14, repr.; Prague, 1968, no. 41, repr.
Stockholm—Göteborg, 1973, no. 89

Kupka's biographer Siblík (1929) and other writers such as Turpin (1931) state that *Family Portrait* was executed before *Planes by Colors: Large Nude.* This seems implausible for a number of reasons. A small sketchbook of 1909-10 (Private Collection, Paris) contains drawings related to the final and most stylistically advanced formulation of the *Large Nude* and a single drawing for *Family Portrait* which appears to be one of its first tentative sketches. Secondly, a preliminary pastel for *Family Portrait* (cat. no. 43) shows the unusual color combinations—predominantly orange, purple, green—which were developed only in the last versions of the *Large Nude.* Finally, Kupka himself dated *Large Nude* 1909 and *Family Portrait* 1910. Although the dates were added in pencil probably many years after the paintings' completion and therefore cannot be considered completely reliable, presumably the artist remembered the order in which the paintings were done.

Family Portrait is a more complex painting stylistically, showing two different, almost opposed, manners of dealing with color, form and light. In Kupka's 1912-13 manuscript he wrote: "The painter can animate the surface according to the nature of his vision. From the most imposing mass of cyclopean planes, he can pass to the most subtle flickering of smaller planes."[1]

When this painting was first exhibited in 1911, Gustave Kahn spoke of the beauty and accomplishment of this "portrait of young girls, sparkling and infused with light."[2] The "young girls" are of course Madame Kupka and her daughter Andrée.

For a more extensive stylistic discussion of this painting, see pp. 69-70.

1 Manuscript II, p. 45.
2 *Mercure de France,* October 16, 1911,
p. 872.

45   Study after *Girl with a Ball*. 1909

Colored crayons on paper, 8¼ x 4″
(20.6 x 10.2 cm.)

Stamped ll "Kupka"

Collection The Museum of Modern
Art, New York, Gift of Mr. and Mrs.
František Kupka, 1956 (568.56.6)

PROVENANCE:

the artist
to present owner, gift

For the complete sequence of these
works, see cat. nos. 32, 61-62.

46   *Woman Picking Flowers I (Femme
cueillant des fleurs I).* 1909-10

Pastel on paper, 17¾ x 18¾″
(45 x 47 cm.)

Signed lr "Kupka"

Fédit, no. 42, repr.
Vachtová, addenda cat. no. 40

Musée National d'Art Moderne,
Paris (AM 2776-D)

PROVENANCE:

the artist
Eugénie Kupka
to present owner, gift, 1963

Kupka, Study related to *Woman Picking
Flowers I*, c. 1908.

47 *Woman Picking Flowers II*
    (Femme cueillant des fleurs II).
    1909-10

Pastel on paper, 18⅞ x 19½″
(48 x 49.5 cm.)

Signed lr "Kupka"

Fédit, no. 43, repr.
Vachtová, addenda cat. no. 43

Musée National d'Art Moderne,
Paris (AM 2777-D)

PROVENANCE:

the artist
Eugénie Kupka
to present owner, gift, 1963

Visitors to Kupka's studio in the fifties remember seeing at least fifteen pastel studies on this theme. Photographs of numerous drawings have also been found (figs., pp. 136, 141). The whereabouts of most of these are unknown today.

It has been suggested that the source of this series was a multiple-exposure photograph of Madame Kupka in the garden (see p. 62). Unfortunately no photographs have been found. The model, as she is most clearly seen in the earlier versions, appears closer to the model in *Portrait of a Lady* (cat. no. 27) than to Madame Kupka,

48 *Woman Picking Flowers (Femme cueillant des fleurs)*. 1909-10

Pastel on gray paper, 21¼ x 20⅜″
(54 x 51.8 cm.)
Signed lr "Kupka"
Private Collection

PROVENANCE:

the artist
to present owner

but this is essentially unimportant since Kupka often combined models and visual sources into composite images. The two kinds of garden chairs in this series of pastels are found in photographs of Kupka's garden, as well as in other subjects painted after the artist's 1906 move to Puteaux.

For an extensive discussion of this series, see pp. 60-61.

49   *Woman Picking Flowers III*
     (Femme cueillant des fleurs III).
     1909-10

Pastel on cream paper, 17⅛ x 20⅞″
(43.5 x 53 cm.)

Signed ll "Kupka"

Fédit, no. 40, repr.
Vachtová, addenda cat. no. 40

Musée National d'Art Moderne,
Paris (AM 2775-D)

PROVENANCE:

the artist
Eugénie Kupka
to present owner, gift, 1963

49   *Woman Picking Flowers III*

50   *Woman Picking Flowers IV*
      (Femme cueillant des fleurs IV).
      1909-10

Pastel on gray paper, 16½ x 15⅜"
(42 x 39 cm.)

Signed lr "Kupka"

Fédit, no. 41, repr.
Vachtová, addenda cat. no. 41

Musée National d'Art Moderne,
Paris (AM 2757-D)

PROVENANCE:

the artist
Eugénie Kupka
to present owner, gift, 1963

Kupka, Study related to *Woman Picking
Flowers IV*, c. 1909.

51 *Woman Picking Flowers V*
    (Femme cueillant des fleurs V).
    1909-10

Pastel on paper, 18⅞ x 20½″
(48 x 52 cm.)

Signed lr "Kupka"

Fédit, no. 44, repr.
Vachtová, addenda cat. no. 44

Musée National d'Art Moderne,
Paris (AM 2778-D)

PROVENANCE:

the artist
Eugénie Kupka
to present owner, gift, 1963

52   Study for *The Oval Mirror* (Etude pour *Le Miroir ovale*). 1909-10

Colored pencils on beige paper,
4⅛ x 4¾" (10.5 x 12 cm.)

Signed lr "Kupka"

Fédit, no. 37, repr.
Musée National d'Art Moderne,
Paris (AM 2754-D)

PROVENANCE:

the artist
Eugénie Kupka
to present owner, gift, 1963

53 *The Oval Mirror (Le Miroir ovale).* 1910

Oil on canvas, 42⅝ x 34⅞"
(108.3 x 88.6 cm.)

Signed and dated ll "Kupka//1910"

Vachtová, no. 90, repr. p. 82 (dated 1911)

Collection The Museum of Modern Art, New York, Hillman Periodicals Fund, 1956 (565.56)

PROVENANCE:

the artist
to present owner

EXHIBITIONS:

Paris, *Salon des Indépendants,* 1912, no. 1833, 1834, or 1835
*Prague, 1946, Mánes, no. 32 (dated 1911)
New York, 1957
*New York, 1961, Royal S. Marks, no. 4
*New York, 1964, Royal S. Marks, no. 5
New York, 1965; 1966; 1968, MOMA

In contrast to the distinctly defined contours and sharply contrasted color planes of *Large Nude* and *Family Portrait, The Oval Mirror* is a somewhat blurred and structurally undefined image. Nonetheless Kupka has retained some of the formal characteristics of the other two works: the *plans-souchettes* of color (see discussion p. 130), here impastoed and much enlarged; and the reversal of the usual chromatic roles (see pp. 69-70), here a purple which advances and a green which recedes to yellow. The small sketch (cat. no. 52) shows these formal concerns more clearly.

The subject of a woman looking in a mirror, one which Kupka had used before (see cat. no. 12) lent itself to a more ambiguous image. On the basis of his experiments in the *Woman Picking Flowers* series (cat. nos. 46-51), Kupka now tried to dissolve the focal image, not through sequential motion but through reflection of a single body in space. This is consistent with the artist's ideas c. 1909-10 when he began exploring the distinction between movement in three-dimensional as opposed to four-dimensional space. An inscribed colored crayon drawing defines and illustrates the two notions (fig., p. 65; see discussion pp. 65-66).

Although Kupka may have thought that the rippling contours effected by a mirror image would generate a kinetic dimension, the painting *The Oval Mirror* (as well as the preliminary sketch) is essentially static. Yet in the two-sided drawing inspired by the painting (cat. no. 54) almost imperceptibly the figure begins to turn, progressing from a full rear view to that of a silhouette turning toward the right. This rotational movement, derived from the elliptical curves of the painting, will lead Kupka to the subtle, more tangible shifting in space seen in *The Musician Follot* and *Planes by Colors* which immediately follow.

54   *Untitled* (Study after *The Oval Mirror* leading into *Planes by Colors*). 1910

Charcoal on paper, 12¼ x 9″
(31 x 23 cm.)
Stamped ll "Kupka;" inscribed ll in
unknown hand "199"
on reverse, pastel
Stamped ll "Kupka"
Collection Karl Flinker

PROVENANCE:
the artist
Eugénie Kupka
to present owner

55 *Portrait of The Musician Follot*
(Portrait du musicien Follot).
1910-11

Oil on canvas, 28½ x 26⅛"
(72.4 x 66.3 cm.)

Inscribed, signed and dated lr "A
mon ami//G. Follot//Kupka//
1910"

Collection The Museum of Modern
Art, New York, Hillman Periodicals
Fund, 1956 (564.56)

PROVENANCE:

the artist
to present owner

EXHIBITIONS:

Paris, 1912, *Salon des Indépendants*,
no. 1833, 1834 or 1835
*Paris, 1936, Jeu de Paume, no. 18
(as *Portrait*, dated 1910-11)
*Prague, 1946, Mánes, no. 31 (dated
1911)
New York, 1957, MOMA
New York, MOMA, May 4-July 5,
1960, *Portraits from the Museum
Collection*. Traveled throughout the
United States, February 15, 1961-
February 28, 1964.
New York, 1964, Royal S. Marks
(not on checklist)
New York, 1968, MOMA

1 Quoted by Fédit, in conversation with
the author, 1974.

Apparently Kupka said in reference to this picture that he was trying to abolish the
notion of time.[1] In the context of his work and thinking of this period, one can
understand his statement to mean an attempt to replace sequential motion by an
almost imperceptible shifting in space which would abolish the notion of consecutive moments in time. This would ultimately lead to his concept of simultaneity
(see discussion pp. 64-65).

In composition and palette, *Follot* is extremely close to *Planes by Colors* (cat. no.
59). However, partly because the subject is less appropriate to the concept, and
partly because this painting was done somewhat earlier, the impression of shifting
in space remains slight.

56   Study for *Planes by Colors* (Etude
pour *Plans par couleurs*). 1909-10

Pastel on paper, 21½ x 18⅛"
(54.6 x 46 cm.)
Signed and dated lr "Kupka//1909"
Private Collection

PROVENANCE:
the artist
to present owner

57 Study for *Planes by Colors* (Etude pour *Plans par couleurs*). 1909-10

Pastel on paper, 22 x 17⅛″
(56 x 45.5 cm.)

Signed lr "Kupka"

Musée National d'Art Moderne,
Paris (AM 2779-D)

PROVENANCE:

the artist
Eugénie Kupka
to present owner, gift, 1963

58 Study for *Planes by Colors* (Etude pour *Plans par couleurs*). 1909-10

Pencil on paper, 8¼ x 4⅞″
(21 x 12.5 cm.)

Stamped lc "Kupka;" signed ll
"Kupka"

Collection Karl Flinker

PROVENANCE:

the artist
Eugénie Kupka
to present owner

59   *Planes by Colors (Plans par couleurs).* 1910-11

Oil on canvas, 43⅜ x 39⅜"
(110 x 100 cm.)

Signed and dated lr "Kupka//
1910-11"

Fédit, no. 48, repr. color
Vachtová, no. 88, repr. p. 111

Collection Musée National d'Art
Moderne, Paris (AM 3549-P)

PROVENANCE:

the artist
Eugénie Kupka
to present owner, 1957

EXHIBITIONS:

Paris, 1912, *Salon des Indépendants,*
no. 1833, 1834 or 1835
*Paris, 1958, MNAM, no. 9
*Cologne, 1967, no. 11, repr. color;
Munich, 1967, no. 11, repr.; Vienna,
1967, no. 13, repr. color; Amsterdam, 1968, no. 16, repr. black and
white, color; Prague, 1968, no. 43,
repr. black and white, color
Milan, 1973, no. 149, repr.

Drawings found among Kupka's personal notes indicate that the three paintings entitled *Plans par couleurs* exhibited at the 1912 *Salon des Indépéndants* were our catalogue numbers 53, 55 and the present painting. Roger Allard, in reviewing the 1912 *Salon* said, "the post-cubist fantasies by Kupka and Juan Gris are rather in-significant."[1] It is worth noting that Juan Gris' "post-cubist fantasy" was his *Hommage à Picasso (Portrait of Picasso,* 1911-12, Art Institute of Chicago).

For a detailed discussion of this painting, see pp. 62-64, 72.

1 *La Revue de France,* March 1912, p. 72.

60 *Chromatic Scale (Gamme chromatique).* 1910-11

Pastel and colored crayons on paper,
9¾ x 8⅛″ (25 x 20.5 cm.)
Signed lr "Kupka"
Lent by Spencer A. Samuels and
Company, Ltd.

PROVENANCE:
the artist
Estate of the artist
Galerie Karl Flinker, Paris
to present owner

Both formally and chromatically, this pastel is related to the *Woman Picking Flowers* series and the pastel studies for *Planes by Colors*. It is an important transitional work exemplifying Kupka's shift of focus from a subject subdivided rhythmically by a vertical grid to an abstract pattern of pure rhythmic planes.

a-c Three studies after *Girl with a Ball* and for *The Fugue* (mounted in a single mat). 1908-09

a. Colored crayons on paper, 10⅝ x 8¼" (27 x 21 cm.) Signed and dated ll "Kupka//1908"

b. Colored crayons on paper, 8¼ x 7½" (20.8 x 19 cm.) Signed and dated ll "Kupka//1908"

c. Colored crayons on paper, 6⅝ x 6" (16.8 x 15 cm.) Signed lc "Kupka"; inscribed lr "origine de la technique//employée à la charpente//de la Fugue."

Collection The Museum of Modern Art, New York, Gift of Mr. and Mrs. František Kupka, 1956 (568.56.8-3-1)

PROVENANCE:

the artist
to present owner, gift

62 Study after *Girl with a Ball* and
    for *The Fugue*. 1909

Colored crayons on paper, 8¼ x 5¼″
(21.2 x 13.5 cm.)

Signed lr "Kupka"; inscribed ll
"Genèse des disques//et de la
‹Fugue› "

Private Collection, New York City

PROVENANCE:

the artist
to present owner, 1955

For the complete sequence of these
works, see cat. nos. 32, 45, 61.

63 *Study for Amorpha, Fugue in Two Colors (Etude pour Amorpha, Fugue à deux couleurs).* 1910-11

Oil on canvas, 44 x 27"
(111.8 x 68.5 cm.)

Signed ll "Kupka"

Contemporary Collection of The Cleveland Museum of Art (69.51)

PROVENANCE:

the artist
Mr. and Mrs. Alexander Liberman, 1950's
to present owner, 1969

EXHIBITIONS:

*Prague, 1946, Mánes (installation photograph)
*New York, 1961, Royal S. Marks, no. 1
*New York, 1964, Royal S. Marks, no. 1
Buffalo-Dayton-Cleveland, 1970 (hors catalogue; shown at Cleveland only)

For a detailed discussion of this painting, see p. 71.

64 Study for *Vertical Planes* (Etude pour *Plans verticaux*). c. 1910-11

Pastel on paper, 8 x 8¾"
(20.3 x 22.3 cm.)
Signed ll "Kupka"
Collection The Solomon R. Guggenheim Museum, New York, Gift of Mr. and Mrs. Alexander Liberman, 1974 (2124)

PROVENANCE:

the artist
Mr. and Mrs. Alexander Liberman, 1950's
to present owner, gift

65   *Arrangement of Verticals (Ordonnance sur verticales)*. 1910-11

Pastel on gray paper, 18⅞ x 19¾"
(48 x 50 cm.)

Signed lr "Kupka"

Fédit, no. 52, repr.

Musée National d'Art Moderne,
Paris (AM 2780-D)

PROVENANCE:

the artist
Eugénie Kupka
to present owner, gift, 1963

66 *Arrangement of Verticals in Yellow (Ordonnance sur verticales en jaune).* 1910-11

Oil on canvas, 27½ x 27½"
(70 x 70 cm.)

Signed and dated lr "Kupka//1913"

Fédit, no. 51, repr.

Musée National d'Art Moderne, Paris (AM 3558-P)

PROVENANCE:

the artist
Eugénie Kupka
to present owner, 1957

EXHIBITIONS:

*Paris, 1958, MNAM (hors catalogue)
Grenoble, 1963, no. 25
*Cologne, 1967, no. 13, repr.;
  Munich, 1967, no. 13, repr.; Vienna, 1967, no. 24, repr. p. 32; Amsterdam, 1968, no. 21, repr.; Prague, 1968, no. 49, repr.

Many of Kupka's abstract paintings derive from a perceptual experience of the real world which, when translated into purely pictorial terms, lose all visible relationship to the original subject matter. It is quite possible that *Arrangement of Verticals in Yellow* and a companion painting simply called *Arrangement of Verticals* (MNAM, Paris) were inspired by the interior of a Gothic cathedral. The thin vertical planes which scan the surface may refer to the closely massed columns of a church interior through which the stained glass windows flicker like shards of purple light. The companion painting is predominantly gray with red and blue accents in the upper part, again evoking stone columns and stained glass windows.

However, as we can see, the perceptual experience was a mere point of departure for a stringently regulated abstract composition. Although there is a definite shifting in space between the planes on the surface and others which appear to recede slightly into depth, the dominant impression is of an even all-over pattern.

Since these paintings derive directly from the *Woman Picking Flowers* series (see cat. no. 51) it is impossible to accept Kupka's 1913 date.

67 Study for *The Language of Verticals* (Etude pour *Le Langage des
verticales*). 1910-11

Brown ink wash on gray paper,
16¼ x 17⅜″ (41.3 x 44.2 cm.)
Signed lr "Kupka"
Private Collection

PROVENANCE:

the artist
to present owner

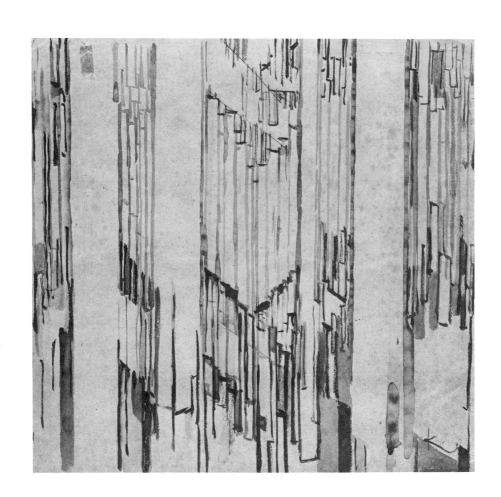

68 *"Copenetrations" ("Conpénétrations").*[1] 1910-11

Oil on canvas, 29¾ x 32½″
(75.5 x 82.5 cm.)
Signed ll "Kupka"
Private Collection, New York City

PROVENANCE:

the artist
to present owner, 1956

1 Owner's title. The title appears
  nowhere on the painting or in any of
  the artist's documentation. The owner
  prefers this spelling. The correct
  French spelling is *Compénétrations*.

The inspiration for *Copenetrations* was probably the same as that of *Arrangement of Verticals in Yellow* (cat. no. 66). Here the treatment is bolder and flatter, and the planes are shorter, more randomly distributed and more aggressively superimposed upon the surface. Furthermore the color is more arbitrary. A continuous arabesque links the bright floral clusters of color which weave in and out between the floating planes. The inner articulation of these color forms evokes the triangulated panes of stained glass, an articulation found again in both the *Amorphas* of 1912 and much other work prior to 1913-14.

This is one of the few paintings one would be tempted to interpret in terms of music: as a melody unfolding in even measures of time. The melody (in a major key) here forecasts *Amorpha, Fugue in Two Colors* of 1912; in fact the continuous arabesque motif appears again in a pastel study for that painting (Cassou-Fédit, *Kupka*, Paris, 1964, repr. p. 23). The stacked planes of color may be read as stacked notes or chords like those seen in *Piano-Keys-Lake* (cat. no. 39); their color implies a minor key.

Aside from this reading however, in strictly formal terms, this painting contains the primary motifs of Kupka's major paintings of 1912: *Vertical Planes, Amorpha, Fugue* and *Amorpha, Warm Chromatics*.

69   Study for *Nocturne* (Etude pour
      Nocturne). 1910-11

Colored pencils on paper, 8⅛ x 5⅛″
(20.5 x 13 cm.)

Stamped lr "Kupka"; inscribed
r margin "dissection du repoussoir"

Fédit, no. 46; repr.

Musée Nationale d'Art Moderne,
Paris (AM 2721-D)

PROVENANCE:

the artist
Eugénie Kupka
to present owner, gift, 1963

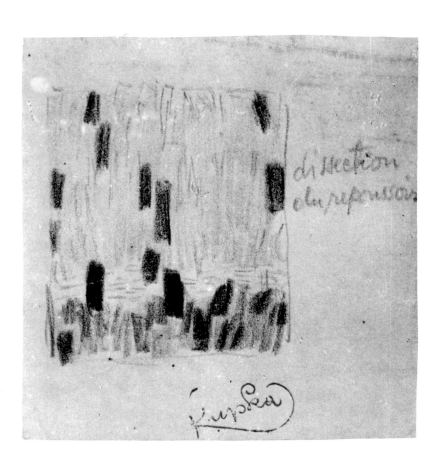

70 *Nocturne (Nocturne).* 1911

Oil on canvas, 26 x 26″ (66 x 66 cm.)

Signed lr "Kupka"

Vachtová, no. 153, repr. p. 109

Collection Museum des 20.
Jahrhunderts, Vienna

PROVENANCE:

the artist
Galerie Louis Carré, Paris
to present owner

EXHIBITIONS:

*Paris, 1936, Jeu de Paume, no. 40
(dated 1911)
*Prague, 1946, Mánes, no. 64 (dated
1911)
Paris, 1949, Maeght, no. 27 (dated
1910)
*New York, 1951, Louis Carré, no. 1,
repr.
*Paris, 1958, MNAM, no. 10 (dated
1910-11), pl. III
Paris, 1960, MNAM, no. 357, repr.
*Paris, 1964, Louis Carré, no. 1
*Vienna, 1967, no. 11, repr. color;
Amsterdam, 1968, no. 22, repr.

1 Manuscript II, p. 11.

An oil study for *Nocturne,* inscribed 1906, shows a blurred nocturnal waterscape in tones of deep blue. Not surprisingly, it is reminiscent of Whistler's famous *Nocturne, Blue and Gold,* exhibited in Paris in 1905 in a large memorial retrospective of the American artist's work. Many of Whistler's paintings bore the title *Nocturne;* many others were simply called *Arrangement,* such as the *Portrait of the Artist's Mother,* otherwise known as *Arrangement in Gray and Black.* Kupka's titles, such as *Arrangement of Verticals in Yellow,* seem to echo Whistler's.

The small drawing for *Nocturne* (cat. no. 69) shows an attempt once again to come to terms with an elimination of perspective. The artist has superimposed large vertical slabs of midnight blue in the frontal plane over a sketchily suggested pond or waterfall (see the Tate Gallery's *Waterfall,* dated 1906). The marginal notes instruct: "dissect the underlying space."

In the final version, the surface is veiled with a screen of blue planes. Kupka wrote in 1912-13: "Look what happens at twilight; when the blue screen of falling night leaves only the luminous values of blues, violets, cold greens, while the complimentaries yellows and reds become shadows."[1] The vertical emphasis of the earlier works (cat. nos. 64-68) has been disarticulated and spread in an all-over pattern. By reducing the palette to the single key of blue, Kupka eliminated contrast and surface-depth illusions. The result is a sheet of vibrating units of light.

71 *Red and Blue Disks (Disques rouges et bleus).* 1911-12

Oil on canvas, 39⅜ x 28¾"
(100 x 73 cm.)

Signed and dated lr "Kupka//
1911-12"

Vachtová, no. 98, repr. p. 83

Collection The Museum of Modern
Art, New York, Purchase, 1951
(141.51)

PROVENANCE:

the artist
Galerie Louis Carré, Paris
to present owner

EXHIBITIONS:

*Prague, 1946, Mánes, no. 131,
  (dated 1911)
Paris, 1949, Maeght, no. 29 (dated
1911)
*New York, 1951, Louis Carré, no. 3
New York, 1952; 1954; 1955; 1957,
MOMA
*New York, 1961, Royal S. Marks,
  no. 5
New York, 1964; 1965, MOMA
New York, 1965, M. Knoedler, no. 26
New York, 1966, Public Education
Association, no. 94
New York, 1966; 1969; July-November 1971; November-December 1971;
1972, MOMA

For an extensive discussion of this
picture, see pp. 72-73.

72   Study for *Disks of Newton* (Etude
      pour *Disques de Newton*).
      1911-12

Pastel on paper, 9½ x 10½"
(24.2 x 26.7 cm.)

Inscribed lr "A mon cher ami//
Lieberman [sic]"; signed and dated ur
(upside down) "Kupka//II//1912"

Collection Mr. and Mrs. Alexander
Liberman

PROVENANCE:

the artist
to present owner, 1950's

72   Study for *Disks of Newton*

73 *Disks of Newton, Study for Fugue
in Two Colors (Disques de Newton, Etude pour la Fugue à deux
couleurs)*. 1911-12

Oil on canvas, 19½ x 25⅝"
(49.5 x 65 cm.)

Dated, signed and inscribed lr
"11-12 Kupka//Etude pour la Fugue
à deux couleurs"

Fédit, no. 62, repr.

Musée National d'Art Moderne,
Paris (AM 3635-P)

PROVENANCE:

the artist
Eugénie Kupka
to present owner, gift, 1959

EXHIBITIONS:

*Paris, 1924, la Boétie, no. 10 or 11
*Prague, 1946, Mánes, no. 132
*Paris, 1953, *Salon des Réalités
    Nouvelles*, no. XLIV-F
Paris, 1954, *Salon des Indépendants*,
no. 1631
São Paulo, 1957, no. 40
*Paris, 1958, MNAM, no. 19, pl. VII
Houston, 1965, no. 51
Buffalo-Dayton-Cleveland, 1970,
no. 22, repr.
San Diego-Oakland-Seattle, 1971,
no. 40, repr. color (inaccurate)
Milan, 1973, no. 148, repr.

For discussion, see p. 73.

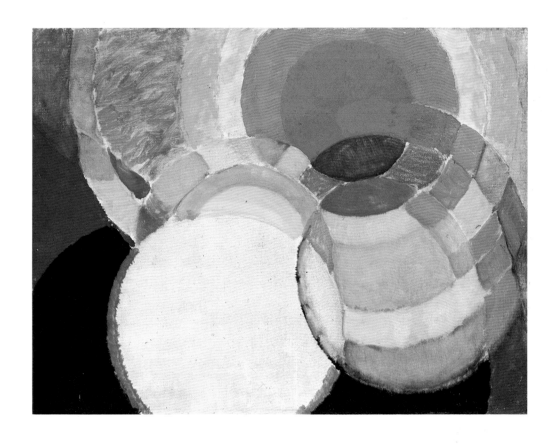

74   Study for *Disks of Newton* (Etude
     pour *Disques de Newton*).
     1911-12

     Gouache on paper, 12⅝ x 9⅞″
     (32 x 25 cm.)
     Signed l of c "Kupka"
     Fédit, no. 63, repr.
     Musée National d'Art Moderne,
     Paris (AM 2789-D)

     PROVENANCE:

     the artist
     Eugénie Kupka
     to present owner, gift, 1963

75 *Disks of Newton, Study for Fugue in Two Colors (Disques de Newton, Etude pour la Fugue à deux couleurs).* 1911-12

Oil on canvas, 39½ x 29″
(77.5 x 73.6 cm.)

Signed ll "Kupka"

Philadelphia Museum of Art, The Louise and Walter Arensberg Collection

PROVENANCE:

the artist
Walter Arensberg, 1937
to present owner

EXHIBITIONS:

*Paris, 1924, la Boétie, no. 10 or 11
New York, 1936, no. 114, fig. 60
Chicago, 1949, no. 128, repr.
Philadelphia, 1954, no. 123, repr.
Newark, 1956, no. 35
New York, 1961, SRGM
*New York, 1968, Spencer A.
  Samuels, no. 26, repr.
Buffalo-Dayton-Cleveland, 1970,
no. 23, repr. (shown at Buffalo only)
San Diego-Oakland-Seattle, 1971,
no. 42, repr. color (inaccurate)
New York, October 1972-January
1973, MOMA, no. 46

For discussion, see p. 74.

76 *Study.* 1910-11

Watercolor on paper, 4½ x 7″
(11.6 x 17.8 cm.)
Signed lr "Kupka"
Private Collection, New York City

PROVENANCE:

the artist
to present owner

77 Study for *Cosmic Spring I* (Etude pour *Printemps cosmique I*). 1911

Watercolor on paper, 9⅛ x 9⅛″ (23.3 x 23.3 cm.)
Signed ll "Kupka"
Private Collection

PROVENANCE:
the artist
previous owner
to present owner

This is obviously a study for *Cosmic Spring I* (fig.). Yet structurally it forecasts *Amorpha, Warm Chromatics* in its intertwined arcs on the left and the curving bands and small dappled motifs on the right. It anticipates *Amorpha, Fugue in Two Colors* in somewhat similar formal concerns. The genesis of these varied themes in a single work of this kind gives some insight into the complexity of Kupka's creative process.

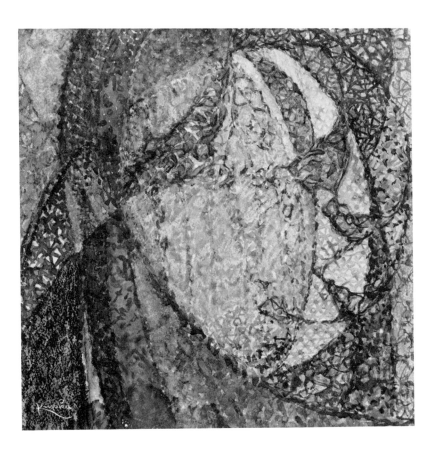

Kupka, *Cosmic Spring I,* 1911-20, oil, NG, Prague.

78 Study for *Cosmic Spring* and
Amorpha, Fugue in Two Colors
(Etude pour *Printemps cosmique*
et pour *Amorpha, Fugue à deux
couleurs*). 1911-12

Gouache on paper, 13¾ x 14½″
(35 x 36.8 cm.)
Signed lr "Kupka"
Collection Mr. and Mrs. Alexander
Liberman

PROVENANCE:

the artist
to present owner, 1950's

79 *Irregular Forms: Creation
(Formes irrégulières: Création).*
1911

Oil on canvas, 42½ x 42½″
(108 x 108 cm.)
Signed lr "Kupka"; inscribed
ll "FORMES IRRÉGULIÈRES// CRÉATION"
Los Angeles County Museum of Art,
Estate of David E. Bright
(M.67.25.10)

PROVENANCE:

the artist
Eugénie Kupka
Richard L. Feigen, Inc., Chicago
David E. Bright, Los Angeles
to present owner from Estate of
David E. Bright, 1967

EXHIBITIONS:

São Paulo, 1957, no. 42
*Paris, 1958, MNAM, no. 16
Los Angeles, Ambassador Hotel,
February 1961, *Living with Famous
Paintings*
Los Angeles, 1967, repr. color
*New York, 1968, Spencer A.
  Samuels, no. 23, repr.
San Diego-Oakland-Seattle, 1971,
no. 38, repr. color, p. 69
Pittsburgh, 1974, no. 41, repr.
Los Angeles County Museum of Art,
October 17-December 17, 1967,
David E. Bright Collection

Kupka's cosmic themes and those alluding to primordial genesis such as seen in this painting, are among the earliest of what the artist called his "imaginary" or "created" motifs. Kupka described these in the following terms: "Chaotic forms circulating like clouds in spaces of a kind never seen before, bizarre and sometimes monstrous worlds, created from scratch by the painter's poetic imagination."[1] Although the basic theme derived from the artist's imagination rather than from the immediately perceived world, he often used visual documents from the world of nature to support and define his vision. However, this painting appears more visionary than scientific in its vivid and vigorous inchoate forms spiraling around a center of infinite depth and weightless atmosphere.

1 In Edouard-Joseph, *Dictionnaire bio-graphique des artistes contemporains, 1910-1930,* Vol. II, Paris, 1931, p. 286. Text signed by Georges Turpin. This text was essentially dictated by Kupka.

80 *Creation (Création).* 1911-20

Oil on canvas, 45¼ x 49¼"
(115 x 125 cm.)

Signed lr "Kupka"

Vachtová, no. 189, color pl. XVII

Collection Národní Galerie, Prague
(o 3837)

PROVENANCE:

the artist
to present owner, 1946

EXHIBITIONS:

*Paris, 1924, la Boétie, no. 1
*Paris, 1936, Jeu de Paume, no. 19
*Prague, 1946, Mánes, no. 33
Paris, 1949, Maeght, repr. p. 194
*Paris, 1958, MNAM, no. 18
*Písek—České Budějovice,   'ou '1961
    12, repr.
Dobruška, 1962
*Paris, 1964, Louis Carré, no. 11
    (as *Création I,* dated 1920)
*Prague, 1965, no. 7
*Ustí nad Orlicí, 1965, no. 1, repr. 2
Hluboké-Brno, 1966, no. 230, repr.
    color
*Cologne, 1967, no. 69, repr. color;
    Munich, 1967, no. 69, repr.; Vienna,
    1967, no. 14, repr. no. 17, color;
    Amsterdam, 1968, no. 49, repr.
    black and white, color; Prague,
    1968, no. 53, repr. color
Geneva, 1970, no. 69, repr. color on
    cover; Zurich, 1970, no. 69, repr.
    color on cover
Turin, 1971, p. 272, repr.
Stockholm-Göteborg, 1973, no. 91,
repr. color (on its side)

Conceived in 1911, this painting was reworked in 1920. Although the formal structure remains essentially the same as that of *Irregular Forms: Creation* (cat. no. 79) the individual motifs have been hardened, and the central spatial thrust extended to infinity, thus making the whole composition more dramatic. The chiseled silhouettes of the foreground shapes and their curved arrangement around an undulating blue ground suggest that Kupka may have been referring to geological configurations seen in Brittany, where he vacationed over the years and returned in 1920 (fig.). Whatever the inspiration, the highly contrasted forms and dramatic thrust into infinite space create a vertiginous impression of the emergent cosmos.

Postcard sent by Kupka from Brittany to
Gallien, July 5, 1927.

81 *Irregular Forms: Release (Formes irrégulières: affranchissement).* 1911-20

Oil on canvas, 29½ x 33¼″ (75 x 84.4 cm.)

Signed lr "Kupka;" inscribed ll "FORMES IRREGULIERES//AFFRAN-CHISSEMENT"

Collection Mr. and Mrs. Arnold A. Saltzman, Great Neck, New York

PROVENANCE:

the artist
grandfather of previous owner
previous owner
to present owner, October 1971

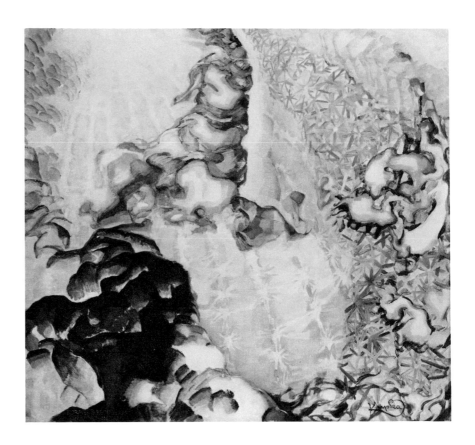

82 *Cosmic Spring II (Printemps cosmique II).* 1911-20; repainted 1934?

Oil on canvas, 45¼ x 49¼″ (115 x 125 cm.)

Signed lr "Kupka"

Vachtová, no. 192, repr. p. 152; color pl. XVI

Collection Národní Galerie, Prague (o 3820)

PROVENANCE:

the artist
to present owner, 1946

EXHIBITIONS:

*Paris, 1924, la Boétie, no. 3
*Paris, 1936, Jeu de Paume, no. 20
*Prague, 1946, Mánes, no. 34
*Paris, 1958, MNAM, no. 17
*Písek–České Budějovice, 1961, no. 11, repr.
Hluboké-Brno, 1966, no. 229
London, 1967, no. 76
Brussels-Rotterdam, 1967, no. 76, repr.
*Prague, 1968, no. 55, repr.
Rome, 1969, no. 1, repr. (on its side)
Stockholm-Göteborg, 1973, no. 92

Although reworked in 1920 and perhaps again c. 1934 (see Vachtová, p. 276), *Cosmic Spring II* retains much of the basic structural composition of its initial conception which was close to that of its pendant *Cosmic Spring I* (NG, Prague, fig., p. 169). The 1920 modifications may have included a brightening of the palette, a tightening of the forms and superficial bands of shadow on either side (see Vachtová, p. 278). In the final version, Kupka darkened the bands of shadow and obliterated the cloud and crystalline motifs in the lower central portion.

Kupka liked to maintain that these images were the pure fruits of his imagination. Yet it is obvious that he drew on photographs or models of the moon for their formulation. In *Cosmic Spring II,* the deep grooves of the lunar surface fan out from a large volcanic crater or *cirque* in the upper left corner (see fig.).

Janssen, Photograph of the moon, taken at the Meudon Observatory, January 1881.

83 *Study for Amorpha, Fugue in Two Colors and Amorpha, Warm Chromatics (Etude pour Amorpha, Fugue à deux couleurs et pour Amorpha, Chromatique chaude).* 1911-12

Oil on canvas, 33½ x 50⅜"
(85 x 128 cm.)

Signed ll "Kupka"

Fédit, no. 61, repr.

Musée National d'Art Moderne, Paris (AM 4173-P)

PROVENANCE:

the artist
Eugénie Kupka
to present owner, gift, 1963

EXHIBITIONS:

*Paris, 1924, la Boétie, no. 8 or 9
*Prague, 1946, Mánes, no. 133 (dated 1911-12)
*Paris, 1953, *Salon des Réalités Nouvelles* (hors catalogue)
São Paulo, 1957, no. 39 (as *Estudo*)
*Paris, 1958, MNAM, no. 20
Grenoble, 1963, no. 22
*Cologne, 1967, no. 18, repr.; Munich, 1967, no. 18, repr.; Vienna, 1967, no. 19; Amsterdam, 1968, no. 19, repr. twice; Prague, 1968, no. 42a, repr.

It is difficult to situate this work in Kupka's progression from the first studies of rotation (1908-09) to the two *Amorpha* paintings of 1912. One may merely identify it as a study of motion, light and color, parallel to the *Disks of Newton* series and the cosmic themes. Yet it would be tempting to define this image as an unfolding of consecutive phases of motion moving toward its synthesis, a synthesis which will be achieved in the two *Amorphas* where movement is not overtly demonstrated but contained.

84 Study related to *Amorpha, Fugue in Two Colors* and *Amorpha, Warm Chromatics*. 1911-12

Pastel on paper, 8¼ x 8¼″
(21 x 21 cm.)
Signed ll "Kupka"

Collection The Solomon R. Guggenheim Museum, New York, Gift, Mr. and Mrs. Alexander Liberman, 1974 (2123)

PROVENANCE:

the artist
Mr. and Mrs. Alexander Liberman, 1950's
to present owner, gift

85 Study related to *Amorpha, Warm Chromatics.* 1911-12

Pastel on paper, 9¾ x 8¼″
(24.8 x 20.6 cm.)
Signed lr "Kupka"
Private Collection

PROVENANCE:

the artist
Galerie Karl Flinker, Paris
Saidenberg Gallery, New York
to present owner, October 1970

86 *Amorpha, Warm Chromatics
(Amorpha, Chromatique chaude).*
1911-12

Oil on canvas, 42½ x 42½″
(108 x 108 cm.)
Signed lr "Kupka;" inscribed and
dated ll "Amorpha—chromatique
chaude//1912"
Vachtová, no. 141, color pl. IV
Private Collection

PROVENANCE:

the artist
Eugénie Kupka
to present owner

EXHIBITIONS:

Paris, 1912, *Salon d'Automne,* no. 926
*Prague, 1946, Mánes, no. 134 (dated
1911-12)
Paris, 1947, *Salon des Réalités
Nouvelles*
Houston, 1965, no. 50
São Paulo, 1957, no. 41
*Paris, 1958, MNAM, no. 23

Amorpha, Warm Chromatics, like *Amorpha, Fugue,* is a composite image deriving from diverse sources, images and impressions. The general organization is very close to a work which precedes it slightly (cat. no. 83). One may also relate it chromatically to still earlier works, the artist's studies of church interiors (cat. no. 66)—here enhanced by the vaulted patterns—and his studies of cosmic space (cat. no. 77) which foreshadow this configuration in formal terms. The intellectual and pictorial processes by which Kupka arrived at this purely abstract composition are indicative of his fundamental aesthetic which is based on an attempt to depict the laws of the macrocosm through microcosmic phenomena. Here he has identified the simplified formal patterns of the vaulted church interior with the rotational patterns and forms of the cosmic order.

In *Amorpha, Fugue* of the same year, Kupka was concerned with pure color refracting light. In *Amorpha, Warm Chromatics,* however he uses mixed colors in a more conventional fashion to produce the illusion of light. For this reason, one may suggest that *Amorpha, Warm Chromatics* is the earlier of the two paintings.

87   Study for *Amorpha, Fugue in Two Colors*. 1911-12

Pastel on paper, 12¼ x 12¾"
(31.1 x 32.4 cm.)
Signed lr "Kupka"
Private Collection, New York

PROVENANCE:
the artist
Eugénie Kupka
to present owner

Like the early studies for *Cosmic Spring* to which it is related (cat. nos. 77, 78), this pastel maintains the primary emphasis in the left foreground of the composition. However the intersecting zones of dappled light and shadow in the earlier studies have here been distilled into unified ribbons of color intertwined in a rotational movement.

During the period 1911-12, Kupka did a large number of preparatory studies for *Amorpha, Fugue* in which the interlaced arabesque motif appears on the right or the left interchangeably (see cat. nos. 88-91).

88 Study for *Amorpha, Fugue in Two Colors*. 1912

Gouache on paper, 8⅜ x 9″
(21.4 x 22.8 cm.)

Signed ll "Kupka"

Collection The Museum of Modern
Art, New York, gift of Mr. and Mrs.
František Kupka, 1956 (569.56.13)

PROVENANCE:

the artist
to present owner, gift

89 Study for *Amorpha, Fugue in Two Colors*. 1912

Gouache on paper, 8⅜ x 9″
(21.4 x 22.8 cm.)

Signed lr "Kupka"

Collection The Museum of Modern
Art, New York, gift of Mr. and Mrs.
František Kupka, 1956 (569.56.14)

PROVENANCE:

the artist
to present owner, gift

90 Study for *Amorpha, Fugue in Two Colors.* 1912

Gouache on paper, 8⅜ x 9″
(21.4 x 22.8 cm.)

Signed ll "Kupka"

Collection The Museum of Modern
Art, New York, gift of Mr. and Mrs.
František Kupka, 1956 (569.56.15)

PROVENANCE:

the artist
to present owner, gift

91   Study for *Amorpha, Fugue in Two Colors*. 1912

Gouache on paper, 8⅛ x 8⅞″
(20.8 x 22.5 cm.)

Signed lr "Kupka"

Collection The Museum of Modern
Art, New York, gift of Mr. and Mrs.
František Kupka, 1956 (569.56.16)

PROVENANCE:

the artist
to present owner, gift

92 *Amorpha, Fugue in Two Colors (Amorpha, Fugue à deux couleurs).* 1912

Oil on canvas, 83⅜ x 86⅝"
(211 x 220 cm.)

Signed lr "Kupka;" inscribed ll
"fugue à deux couleurs"

Vachtová, no. 139, repr. p. 281;
color pl. V

Collection Národní Galerie, Prague
(O 5942)

PROVENANCE:

the artist
Picture Gallery of Prague Castle
to present owner, 1953

EXHIBITIONS:

Paris, 1912, *Salon d'Automne,* no. 925
*Paris, 1924, la Boétie, no. 7 (dated
  1912)
Lille, 1925, no. 1
*Paris, 1936, Jeu de Paume, no. 32
*Prague, 1946, Mánes, no. 130 (dated
  1910-12), pl. VIII
*Paris, 1958, MNAM, no. 22, pl. VIII
*Písek—České Budějovice, 1961, no. 8,
  repr.
*Prague, 1968, no. 42, repr. black and
  white, color

1 Handwritten manuscript in French.
  Long, wordy and written in Kupka's
  sometimes byzantine style, some parts
  will be paraphrased here. Kupka wrote
  many autobiographical texts such as
  this one, in the third person, in which
  numerous disparities are found. Dates
  are often cited incorrectly, as are
  sequences of paintings and events.
  Furthermore, at times one can see a
  tendency to romanticize his own
  development. Nonetheless, despite the
  lack of reliability, this text shows how
  Kupka saw his own development at a
  given time.

2 Manuscript I, 1910-11.

3 *Mercure de France,* November 1, 1912,
  p. 181.

In an autobiography written around 1926-27, Kupka described his transition to abstraction and his development to *Amorpha, Fugue* of 1912.[1] In 1911, during a critical period in his art, a musician friend Morse-Rummel, an admirable interpretor of Bach fugues, used to come to visit him. "Yes, fugues," wrote Kupka, "where the sounds evolve like veritable physical entities, intertwine, come and go." Could one not conceive a painting of similarly orchestrated visual terms, Kupka wondered, a painting where subject matter is eliminated and only the painter's understanding and interpretation of a theme remains? The artist's first experiments showed "masses of clouds with the colors of flowers, forms reminiscent of marine flora, interpenetrations of many colored disks. These laborious beginnings produced monstrosities, resembling a madman's imaginary visions. So Kupka attempted to discipline them according to the implacable logic of the painted canvas." Seeking to translate them in more "absolute" terms, he could only resort to "a kind of geometrization, eliminating the trompe-l'oeil of perspective. Thus the third dimension fell by the wayside, that third dimension against which Maurice Denis had revolted and Odilon Redon in part as well. As for color, sometimes prismatic, sometimes recalling the eighteenth century—an analogy between the fugues Rummel played or others by Seurat, Signac, Debussy, Déodat de Séverac—color must speak as forcibly as form, that is if color itself does not determine the whole construction of the painting."

Further on, Kupka added that since his canvases were rhythmic, the analogy between music and painting seemed obvious, particularly in view of the musical reference in the title of the *Fugue.* Yet, according to Kupka, he chose this title after the fact, almost by default, for lack of a better one.

This account of Kupka's development from a figurative to an abstract idiom is the fullest we have from his hand. At one point, he says that the *Fugue* came from the reds and blues of *Family Portrait* (cat. no. 44). On other occasions, Kupka attributed his inspiration to stained glass windows, and indeed his preoccupation with light reflection and refraction is paramount throughout this period, inspired by his visits to Gothic cathedrals. He even mentions that the best solution for what he is seeking would be achieved by painting on glass.[2] Finally the abundant studies show still other formal preoccupations: separate yet interlacing strands of color, kaleidoscopic patterns, cosmic rhythms, disjointed and overlapping rhythmic silhouettes. And of course the diagrams after the *Girl with a Ball* and their extension into rotational figures and cosmic disks cannot be overlooked as another dimension of his inspiration. However, whether based on human rhythms, stained glass patterns, cosmic rotation or another source, in its final form, *Amorpha, Fugue* shows a consummate synthesis of intellectual, instinctive and pictorial ideas.

Exhibited in 1912 alongside Matisse's *Nasturtiums and "Dance"* (Pushkin Museum, Moscow), Picabia's *Procession* and Cubist paintings by Gleizes, Metzinger and La Fresnaye, it is not surprising that *Amorpha, Fugue* provoked general dismay or hilarity on the part of critics and general public alike. Gustave Kahn, who had been sympathetic to Kupka's earlier work was disconcerted: "the elegant chromatic arabesques based on feminine lines by Mr. Kupka are games which are not within everyone's reach. Even with the greatest sympathy for the Cubist effort, one cannot yet admire these works."[3]

Amorpha, Fugue in Two Colors was the first purely abstract painting exhibited in Paris.

93 Etching related to *Amorpha,*
    Fugue in Two Colors. 1913

    Color etching, 9½ x 6⅜″
    (24 x 16 cm.)

    Signed and dated in plate ll "Kupka"
    lr "1913"

    Collection Karl Flinker

    PROVENANCE:

    the artist
    Eugénie Kupka
    to present owner

94 *Elevation (Elévation).* 1911-12

    Colored crayons on paper,
    11⅜ x 8½″ (29 x 21.5 cm.)

    Signed ll "Kupka"

    Courtesy Galerie Denise René, Paris

    PROVENANCE:

    the artist
    Eugénie Kupka
    Karl Flinker
    to present owner

95   *Study.* 1911-12

Pastel on brown paper, 16 x 8⅞″
(40.6 x 22.5 cm.)

Signed ll "Kupka"

Collection The Museum of Modern
Art, New York, The Joan and Lester
Avnet Fund, 1967

PROVENANCE:

the artist
Private Collection
Graham Gallery, New York
to present owner

96 *Vertical Planes I (Plans verticaux I)*. 1912

Oil on canvas, 59⅛ x 37"
(150 x 94 cm.)

Signed and dated ll "Kupka//1912"

Fédit, no. 55, repr.

Musée National d'Art Moderne,
Paris (J. de P. 807)

PROVENANCE:

the artist
Musée des Ecoles Etrangères
Contemporaines (Musée du Jeu de
Paume), 1936
to present owner, transferred, 1945

EXHIBITIONS:

*Paris, 1924, la Boétie, no. 12 (dated
 1912-13)
*Paris, 1936, Jeu de Paume, no. 40
 (dated 1912-13)
Paris, 1937, no. 163
Paris, 1949, Maeght, repr. p. 197 (as
 Plans verticaux no. 2)
Birmingham, 1956
London, 1956
*Paris, 1958, MNAM, no. 24, pl. V
*Cologne, 1967, no. 14, repr. color;
 Munich, 1967, no. 14, repr.; Vienna,
 1967, no. 18, repr. color; Amster-
 dam, 1968, no. 28, repr. black and
 white, color; Prague, 1968, no. 45,
 repr. black and white, color
San Diego-Oakland-Seattle, 1971,
no. 43, repr. color (inaccurate)

Just as *Amorpha, Fugue* is the culmination of Kupka's studies of color and rotational movement, *Vertical Planes I* and *III* are the consummate expression of the
theme of verticality which started to emerge in his work as early as 1906. Whereas
the paintings of 1909-1911 showed broad impastoed brushstrokes superimposed
on the surface and enmeshed in a closely woven fabric of planes, in *Vertical Planes I*
the planes relate to an entirely different level of experience. Earlier, Kupka referred
to his perceptual experience; here he is attempting to illustrate the abstract idea of
verticality itself.

In 1912-13, Kupka evoked the "rectilinear world" as abstract and immaterial:
"A rectilinear order appears as the most energetic, abstract, elegant, absolute order
. . . The vertical line is like a man standing erect, where the above and the below,
top and bottom are suspended and, since they stretch from one to the other, they
are united, identical, one." He concludes, "Profound and silent, a vertical plane
helps the whole concept of space to emerge."[1]

In contrast to the earlier pictures noted above, these planes are suspended on a
thinly painted ground which connotes an infinite spatial continuum. Free from contours, their diagonally sliced upper and lower edges produce an effect of floating
and a slight turning in space. The delicate colors and their relationships emphasize
the ephemeral elusive quality of the composition.

Finally, in the same text, Kupka says: "Have you never had the experience of
having a 'vertical' intrude upon your vision? It is the shadow of an eyelash which
has fallen before the eye and divides the field of sight."[2] Kupka returned to this
analogy time and again. This reference to personal physiological experience reveals
almost a mystical, visionary dimension in his pictorial investigations—as concentrated physiological experience is sublimated into mystical experience in many
disciplines. This dimension cannot be overlooked, but should not be overempha-
sized. The pictorial objective had priority. On a small study, Kupka wrote: "Syn-
thesis/ the pre-existing form/ the elementary through vertical planes/ planes of
force:/ verticals/ vertical symmorphy."[3]

Just as the *Amorpha, Fugue* was a "symmorphy of colors," this painting was intended as a "symmorphy" or formal orchestration of planes.

1 Manuscript IV, p. 52.

2 Formulation taken from Manuscript II,
  p. 35.

3 In the MOMA Study Collection.

97 *Vertical Planes III (Plans verticaux
    III).* 1912-13

Oil on canvas, 78¾ x 46½"
(200 x 118 cm.)

Signed lr "Kupka;" inscribed and
dated ll "plans//verticaux//
1912-13"

Vachtová, no. 160, color pl. VIII

Collection Národní Galerie, Prague
(O 3819)

PROVENANCE:

the artist
to present owner, 1946

EXHIBITIONS:

Paris, 1913, *Salon des Indépendants,*
no. 1720
Paris, 1926, Grand Palais, no. 1378
(as *Plans verticaux*)
Paris, 1934, *Salon des Indépendants,*
no. 2443
New York, 1936, no. 116, fig. 62
*Paris, 1936, Jeu de Paume, no. 41
(dated 1912-13)
*Prague, 1946, Mánes, no. 67 (dated
1912-13)
*Písek—České Budějovice, 1961,
no. 9, repr.
*Prague, 1965, no. 4
*Cologne, 1967, no. 70, repr.;
Munich, 1967, no. 70, repr.; Vienna,
1967, no. 21, repr. p. 30; Amster-
dam, 1968, no. 31, repr.; Prague,
1968, no. 46, repr.
Geneva, 1970, no. 68, repr.; Zurich,
1970, no. 68, repr.
Venice, 1972
Stockholm—Göteborg, 1973, no. 93

Vertical Planes II has either been lost or was destroyed by Kupka. *Vertical Planes III* has been identified as the painting exhibited at the 1913 *Indépendants.* However one reviewer of the exhibition described the painting as "several stripes of brown on a gray ground."[1] Either the critic's visual memory failed him, or the painting exhibited was not this picture. Kupka always maintained that it was this one.

In 1936, Alfred Barr exhibited this painting in his epoch-making exhibition *Cubism and Abstract Art.* In the catalogue he wrote: "At the end of the year [1912] Kupka began the final version of *Vertical Planes* the first studies of which had been done in 1911. Its cold gray rectangles sharpened by a single violet plane anticipate the geometric compositions of Malevich, Arp and Mondrian. *Vertical Planes* was exhibited at the *Indépendants* in the spring of 1913. Within a year's time Kupka had painted what are probably the first geometrical curvilinear and the first recti-linear pure-abstractions in modern art. In comparison with these conclusive and carefully considered achievements the slightly earlier abstractions of Kandinsky and Larionov seem tentative."[2]

1 *Intransigeant,* March 1913. Cited in
  Arnould-Grémilly, 1922, p. 73.

2 Barr, Alfred H., Jr., *Cubism and
  Abstract Art,* New York, 1936, pp.
  73-74.

98 *Untitled.* 1913

Etching, 9½ x 6¼" (24 x 16 cm.)
Signed in plate lr "Kupka"
Collection Karl Flinker

PROVENANCE:

the artist
Eugénie Kupka
to present owner

99 *The Cathedral (La Cathédrale).*
1913

Oil on canvas, 70⅞ x 59⅛"
(180 x 150 cm.)
Signed ll "Kupka"

Vachtová, no. 164, repr. p. 140, color
pl. XI

Private Collection

PROVENANCE:

the artist
Galerie Louis Carré, Paris
to present owner, 1975

EXHIBITIONS:

*New York, 1953, Rose Fried, no. 8
Lausanne, 1955, no. 43
*Paris, 1958, MNAM, no. 31 (dated
  1913), pl. XII
*Paris, 1964, Louis Carré, no. 4

100   Study related to *The Cathedral*.
      c. 1913

      Gouache on paper, 26⅝ x 19¾"
      (67.7 x 50.2 cm.)
      Signed lr "Kupka"
      Private Collection

      PROVENANCE:

      the artist
      to present owner

*Vertical and Diagonal Planes
      (Plans verticaux et diagonaux).*
      1913-14

Oil on canvas, 22 x 15¾"
(55.9 x 40 cm.)
Signed ll "Kupka"
Collection McCrory Corporation,
New York

PROVENANCE:
the artist
Marcel Duchamp-Jacques Villon
Spencer A. Samuels and
    Company, Ltd., New York
Suzanne Feigel, Basel
Annely Juda Fine Art, London
to present owner

EXHIBITIONS:
*Paris, 1936, Jeu de Paume, no. 59
  (dated 1913), repr.
Paris, 1949, *Salon des Réalités Nouvelles*, no. 285

102 Study for *Organization of Graphic
Motifs* (Etude pour *Localisations
de mobiles graphiques*). 1911-12

Charcoal on paper, 13 x 12¼″
(33 x 31 cm.)
Signed lr "Kupka"
Courtesy Galerie Denise René, Paris

PROVENANCE:
the artist
Eugénie Kupka
Karl Flinker
to present owner

103 Study for *Organization of Graphic
Motifs* (Etude pour *Localisations
de mobiles graphiques*). 1911-12

Charcoal on paper, 12⅝ x 11¾″
(32 x 30 cm.)
Unsigned
Courtesy Galerie Denise René, Paris

PROVENANCE:
the artist
Eugénie Kupka
Karl Flinker
to present owner

Study for *Organization of Graphic Motifs* (Etude pour *Localisations de mobiles graphiques*). 1912-13

Pastel on paper, 13½ x 13⅛″
(34.3 x 33.3 cm.)
Signed l of c "Kupka"
Private Collection

PROVENANCE:
the artist
Eugénie Kupka
to present owner

105

*Organization of Graphic Motifs I
(Localisations de mobiles graphiques I). 1912-13*

Oil on canvas, 78¾ x 76⅜″
(200 x 194 cm.)
Signed lr "Kupka;" inscribed ll
"LOCALISATIONS DE MOBILES
GRAPHIQUES"
Vachtová, no. 195
Collection Royal S. Marks Gallery,
New York

PROVENANCE:
the artist
Eugénie Kupka
Richard L. Feigen, Chicago
to present owner, 1958

EXHIBITIONS:
Paris, 1913, *Salon d'Automne,*
no. 1149
*Paris, 1936, Jeu de Paume, no. 33
*Paris, 1958, MNAM, no. 26, pl. X
Cleveland, 1960, no. 29, repr.
*New York, 1961, Royal S. Marks,
no. 8
*New York, 1964, Royal S. Marks,
(not on checklist)

The phrase *"localisations de mobiles graphiques"* is developed in two stages in Kupka's writings. The terms *"mobile"* and *"mobile graphique"* occur for the first time in his 1910-11 manuscript. They are defined as the outer expression of the artist's inner motivations (or motives) and identified as *"motifs-mobiles"* (motive-motifs) as opposed to *"motifs-sujets"* (subject-motifs) or the motif derived from a subject in the perceived world. For Kupka, there is no necessity to look for subject matter in perceived objects. The artist's slightest gesture, his style or approach to painting express an intelligence, a mentality, a vision and this is sufficient.[1]

In the same text, Kupka defines the phrase *"localisations des motifs-mobiles graphiques,"* a concept which he will develop more extensively in the years these pictures were done. In his 1912-13 manuscript, Kupka devotes three to four handwritten pages to this concept which we will attempt to summarize here:

In our inner visions, fragments of images float before our eyes. In order to capture these fragments, we unconsciously trace lines between them and by thus setting up a network of relationships, we arrive at a coherent whole. These lines drawn to organize our visions are like "stereoscopic bridges" between fragments in space. . . . The lines of this network define points in space and directions. They provide the scaffolding of the image; they capture the rhythmic relationships between impres-

1 Manuscript I, pp. 30-31.

106

Organization of Graphic Motifs II (Localisations de mobiles graphiques II). 1912-13

Oil on canvas, 78¾ x 78¾″
(200 x 200 cm.)

Signed ll "Kupka"

Vachtová, no. 196

Private Collection

PROVENANCE:

the artist
Eugénie Kupka
to present owner

EXHIBITIONS:

Paris, 1913, *Salon d'Automne,*
no. 1150
Houston, 1965, no. 52

sions. And this is the real subject of the painter: the lyrical or tragic schema of nature poeticized or dramatized. Details, forms, figures, objects may subsequently be added to articulate the image further.[2]

Early sketches for these two paintings[3] show varied approaches to the problem of pure spatial relationships. Probably the earliest show what appears to be a road between houses in which all but the vertical lines are drawn off into a central vanishing point. Other drawings contain what look like railroad tracks or telegraph wires. Still others show small clusters of enigmatic figures scattered at random, and arbitrarily connected by scores of lines. These are the flattest of all the drawings.

However, in keeping with Kupka's notion of "stereoscopic bridges," the final paintings retain a thrust into depth, magnified once again to vertiginous cosmic proportions. After the flat synthesis of contained motion and color of the *Fugue,* Kupka turned to a more overtly dynamic and dramatic imagery. A third painting, *Non-Descriptive Space,* of 1913-14[4] was originally extremely close to *Organization of Graphic Motifs II.* Subsequently, Kupka reworked the painting, leaving only the motifs around the outer edge.

2 Manuscript II, pp. 28-30 *bis.*

3 In MOMA Study Collection.

4 Collection Louis Carré, Paris. See study, cat. no. 107. The painting may be seen in fig. 11, p. 313, second painting from the right.

107 Study for *Non-Descriptive Space*
(Etude pour *Espace non descrip-tif*). 1913-14

Colored crayons on paper, 5¾ x 5½"
(14.5 x 14 cm.)
Signed ll "Kupka"
Collection Karl Flinker

PROVENANCE:

the artist
Eugénie Kupka
to present owner

108 *Solo of a Brown Line (Le Solo d'un
trait brun)*. 1912-13

Oil on canvas, 27½ x 45¼"
(70 x 115 cm.)
Inscribed, dated and signed ll "Le
solo//d'un trait brun//1912-13
Kupka"
Vachtová, no. 232, color pl. XIX
Collection Národní Galerie, Prague
(O 3825)

PROVENANCE:

the artist
to present owner, 1946

EXHIBITIONS:

Paris, 1913, *Salon des Indépendants,*
no. 1721
*Paris, 1924, la Boétie, no. 16 (dated
1913)
Paris, 1926, Grand Palais, no. 1379
*Paris, 1936, Jeu de Paume, no. 64
*Prague, 1946, Mánes, no. 151
Paris, 1949, Maeght, repr. p. 194
*Paris, 1958, MNAM, no. 28, pl. IX
*Písek—České Budějovice, 1961,
no. 10, repr.
Hluboké—Brno, 1966, no. 231
London, 1967, no. 77
Brussels—Rotterdam, 1967, no. 77
*Prague, 1968, no. 56, repr.
Turin, 1971, p. 273, repr.
Stockholm—Göteborg, 1973, no. 94

Kupka's 1910-11 notebook contains a number of short entries concerning "point," "line," "spot," "plane," "space," "light," themes which he would develop in his treatise on the function of painting. On the page devoted to "line," he drew a number of whiplash curves, each representing the characteristic style of a period: "eighteenth century," "Gothic," "Art Nouveau," etc., obviously inspired by his early training in the function of ornamental motifs. On the same page he noted that the autonomous line is the "happiest" line because it serves no master (such as shading, form, color, plane). It generates its own significance through "associations" with forms, volumes, tactility, muscular activity.[1]

By 1912-13, the time of this painting, Kupka's thinking had developed further. In his manuscript of this period he differentiates between line *(la ligne)* and stroke *(le trait),* saying that whereas a line divides space, a stroke acts as an autonomous graphic entity. It is an ideogram: the true expression of an idea. It has nothing to do with geometry, it is not the shortest distance between two points. It possesses its own substance and presence. In support of his theory, Kupka referred to Rembrandt's etchings.[2]

This emphasis on the expressive vitality of a line is reminiscent of van de Velde and other exponents of Art Nouveau. Kupka's early exposure to this idiom made a profound impression on his art and his thinking, traces of which are still seen here in the dynamic trajectory of a line through space. As we have seen elsewhere, Kupka consistently sought to disengage formal motifs from descriptive tasks and make them function according to their own substance. A drawing in The Museum of Modern Art Study Collection bears the inscription: "Solo of a brown sinuous [line], orchestration of spots placed with no motivation, solely to send off and receive the line."

The "spots" or triangular planes on either side of the present work resemble a kaleidoscopic image, even though they are based on the familiar panes of stained glass seen frequently elsewhere. Kupka knew about kaleidoscopes by this time and referred to them in the same manuscript as a mirror technique for decomposing forms and reconstituting them into a new homogenous ensemble.[3] These kaleidoscopic shifting forms are seen in other works of the period.[4]

1 Manuscript I, p. 41.
2 Manuscript IV, p. 58.
3 Ibid., p. 79.
4 See cat. nos. 105 and 109.

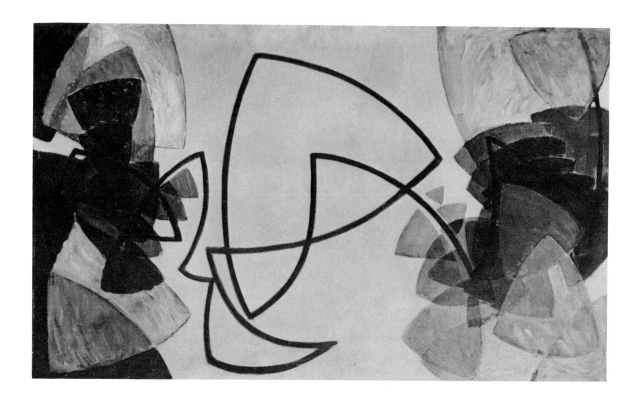

109 *Study.* 1912-13

Pastel on paper, 11¾ x 13½″
(29.9 x 34.3 cm.)

Signed and dated lr "Kupka//13-14"

Collection Mr. and Mrs. Alexander
Liberman

PROVENANCE:

the artist
to present owner, 1950's

110 *Study.* 1912-13

Colored crayons and colored pencils
on paper, 5⅛ x 10⅜″ (13 x 26.5 cm.)

Stamped ll "Kupka"

Collection Karl Flinker

PROVENANCE:

the artist
Eugénie Kupka
to present owner

11 Study for *Lines, Planes, Spaces*
(Etude pour *Traits, plans, espaces*). 1913

Gouache on paper, 11¾ x 9″
(29.9 x 22.9 cm.)
Signed lr "Kupka"
Collection William Zierler

PROVENANCE:
the artist
Estate of the artist
Karl Flinker
Spencer A. Samuels and Co., Ltd.,
New York
to present owner

12 *Untitled.* 1913

Color etching, 6⅛ x 13¾″
(15.5 x 35 cm.)
Signed and dated in plate lr "Kupka"
ll "1913"
Collection Karl Flinker

PROVENANCE:
the artist
Eugénie Kupka
to present owner

During this period, Kupka did a number of etchings on the theme of acrobats or
fairs. Although this etching is on the borderline between figuration and abstraction, it captures the spirit of a circus; one is reminded for example of Toulouse-
Lautrec's circus series, particularly the painting *Au cirque Fernando* of 1888 (Art
Institute of Chicago), and of Kupka's own lithograph of 1899, *The Fools,* (fig. 3,
p. 307). Yet despite the barely discernible silhouettes of figures, the dynamic sweep
of circular rhythms, strong directional lines and dramatic composition endow the
subject with a cosmic dimension.

113 *Untitled.* 1913

Color etching, 6¼ x 9½"
(16 x 24 cm.)
Signed in plate ll "Kupka"
Collection Karl Flinker

PROVENANCE:

the artist
Eugénie Kupka
to present owner

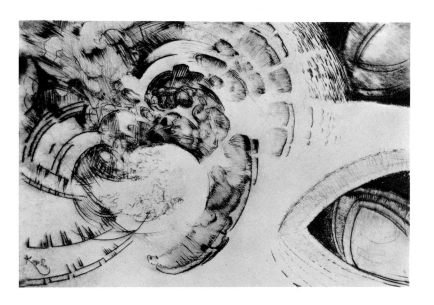

1 One might look for their source in
  Kupka's early illustrations for
  L'Homme et la terre (see fig. 4, p. 308).

The cosmic dimension seen emerging in the preceding etching is here fully developed. At least two motifs appear in this work which, although conceived as early as 1912, will only be fully elaborated after World War I. The large circular configuration on the left anticipates the series *Around a Point* (cat. nos. 152-160) for which preliminary watercolors were probably executed at around this time. However the loose floral arrangement in the sketches is translated here into a more geometric configuration because of both the altered context and the constraints of the etching technique. The motifs on the right were first formulated in the two paintings *Organization of Graphic Motifs* of 1912-13.[1] Again they appear in the etching in the tighter, stricter form of Kupka's later work.

14   *Evidence (Evidence).* 1914-1919?

Watercolor on paper, 10⅝ x 8¼″
(27 x 21 cm.)
Signed ll "Kupka"
Collection Royal S. Marks Gallery,
New York

PROVENANCE:
the artist
Estate of the artist
Karl Flinker
Galerie Denise René, Paris
to present owner

Usually dated 1914, the type of organic forms depicted here did not appear in
Kupka's work until after 1919. It is conceivable that this might be an early variation
on the theme *Tale of Pistils and Stamens.*

115 Study for *The Colored One* (Etude pour *La Colorée*). 1911-19?

Pastel on paper, 10 x 9″
(25.4 x 22.9 cm.)
Signed ll "Kupka"
Private Collection

PROVENANCE:

the artist
Eugénie Kupka
to present owner

Kupka, *Black Accent,* c. 1919, oil, Private Collection.

6 *The Colored One (La Colorée).*
1919

Oil on canvas, 25⅝ x 21¼"
(65 x 54 cm.)

Signed ll "Kupka"

Collection The Solomon R.
Guggenheim Museum, New York,
Gift of Mrs. Andrew P. Fuller, 1966
(1810)

PROVENANCE:

the artist
Eugénie Kupka
Richard L. Feigen, Inc., New York,
1958
Mr. and Mrs. Andrew P. Fuller,
December 1961
to present owner, gift

EXHIBITIONS:

New York, 1966, SRGM
New York, May-June 1967, SRGM
New York, June-October 1967,
SRGM
*New York, 1968, Spencer A.
  Samuels, no. 40, repr.
New York, 1969, SRGM
New York, 1970, SRGM, p. 257, repr.
New York, 1971, SRGM, p. 257, repr.
New York, 1973, SRGM

1 In his 1910-11 manuscript (Manuscript
I, p. 6), Kupka quoted Delacroix: "For
the artist, nature is only a dictionary."

The Colored One is a problematic picture. The subject of a woman lying on her back with a sun-disk between her open thighs is unique in Kupka's oeuvre. It seems incongruous that Kupka would have reverted to such a sensuous and symbolic figurative subject after his bold pure abstractions of 1911-13. Yet the brushwork and palette relate it unmistakably to the period 1919.

In 1919, after the war, when Kupka began painting seriously again, he returned once more to nature for his vocabulary and syntax.[1] At this time he did a number of experimental paintings in which the subject of nature plays a prominent role. The first series, *Tale of Pistils and Stamens* (cat. nos. 117-122) shows obvious and direct references to nature and biological processes. However this series also contains an explicit symbolic dimension which will subsequently be eliminated in favor of more purely formal concerns (see discussion, cat. no. 120).

Kupka produced a number of preliminary paintings before arriving at the definitive formulation of this theme. One of the pictures shows brightly colored human silhouettes massed together in a rhythmic organic image (fig., p. 208). This motif will emerge as the core of two of the *Pistils* paintings, where it will illustrate the erotic dimension of Kupka's symbolism. *The Colored One* can be related to this cycle; it appears as a first attempt to illustrate Kupka's allegory of floral fecundation.

117　Study for *Tale of Pistils and*
Stamens (Etude pour *Conte de*
pistils et d'étamines). 1919?

Light gray chalk or charcoal on
paper, 17 x 17¼″ (43 x 44 cm.)
Stamped lr "Kupka"
Courtesy Galerie Denise René, Paris

PROVENANCE:

the artist
Eugénie Kupka
Karl Flinker
to present owner

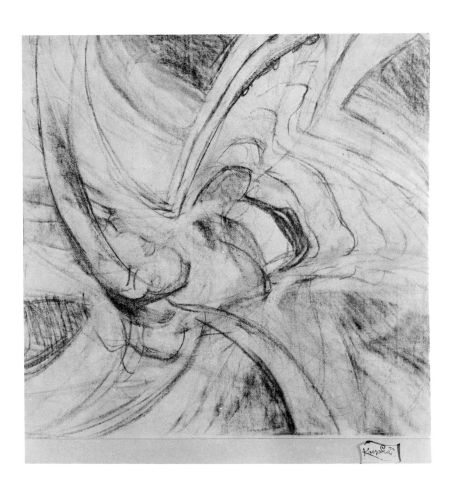

18 Study for *Tale of Pistils and Stamens* (Etude pour *Conte de pistils et d'étamines*). 1919

Watercolor on paper, 10¾ x 9⅜" (27.5 x 24 cm.)

Signed lr "Kupka"

Collection The Solomon R. Guggenheim Museum, New York (1704)

PROVENANCE:

the artist
Eugénie Kupka
Karl Flinker
to present owner, 1964

EXHIBITIONS:

New York, June-October 1967, SRGM
*New York, 1968, Spencer A. Samuels, no. 41
New York, July-September 1969, SRGM, p. 50, repr. color
New York, December 1969-January 1970, SRGM
New York, 1970, p. 256, repr.
New York, 1971, SRGM, p. 256, repr.

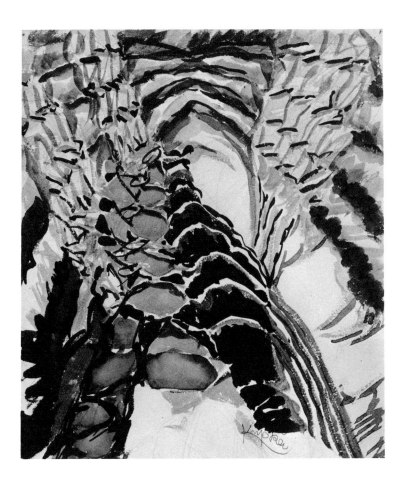

119 Study for *Tale of Pistils and Stamens* (Etude pour *Conte de pistils et d'étamines*). 1919

Watercolor on paper, 12⅜ x 10⅝″ (31.5 x 27 cm.)
Signed ll "Kupka"
Private Collection

PROVENANCE:

the artist
Eugénie Kupka
to present owner

120 *Tale of Pistils and Stamens I (Conte de pistils et d'étamines I)*. 1919

Oil on canvas, 33½ x 28¾″ (85 x 73 cm.)
Signed and dated lr "Kupka//$\overline{23}$"
Fédit, no. 72, repr.
Vachtová, no. 206, repr. p. 303
Musée National d'Art Moderne, Paris (AM 4181-P)

PROVENANCE:

the artist
Eugénie Kupka
to present owner, gift, 1963

EXHIBITIONS:

Paris, 1919, *Salon d'Automne*, no. 1035
*Paris, 1924, la Boétie, no. 24 (dated 1919-20)
*Prague, 1946, Mánes, no. 52 (dated 1923)

Tale of Pistils and Stamens is probably Kupka's first significant post-war series. As mentioned elsewhere, it shows a renewed interest in biological processes. This interest had been formulated in Kupka's mind by 1912-13. In the manuscript for his book he wrote: "In broad daylight, every plant raises its flowers to the heights. The stamens, with their joyous phallic forms fecundate the gracious pistils. It is a real pollen festival in the gynoecium bathed in sunlight, and surrounded by the petals which unfold to protect the event of conception."[1] This baroque "tale" is as imaginative an interpretation of biological facts as are the artist's paintings on the same theme.

1 Manuscript IV, pp. 80-81.

2 It is possible that the fourth work in this group is a gouache, visible in the installation photograph (fig. 11, p. 313). However, this cannot be taken for granted as the gouache may be one of the unidentified "studies" also shown in the exhibition (la Boétie, cat. nos. 70-101: *Etudes* 1919-24").

Three paintings from this cycle are known today, although four were exhibited at la Boétie in 1924, all dated 1919-20, which seem to be the proper dates.[2] The present version appears to be the earliest one. Cat. no. 121, like cat. no. 122, shows a cluster of anthropomorphic forms in the center, and thereby illustrates Kupka's "tale" more literally.

In addition to the biological inspiration, the vigorous thrust in depth, vertiginous motion and vivid colors which provoke associations with nature, endow these paintings with a true cosmic sense.

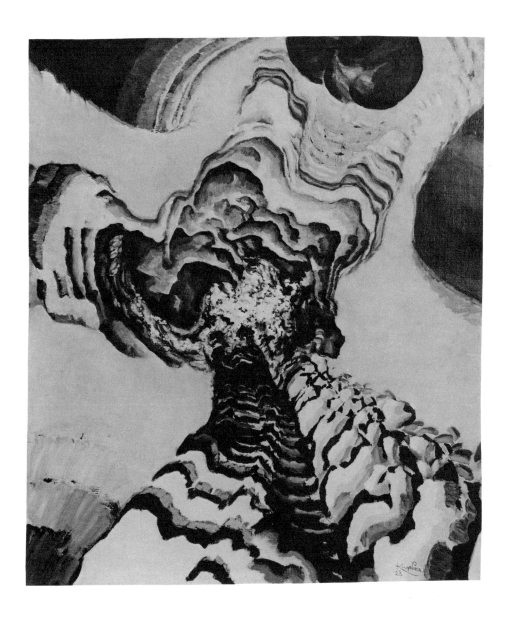

121 *Tale of Pistils and Stamens (Conte de pistils et d'étamines)*. 1919-20

Oil on canvas, 43¼ x 36¼"
(110 x 92 cm.)

Dated and signed lr "1920//Kupka"

Vachtová, no. 205, repr. pp. 161-162

Collection Národní Galerie, Prague
(O 11163)

PROVENANCE:

the artist
intervening history unknown
on deposit at Ministry of Foreign
Affairs
to present owner, 1965

EXHIBITIONS:

*Paris, 1924, la Boétie, one of nos.
   25-27
*Prague, 1946, Mánes (hors
   catalogue; installation photograph)
*Paris, 1958, MNAM, no. 35
*Ústí nad Orlicí, 1965
*Prague, 1965, no. 6
London, 1967, no. 79, repr.
Brussels-Rotterdam, 1967, no. 79
*Prague, 1968, no. 66, repr.
*Belgrade, 1969, no. 11, repr.

122 *Tale of Pistils and Stamens II or III (Conte de pistils et d'étamines II ou III).* 1919-20

Oil on canvas, 31½ x 35½"
(80 x 90 cm.)
Signed ll "Kupka"
Collection Wilhelm Hack, Cologne

PROVENANCE:

the artist
Eugénie Kupka
to present owner

EXHIBITIONS:

*Paris, 1924, la Boétie, no. 25, 26 or 27 (dated 1919-20, installation photograph)
*Paris, 1936, Jeu de Paume, no. 25 (installation photograph)
*Prague, 1946, Mánes, no. 53 (dated 1923, installation photograph)
Cologne, Kölnischer Kunstverein, November 12-December 20, 1964, *Kunst des 20. Jahrhunderts in Kölner Privatbesitz,* no. 55, repr.
Frankfurt, Kunstverein, June 25-August 7, 1966, *Vom Impressionismus zum Bauhaus: Meisterwerke aus deutschem Privatbesitz.* Traveled to Hamburg, Kunstverein, August 27-October 16, 1966, no. 38, repr.
Dusseldorf, Kunstverein für die Rheinlande und Westfalen, April 23-June 29, 1969, *Sammlung Wilhelm Hack,* no. 96, repr.

Although listed by Kupka in his 1946 retrospective as the second painting in this cycle, it was perhaps so designated for the needs of the exhibition, the catalogue for which contained only two works of this title. The Národní Galerie painting (cat. no. 121), which was shown *hors catalogue* in 1946, seems stylistically to belong between this painting and cat. no. 120. It has essentially the same composition and loosely painted forms as *Pistils I,* and contains the same anthropomorphic central motif as the present painting, which we would tend to identify as *Pistils III.*

The composition of this painting is quite different from the other two. It is extremely close to a painting of 1920-21, *Crystal,* from the *Gothic Contrasts* series which Kupka developed immediately after this cycle, and in which he used some of the same burgeoning motifs, natural colors, and even the central configuration of writhing bodies within the framework of a stained glass window. *Pistils III* also shows a flatter brushstroke than that found in the two earlier versions, tauter forms, more controlled rhythms and a more nuanced chromatic progression, once more relating it to slightly later works.

123 *Gothic Contrasts (Contrastes gothiques)*. c. 1920

Oil on canvas, 26 x 28″ (66 x 71 cm.)
Signed ll "Kupka"
Collection Camille Renault

PROVENANCE:
the artist
to present owner

It is tempting to compare this painting with Delaunay's *St. Séverin* series of 1909-10 and thereby situate it earlier in Kupka's oeuvre. One might also be tempted to consider it an early study of a Gothic interior and attribute it to the artist's early figurative period. Yet the facture indicates a later dating. One can only conclude that this was one of Kupka's experimental post-war paintings in which he returned briefly to figurative themes in order to work out problems of color and form. In fact the subject of Gothic vaulting and windows led Kupka to produce a unique figurative cycle on which he worked between c. 1920-25. He elaborated the theme so as to accentuate the optical illusions of perspective as seen through the complex network of vaulted arcades in a church. Sometimes he borrowed the dynamic motion and biological forms and palette from the immediately preceding *Pistils* cycle (see cat. nos. 120-122). Eventually, the connected arabesques of pointed arches would lead him to the undulating rhythms of the paintings *Moving Blues* of 1923-24 (see cat. nos. 148-150).

Three other paintings of this cycle are known: *Crystal*, c. 1920-21 (Collection Gallien); *Gothic Contrast*, c. 1921-22 (Museum of Art, Rhode Island School of Design, Providence); *Gothic Contrasts*, c. 1925 (MNAM, Paris).[1]

1 The latter painting was dated 1925 by Kupka. However, on stylistic grounds, the author would prefer to date it 1921-22, like the Providence painting.

124 *Essay, Vigor (Essai, robustesse).*
1920

Oil on canvas, 59⅛ x 39⅜″
(150 x 100 cm.)
Signed and dated lr "Kupka//1920"
Vachtová, no. 215, repr. p. 149
Collection Margit Chanin, Ltd.

PROVENANCE:

the artist
Galerie Louis Carré, Paris
to present owner

EXHIBITIONS:

*Prague, 1946, Mánes, no. 44
*Paris, 1958, MNAM, no. 38
*Paris, 1964, Louis Carré, no. 10

In 1920, Kupka spent the summer in Brittany, as he had done many times before, starting at least as early as 1900. The curious rock formations found on the Brittany coast are seen in much of his work, particularly between 1900 and 1904.[1] The dramatic monolithic shapes in the present painting echo this familiar motif.

The upward thrust of rounded vertical forms crowned by an agitated mass of clouds reveals one source of Kupka's inspiration for the *Hindu Motifs* cycle (cat. nos. 125, 128, 137).[2] However, while the present image derives from the perceived world, in the ensuing years the motifs will be translated into a progressively more imaginary landscape.

The title implies that this work may be a first attempt to formulate a theme. In fact, a painting, *Facture robuste (Vigorous Brushwork)* of 1920 (MNAM, Paris) contains the same bold forms and colors and is visibly based on the same pictorial ideas. Since it shows definite similarities with the *Pistils* series, appearing more advanced than the first, and less than the last version shown here, it seems safe to maintain the date of 1920 for these two paintings.

Fédit relates *Vigorous Brushwork* to the *Creation* series[3] and says it shows an attempt to depict the birth of the world from its original chaos.

1 See cat. no. 5 for example. Also, *Window on the Beach*, c. 1901, MOMA, The Joan and Lester Avnet Collection. The rocks appeared in the first version of *Ballad-Joys* (cat. no. 8; see discussion). See also Vachtová, p. 148.

2 Also *Motif hindou* or *Dégradés rouges*, 1920 *(Hindu Motif* or *Red Gradations)*, MNAM, Paris.

3 Fédit, cat. no. 69, p. 86.

125 *Blue Scaffolding (Charpente bleue).* 1919

Oil on canvas, 29½ x 33½"
(75 x 85 cm.)

Signed ll "Kupka"

Vachtová, no. 217, repr. p. 150,
color pl. XIII

Collection Národní Galerie, Prague
(O 3828)

PROVENANCE:

the artist
to present owner, 1946

EXHIBITIONS:

Paris, 1919, *Salon d'Automne*, no.
1036 (as *Armature bleue*)
*Paris, 1924, la Boétie, no. 39 (dated
1921)
*Paris, 1936, Jeu de Paume, no. 28
*Prague, 1946, Mánes, no. 48 (dated
1920)
*Ústí nad Orlicí, 1965, no. 6
*Cologne, 1967, no. 72, repr.;
Munich, 1967, no. 72, repr.;
Vienna, 1967, no. 29; Amsterdam,
no. 50, repr.; Prague, 1969, no. 68,
repr.
*Belgrade, 1969, no. 13, repr.

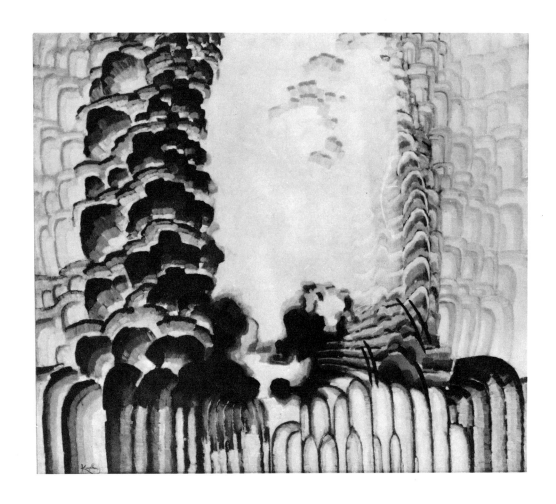

26 *Untitled.* 1919

Gouache on paper, 8¾ x 6″
(22.3 x 15.2 cm.)
Signed lr "Kupka"
Collection Mr. and Mrs. M. A. Gribin

PROVENANCE:

the artist
Robert Elkon Gallery, New York
to present owner

27 *Chromatic Vibrations (Vibrations
chromatiques).* 1919-20

Gouache on paper, 9⅝ x 10″
(24.5 x 25.2 cm.)
Signed lr "Kupka"
Collection Peter Gimpel

PROVENANCE:

the artist
Eugénie Kupka
Karl Flinker
to present owner

128 *Intensifications (Intensifications).*
1921

Oil on canvas, 31 x 31"
(78.7 x 78.7 cm.)
Signed lr "Kupka"
Private Collection, New York

PROVENANCE:

the artist
Eugénie Kupka
Rose Fried Gallery, New York,
June 1958
to present owner, December 1958

EXHIBITION:

*Paris, 1924, la Boétie, no. 38 (dated
1921)

The *Hindu Motif* or *Scaffolding* series evolved from a number of themes which Kupka was exploring c. 1919-20. Obviously deriving initially from the pre-war paintings *Creation* and *Cosmic Spring* (cat. nos. 80, 82), Kupka's reworking of these early paintings in 1919-21 may have acted as a catalyst in the elaboration of this series. Formal innovations developed in the diverse cycles of *Tale of Pistils and Stamens* (cat. nos. 117-122), *Essay, Vigor* and *Vigorous Brushwork* (see cat. no. 124), *Gothic Contrasts* (cat. no. 123) and studies of marine life (cat. no. 126) contributed to its formulation. It should be noted that all of these cycles except the *Gothic Contrasts* series are interpretations of biological growth and vitality. The *Gothic Contrasts* series contributes the dimension of architecture applied to organic life.

The *Hindu Motif* or *Scaffolding* cycle includes four paintings and a number of gouaches and watercolors. The Národní Galerie, Prague, version, *Blue Scaffolding* (cat. no. 125) is probably the earliest, dating from 1919. The left side contains motifs which are extremely close to those found in *Cosmic Spring II* (cat. no. 82). *Hindu Motif* or *Red Gradations* is probably the second version (MNAM, Paris; see Fédit, cat. no. 73, p. 91). Dated 1919 by Fédit, its close similarity to *Essay, Vigor* argues for a 1920 dating.

Intensifications is probably the third in the series. Dated 1921 by Kupka for his 1924 exhibition at la Boétie, the more evenly regulated progression of growth, and the more clear cut stylized forms confirm this later dating. Finally *Green and Blue* (cat. no. 137) is the last in the series, by which time the theme has been transformed into a visionary architecture.

A photograph found among Kupka's possessions shows either a study or an early version of *Intensifications* which would subsequently have been repainted (fig.). The initial inspiration from natural floral growth is clearly visible. The vertical planes framing the composition, seen in this version and not in the others, make it closer in feeling to *Gothic Contrasts* (cat. no. 123).

Kupka, early version of *Intensifications*.

129 *Flaccid Forms (Formes flasques).*
1921-23

Oil on canvas, 25¾ x 25¾"
(65.5 x 65.5 cm.)
Signed lr "Kupka"
Collection Joseph H. Hazen

PROVENANCE:

the artist
Richard L. Feigen, Inc., New York
Royal S. Marks, New York
to present owner

EXHIBITIONS:

*Prague, 1946, Mánes, no. 56 (dated
  1925)
*New York, 1961, Royal S. Marks,
  no. 6
*New York, 1964, Royal S. Marks,
  entry C
Cambridge, 1966; Los Angeles, 1967;
Berkeley, 1967; Houston, 1967;
Honolulu, 1967

A list of paintings compiled by Eugénie Kupka in 1956 includes the entry: *"Formes flasques (motif indou)* [sic] *1925."* Kupka dated the painting 1925 in his 1946 Prague catalogue. However due to its inspiration, facture, palette and attribution as a *Hindu Motif,* one is inclined to think it was started c. 1921, and there is nothing that points to it being reworked after 1923.

The dominant motifs of *Flaccid Forms* are the stylized anvil-shaped clouds seen as early as 1911-20 in *Cosmic Spring II* (cat. no. 82), reproduced in more stylized form in Kupka's black and white gouache on the same theme (cat. no. 130). Clearly, in composition and palette, this is a variation on the *Cosmic Spring* theme. Another painting, *Debris* of 1920 (Private Collection, Switzerland), shows the same loose composition, brilliant palette and nebulous forms.

The revisions up to 1923 may include a reinforcing of the central nimbus. This nimbus occurs in paintings of the 1919-23 period of a cycle called *The Form of Yellow* (see Vachtová, p. 195, for example). The configuration has an interesting history. It is derived from Kupka's 1917-18 illustrations for *The Song of Roland.* One of these academic illustrations done during the war shows the same haloed light and nebulous forms as found in this painting (fig. 9, p.312). It also contains similar superpositions of foreground and background motifs.

30　*Cosmic Spring (Printemps cosmique).* 1921

Gouache on paper, 15¾ x 12⅛″
(40 x 30.8 cm.)
Signed r of c "Kupka"
Collection Karl Flinker

PROVENANCE:

the artist
Eugénie Kupka
to present owner

131 Study after *The Language of Verticals*. 1921

Gouache on paper, 15⅜ x 13⅜"
(39 x 34 cm.)
Signed ll "Kupka"
Private Collection

PROVENANCE:

the artist
to present owner

1 *Cosmic Spring*, started 1911, see cat.
  no. 82; Study for *The Language of
  Verticals*, c. 1911, Collection Louis
  Carré, Paris; see also cat. no. 67.

2 Arnould-Grémilly, 1922, p. 15. This
  study is not identical to the final
  version.

3 *La Création dans les arts plastiques*,
  p. 104.

4 See window curtains in fig., p. 6.

In 1920-21, Kupka prepared the woodcut illustrations for two books which appeared in 1922 and 1923 respectively: Arnould-Grémilly's monograph and the artist's own treatise on painting. Most of the illustrations were drawn from earlier existing works. The two exhibited here were inspired by paintings of the same title which were conceived prior to World War I.[1]

The black and white rendering of *Cosmic Spring* served as the frontispiece for Kupka's book, *La Création dans les arts plastiques*. Study after *The Language of Verticals* was used as an illustration for the monograph.[2] A long horizontal version of the same motif is also found in Kupka's book.[3]

The inspiration for the tightly pleated vertical motifs which Kupka developed at an early date has sometimes been attributed to the mottled patterns of light through the embroidered window curtains at Puteaux.[4]

Many of the black and white motifs Kupka developed in 1921 would be taken up again in his 1926 album of woodcuts (cat. no. 165).

Unsteady Planes (Plans instables).
1921

Oil on paperboard, 18½ x 30″
(43 x 76 cm.)
Signed ll "Kupka;" inscribed lr
"PLANS INSTABLES"
Courtesy Galerie Denise René,
New York

PROVENANCE:

the artist
Andrée Martinel-Kupka
Karl Flinker-Daniel Gervis, Paris
to present owner

EXHIBITIONS:

*Paris, 1921, Povolozky, no. 16
*Paris, 1936, Jeu de Paume, no. 34
  (as *Plans en mouvement*)
*Paris, 1964, Karl Flinker, no. 102
*Cologne, 1967, no. 100, repr.;
  Munich, 1967, no. 100, repr.;
  Vienna, 1967, no. 32; Amsterdam,
  1968, no. 55, repr.; Prague, 1968,
  no. 72, repr.
Krefeld, 1969 (cat. not located)

In 1920-21, Kupka did a large series of works exclusively in black and white. These were exhibited at the Galerie Povolozky in 1921. At the same time he was preparing woodcut illustrations for two books (cat. nos. 130, 131). It is hard to say whether the work for the illustrations inspired the black and white paintings or whether they evolved independently from other sources. Kupka's friendship with the master wood-block printer and painter A. P. Gallien, who had been painting black and white abstract subjects on canvas since 1920, should be mentioned in this context. It is plausible that Gallien's example was one factor in Kupka's decision to work in black and white.

Unsteady Planes is an excellent example of Kupka's autonomous black and white style. Possibly inspired in its organic forms by a detail of a cosmic composition, and in its formal repetition by the various studies of "pleated" vertical planes, the cadenced progression of forms through space echoes the artist's earlier investigations of consecutive motion (cat. nos. 9, 46-51).

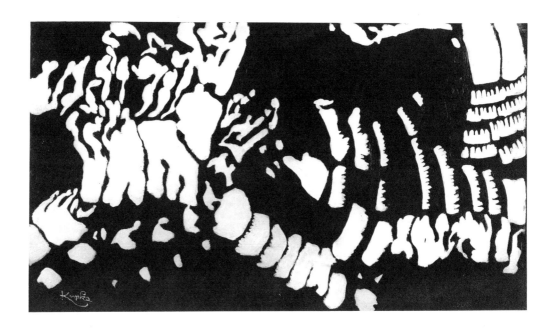

133 *The Fair* or *The Quadrille (La Foire* ou *La Contredanse).*
1920-21

Oil on canvas, 28¾ x 93⅝″
(73 x 238 cm.)

Signed lr "Kupka"

Vachtová, no. 222, repr. p. 176

Private Collection

PROVENANCE:

the artist
Galerie Louis Carré, Paris
to present owner, 1975

EXHIBITIONS:

*Paris, 1921, Povolozky, no. 28 (as
  La Contredanse)
*Paris, 1924, la Boétie, no. 30 (as
  La Contredanse, dated 1920-21)
*New York, 1951, Louis Carré, no. 7,
  repr.
*Paris, 1958, MNAM, no. 39 (dated
  1921)
*Paris, 1964, Louis Carré, no. 12
  (dated 1921)

1 See *The Fools,* fig. 3, p. 307.

2 See cat. nos. 112, 113.

3 Busch-Reisinger Museum, Cambridge,
  Mass.

4 MNAM, Paris; Fédit, cat. no. 95,
  p. 108; Fédit relates this painting to
  stroboscopic images.

5 Published in *La Vie des lettres,* October
  1921, pp. 670-686. Reprinted in book
  form 1922 (see bibliography). Present
  quote, p. 680.

Since it was purchased by Louis Carré in 1951, this painting has been exhibited and reproduced under the title *La Foire.* Because the theme of a fair or circus was one which Kupka treated as early as 1899[1] and returned to intermittently throughout his career,[2] this title seems logical and appropriate, even though it is difficult to determine its source.

The installation photograph of Kupka's 1924 la Boétie retrospective shows that this painting was exhibited there. However the title *La Foire* is not included in the catalogue, and the only title which seems to correspond to this painting is *La Contredanse,* dated 1920-21. The title *La Contredanse* appears in the Povolozky catalogue of 1921, the year in which Kupka finished the painting.

There are several reasons for believing that this canvas was originally called *La Contredanse (The Quadrille).* The first is the imagery itself. A quadrille is a French country dance, like a square dance, in which four couples face and bow off from one another. Although the present painting is essentially abstract, it is obviously about measured rhythms and consecutive motion, and in certain areas one can even decipher human silhouettes shuffling and bowing in evenly cadenced rhythms. These silhouettes are related to Kupka's paintings of 1919-20, *The Colored One* (cat. no. 116) and *Black Accent* (fig., p. 208).

The decomposition of movement across a horizontal field may be loosely compared to that in *Unsteady Planes* (cat. no. 132), also shown at Povolozky in 1921. Yet the shattered and spliced effect of the motion goes back to Kupka's early drawing, *The Horsemen* (cat. no. 9), inspired by the Praxinoscope. There seems no doubt that Kupka was involved with the representation of movement in time and space during this period. In fact, one painting dated 1920, *L'Heure (The Hour),*[3] and a second dated 1925, *Le Temps passe* or *L'Instant (Passing Time or The Moment)*[4] which was probably painted closer to 1921, confirm this preoccupation with stroboscopic images unfolding in time.

At the opening of Kupka's 1921 exhibition, Arnould-Grémilly gave a lecture about the artist's work in which he seems to refer precisely to this painting: "In order to achieve a florid counterpoint, a fugue, or a free style, mustn't one turn to cinematographic projection? The latter alone can endow the simultaneously presented two dimensions of the canvas with a third more musical dimension, progression in duration, measured rhythm, cadenced movement, repetition in time."[5]

134 *Triangular Composition (Composition triangulaire).* 1920-21

Oil on canvas, 26 x 27⅛″
(66 x 70 cm.)

Signed lr "Kupka"

Private Collection

PROVENANCE:

the artist
Eugénie Kupka
Rose Fried Gallery, New York
to present owner

This work may be related to two other known paintings of c. 1920-22: *Compliment*[1] and *En dégradés* (*Gradations,* fig.; present whereabouts unknown). *Compliment* is probably the earliest of the three and may be dated c. 1919-20. In *Compliment,* the dynamic organic rhythms on the left are related to *Tale of Pistils and Stamens II or III* (cat. no. 122), whereas the "bowing," shuffling planes on the right, although completely abstract, evoke not only the rhythms of the *Women Picking Flowers* series (cat. nos. 46-51) but relate to *The Quadrille* (cat. no. 133). The burgeoning motifs on the left are also close in treatment to those in other 1920 paintings such as *Essay, Vigor* (cat. no. 124).

Triangular Composition like *The Quadrille* (cat. no. 133) retains the same bright palette as *Compliment,* and a somewhat similar grouping of motifs. However here the rippling forms and organic rhythms are translated into more distinctly and evenly defined and graded planes. These planes, which still show loose vibrant brushwork, are close to those in the first version of *Animated Lines* (cat. no. 135)[2] which was exhibited in 1920 in its first state.

Gradations, last of the three, shows the even shading and flatter brushwork which Kupka developed between 1920 and 1922. This painting was exhibited at la Boétie as *Dégradés,* dated 1920-22 (la Boétie, cat. no. 37).

The curved forms in all three of these paintings anticipate the final stricter rendering of the same theme: *Planes by Curves* of 1926-30 (cat. nos. 161, 162).

1 MNAM, Paris; Fédit, cat. no. 82, p. 98. The painting is inscribed 1912. However Fédit finds this stylistically improbable and refers to Kupka's 1951 inventory in which he dated it 1919.

2 See Fédit, cat. no. 75, p. 94 for photograph of initial version.

Kupka, *Gradations,* 1920-22, oil, present whereabouts unknown.

135 *Animated Lines (Lignes animées).*
1920-21; reworked between
1924-33

Oil on canvas, 76 x 78¾″
(193 x 200 cm.)

Signed and dated lr "Kupka 2̅1̅;"
ll "LIGNES//ANIMEES"

Fédit, no. 75, repr.

Vachtová, no. 212 (dated 1919-34),
pl. XV

Musée National d'Art Moderne,
Paris (AM 3565-P)

PROVENANCE:

the artist
Eugénie Kupka
to present owner, 1957

EXHIBITIONS:

Paris, 1920, *Salon d'Automne,*
no. 1249 (first state)
*Paris, 1924, la Boétie (dated 1920-21)
*Paris, 1936, Jeu de Paume, no. 37
*Prague, 1946, Mánes, no. 140 (dated
   1919-21)
Paris, 1948, *Salon des Réalités
Nouvelles* (hors catalogue)
*Paris, 1953, *Salon des Réalités
   Nouvelles* (hors catalogue)
Paris, 1954, *Salon des Réalités
Nouvelles,* no. 345
*Paris, 1958, MNAM, no. 41, pl. XV
Rennes, 1961
Vienna, 1962, no. 111 (as *Beseelt
Linien),* repr. (on its side)
*Cologne, 1967, no. 26, repr.;
   Munich, 1967, no. 26, repr.;
   Vienna, 1967, no. 31, repr.;
   Amsterdam, 1968, no. 52, repr.;
   Prague, 1968, no. 70, repr.

Obviously based on the idea of cosmic rotation, this painting presents analogies with three of Kupka's pictorial themes: *Organization of Graphic Motifs* (cat. nos. 102-106), *Tale of Pistils and Stamens* (cat. nos. 117-122) and *Around a Point* (cat. nos. 152-160). In its original state, the present painting showed a more organic center, closer to the *Pistils and Stamens* series, and the more fluid forms characteristic of Kupka's 1920 work. Sometime between 1924 and 1933, the canvas was reworked and brought to its present state.[1]

In 1910-11, Kupka wrote: "A point which acts as a nucleus. Concentration of rays. It is determined by the centrifugal directions of lines or planes. Converging rays, converging lines, which then reach outward to infinity."[2]

1 See discussion and photograph of
   original state in Fédit.

2 Manuscript I, p. 40.

136 *Lines, Planes, Depths (Traits, plans, profondeurs).* 1920-22

Oil on canvas, 31½ x 28½"
(80 x 72 cm.)
Signed lr "Kupka"
Collection Lucy Delmarle

PROVENANCE:
the artist
Félix Del Marle
to present owner

EXHIBITIONS:
*Paris, 1924, la Boétie, no. 31?
Lille, 1925, no. 4
*Paris, 1958, MNAM, no. 53 (as *Dominante bleue*)

Five paintings on this theme are known today. The earliest version (MNAM, Paris; Fédit, cat. no. 74, pp. 92-93), dated 1918-20 by Fédit, is the most heavily painted and emphasizes a biological inspiration. Indeed, in its brooding blues, purples, blacks and grays, it evokes a species of marine flora. A second version (NG, Prague) shows the same dense brushwork and tonalities. In contrast to these, three somewhat later versions (probably 1920-23)[1] in their transparency of color and overlapping forms, no longer call to mind biological life, but an ephemeral shifting of light through panes of glass. Kupka had a carved wooden panel in his studio, cut out and glazed with a similar stylized floral motif.[2] The backdrop for these panes was a rich resonant blue which filtered through the glass in different azure tones. Although Kupka's painting once again depicts rotation, even arterial circulation,[3] and refers distantly to organic life, this openwork panel in Kupka's house was obviously one of several sources of inspiration for the final pictorial idea.

One of the series (which one is unclear) was exhibited at the *Salon des Indépendants* of 1923. Another, dated 1913-22, was exhibited at la Boétie (la Boétie cat. no. 31). Possibly it was this one, since the artist Del Marle helped finance this exhibition and Kupka was "very grateful to Del Marle for his help and support."[4] According to Fédit, the first studies for this theme were done before World War I, which explains the la Boétie dating.

1 Collection Joseph H. Hazen, New York; NG, Prague; and the present painting.

2 Seen on a color slide taken by Alexander Liberman in preparation for *The Artist in his Studio*, n.d.; see bibliography.

3 See Fédit's discussion, her cat. no. 74, p. 92.

4 Andrée Martinel-Kupka (in conversation with the author), 1974.

137   *Green and Blue (Vert et bleu).*
1921-23

Oil on canvas, 52½ x 32"
(133.3 x 81.2 cm.)
Signed and dated lr "Kupka//23"
Collection Mr. and Mrs. M. A. Gribin

PROVENANCE:

the artist
Mr. and Mrs. Alexander Liberman,
1950's
Robert Elkon Gallery, New York
to present owner

EXHIBITIONS:

*Paris, 1924, la Boétie, no. 40 (as
  Charpente bleue II, dated 1921,
  subsequently reworked and redated)
*Paris, 1936, Jeu de Paume, no. 29
*Prague, 1946, Mánes, no. 50 (dated
  1923)
*New York, 1964, Royal S. Marks,
  no. 2
New York, Robert Elkon Gallery,
September 30-November 2, 1972,
Twentieth Century Masters, no. 20,
repr. (as *Untitled,* dated 1923)

1 See discussion of this series, cat. no.
  128.

2 The la Boétie catalogue lists *Charpente
  bleue I* and *II,* cat. nos. 39 and 40, both
  dated 1921. The painting *Blue Scaffolding* (cat. no. 125) is usually identified
  as *Blue Scaffolding II,* 1920-21. However the Prague painting was exhibited
  in the 1919 *Salon d'Automne* (as
  Armature bleue, no. 1036). This painting is obviously the later of the two.

Green and Blue, also known as *Green and Blue Scaffolding (Charpente verte et
bleue)* (see Prague, 1946, cat. no. 50) is the last of the *Scaffolding* or *Hindu Motif*
series. In contrast to the earlier works in this group[1] based on biological forms and
cosmic landscapes, *Green and Blue* shows an extension of these pictorial ideas into
a mystical architecture. This dimension is achieved through the vertical format of
the painting which accentuates its upward thrust. It is reinforced by the pale
ephemeral colors, applied in evenly graded planes which no longer connote the
dynamic surge of organic growth but instead evoke a celestial architecture. Thus,
the present picture marks a transition between the earlier works in the series and
the paintings known as *Upward Thrust* of 1922-23 (cat. nos. 139-140).

   Green and Blue was exhibited at la Boétie in 1924, as *Charpente bleue II,* dated
1921 (la Boétie cat. no. 40). In the context of the other related pictures, a 1921-23
date appears preferable.[2]

38   Study for *Upward Thrust* (Etude
     pour *Le Jaillissement*). 1921-22

Gouache on paper, 10¾ x 6½"
(27.3 x 16.5 cm.)

Signed lr "Kupka"

Collection The Solomon R.
Guggenheim Museum, New York,
Gift of Galerie Karl Flinker, Paris,
1964 (1705)

PROVENANCE:

the artist
Eugénie Kupka
Galerie Karl Flinker, Paris
to present owner, gift

139 *Upward Thrust I (Le Jaillissement I).* 1922-23

Oil on canvas, 47⅝ x 32⅝"
(121 x 83 cm.)

Signed and dated lr "Kupka//1923"

Vachtová, no. 167 (as *Outspurt II),* color pl. XII

Collection Národní Galerie, Prague (O 5944)

PROVENANCE:

the artist
to present owner, 1953

EXHIBITIONS:

*Paris, 1936, Jeu de Paume, no. 26 (as *Jaillissement,* either present work or another of series)
*Prague, 1946, Mánes, no. 118
*Paris, 1958, MNAM, no. 48
*Písek—České Budějovice, 1961, no. 18.
Hluboké-Brno, 1966, no. 234
*Cologne, 1967, no. 74, repr.; Munich, 1967, no. 74, repr.; Vienna, 1967, no. 34, repr. no. 38; Amsterdam, 1968, no. 59, repr. black and white, color; Prague, 1968, no. 69, repr.
Stockholm, 1973, no. 97

1 Another painting of 1922-23, called *La Montée (Rising)* (fig.), is related to this series and particularly to *Upward Thrust I* with which it shares the same rounded columnar forms. The explanation for this painting, as given by Eugénie Kupka, was that it was inspired by glasses of fruit preserves set in the sun. The original title for the painting as it was shown in Prague in 1946 was *The Fermentation of Jam* (Prague, 1946, cat. no. 74; see Fédit's discussion, cat. no. 73, p. 91).

The theme of the vertical or upward thrust is a recurrent one in Kupka's oeuvre, found in paintings both earlier and later than these. Before World War I, they were generally inspired by Gothic interiors; after 1919 they expressed biological vitality.

These two paintings, while retaining the vigor of the later works, clearly tend toward the architectural.[1] The billowing shapes of the 1919-22 pictures are gradually transformed into rectilinear planes. Similarly, color, formerly rich and vibrant, shows a new austerity. The effect of bunched columns, and the juxtaposition of neutral tones and brilliant hues are reminiscent of the earlier Gothic interiors, despite the fact that here both the focus and intent are quite different.

Kupka did three paintings on this theme, of which the first and third are exhibited here. The second is in a New York private collection.

Kupka, *Rising,* 1923, oil, Royal S. Marks Gallery, New York.

140 *Upward Thrust III (Le Jaillisse-*
     ment III). 1922-23

Oil on canvas, 43⅜ x 35½"
(110 x 90 cm.)

Signed ll "Kupka"

Vachtová, no. 168, repr. p. 125

Collection Mr. and Mrs. Andrew P.
Fuller

PROVENANCE:

the artist
Galerie Louis Carré, Paris
Margit Chanin, Ltd.
to present owner, 1968

EXHIBITIONS:

*Paris, 1936, Jeu de Paume, no. 26
  (as *Jaillissement,* either present
  work or another of series)
*Prague, 1946, Mánes, no. 120
Turin, 1953, repr.
Vienna, 1962, no. 112, repr.
*Paris, 1964, Louis Carré, no. 14
  (dated 1925)
Lisbon, 1965, no. 72, repr. color

41 *Diagonal Planes I (Plans diagonaux I).* c. 1923

Oil on canvas, 31⅞ x 25⅝"
(81 x 65 cm.)

Signed ll "Kupka"

Vachtová, no. 175, repr. p. 138

Collection Národní Galerie, Prague
(O 3829)

PROVENANCE:

the artist
to present owner, 1946

EXHIBITIONS:

*Paris, 1936, Jeu de Paume, no. 62
*Prague, 1946, Mánes, no. 121
*Písek—České Budějovice, 1961,
  no. 19
*Ústí nad Orlicí, 1965, no. 9
London, 1967, no. 80 (as
Horizontal Planes I)
Brussels-Rotterdam, 1967, no. 80
*Prague, 1968, no. 71, repr.

The Prague 1968 catalogue (cat. no. 71) indicates that this painting was exhibited
at la Boétié in 1924, as cat. no. 21: *Plans verticaux et diagonaux (réminiscences
hivernales).* In view of the austerity of this picture and a complete absence of the
motifs which characterize the *Winter Reminiscences* series (see cat. nos. 143-144),
this appears implausible.

142 *Forms and Structures of Colors*
(*Formes et structures de couleurs*).
1920-23

Oil on canvas, 23 x 32"
(58.4 x 81.2 cm.)
Signed lr "Kupka"
Collection Mr. and Mrs. M. A. Gribin

PROVENANCE:

early history unknown
Gertrude Stein Gallery, New York
to present owner

EXHIBITIONS:

*Paris, 1924, la Boétie, no. 50-56 (one
  of these)
*Paris, 1936, Jeu de Paume, no. 42
  (as *Langage vertical [fond rouge]*)
Riverside, Art Gallery, University of
California, April 25-May 25, 1971,
The Cubist Circle, no. 12, repr.

The groupings of verticals in this painting obviously derive from *The Language of Verticals* theme (see cat. nos. 67 and 131; also Vachtová, cat. no. 157, repr. p. 122). Kupka appears to have reverted to this theme in an attempt to redefine his abstract vocabulary and emphasize the two-dimensionality of the picture plane. Although the format and imagery do not appear again in exactly this form, many of the motifs seen here re-emerge in contemporaneous pictures in somewhat more elaborate rendering (see cat. nos. 143, 144).

Between 1919 and 1923, Kupka painted a series of works on the form and structure of colors, illustrating his belief that every color dictates its own ideal form (see discussion, cat. no. 168). Although the present painting is very different from those in the series, it seems to have borne this title when exhibited in 1924.[1]

Kupka did several small abstract paintings on oval stretchers of which the earliest date from about this time. Most of them were decorative, in shades of yellow and purple, and were conceived for Eugénie Kupka's bedroom. Presumably these inspired him to work in an oval format. Afterwards, in the 1930s and 1940s, and again in the 1950s, he experimented only occasionally with small oval formats.

1 Reproduced with this title in Léon
  Plée, "François Kupka, Le Peintre des
  'Idées-lumières'," *Les Annales,* November 16, 1924. Private notes by the
  painter Gallien concerning the 1924
  retrospective indicate that the painting
  was called *Le Langage des verticales.*
  This title does not appear in the la
  Boétie catalogue, and may be Gallien's
  title for the picture, given its
  resemblance to that series. (Notes
  courtesy Gallien family.)

143 *Reminiscence of a Cathedral* or *Winter Reminiscences (Réminiscence d'une cathédrale* ou *Réminiscences hivernales).* 1920-23

Oil on canvas, 59 x 37″
(149.8 x 94 cm.)

Signed lr "Kupka;" inscribed ll "réminiscence"

Collection Mr. and Mrs. Joseph Randall Shapiro

PROVENANCE:

the artist
Richard L. Feigen, Inc., Chicago, c. 1957
to present owner

EXHIBITIONS:

*Paris, 1924, la Boétie, no. 18-21 (one of these)
*Prague, 1946, Mánes, no. 69 (dated 1920)
Paris, 1950, *Salon des Réalités Nouvelles,* no. 300 (as *Réminiscence,* dated 1913-20)
*New York, 1953, Rose Fried, no. 2
Chicago, Museum of Contemporary Art, December 20, 1969-February 1, 1970, *Selections from the Joseph Randall Shapiro Collection,* no. 39, repr.

In the 1924 la Boétie exhibition, four paintings were exhibited with the title *Plans verticaux et diagonaux (réminiscences hivernales)* (cat. nos. 18-21). Since many of Kupka's titles have changed since that time, it is difficult to identify the corresponding pictures exactly, except from the one existing installation photograph. It is thought however that this painting was among them.

This work was probably painted between 1920 and 1923. It shows the vertical thrust seen in slightly earlier works now congealing into an architecture. The soft floating forms on the frontal plane on the left evoke snow flurries, whereas the background lozenge motifs call to mind leaded glass. The two titles which Kupka used for this painting—referring to winter and the cathedral—are therefore comprehensible.

The braided motif in the lower left and the fluted pianes at the right edge were seen in *Forms and Structures of Colors* (cat. no. 142). The tentative cloudlike forms on the right, subsequently abandoned, and the contradictions of palette—the central panel is executed in mixed muted tones, the sides in primaries and white—suggest that the painting is an early variation on this theme.

†144 *Vertical and Diagonal Planes;*
Winter Reminiscences (Plans
verticaux et diagonaux; rémini-
scences hivernales). 1920-23

Oil on canvas, 70⅞ x 59⅛″
(180 x 150 cm.)

Signed lr "Kupka"

Vachtová, no. 173, repr. p. 126,
color pl. IX

Collection Národní Galerie, Prague
(O 2068)

PROVENANCE:

the artist
Jindřich Waldes
to present owner

EXHIBITIONS:

*Paris, 1921, Povolozky, cat. no. 26
or 27
*Paris, 1924, la Boétie, no. 18-21 (one
of these)
*Prague, 1946, Mánes, no. 116 (dated
1913-29)
*Prague, 1968, no. 61, repr.

1 See p. 230, fn. 5 for complete reference.
Present quote, p. 677.

The larger format, brighter palette and more distinctly determined forms suggest that this painting followed cat. no. 143. The snowflake motifs are again visible, extended in vertical chains across the surface of the canvas. And the background is a complex pattern of transparent lozenges, evoking panes of glass. Curiously, despite the success of *Forms and Structures of Colors* in establishing a two-dimensional continuum, here Kupka reverts to a push-pull relationship between surface plane and background, such as that in paintings executed as early as 1909-11 (see cat. nos. 39, 66, 68). The analogy with *Piano Keys-Lake* (cat. no. 39) is particularly relevant in that the lower area of the present painting is distinctly reminiscent of the inside of a piano.

Arnould-Grémilly, in his speech at the Galerie Povolozky in 1921, described the myriad experiences evoked by Kupka's paintings, among them the sound of organ music: ". . . the chill of abstraction can fall on you like vertical planes, like the pipes of a silver organ within the somber sulkiness of a wood-paneled room."[1] Most of Arnould-Grémilly's remarks referred to paintings in the exhibition. The Povolozky catalogue lists two paintings: *Verticales et diagonales; réminiscences* (Povolozky cat. nos. 26-27). One is tempted to conjecture that the present painting in an earlier state, or one close to it, was shown in 1921.

Small drawings in The Museum of Modern Art Study Collection show the intricately carved posts of a Gothic choir, creating a complex knobbed vertical pattern. A 1913 oil study (fig.) shows a tree (or trees) laden with snow. All of these studies obviously contributed to Kupka's elaborate vision in which winter and the cathedral are combined.

Kupka, Study for *Winter Reminiscences,*
c. 1913, oil, Collection Mr. and Mrs.
M. A. Gribin.

Oil on canvas, 40 x 29″
(101.6 x 73.6 cm.)
Signed lr "Kupka"
Collection Stephen Mazoh & Co.,
Inc.

PROVENANCE:

the artist
Félix Del Marle
Lucy Delmarle
James St. L. O'Toole
Gertrude Stein Gallery, New York
Mr. and Mrs. N. Richard Miller,
New York
to present owner

EXHIBITIONS:

*Paris, 1924, la Boétie, no. 42 or 43,
  probably 43 (installation
  photograph)
*New York, 1968, Spencer A.
  Samuels, no. 36
San Diego-Oakland-Seattle, 1971,
no. 47, repr. color

Untitled is obviously related to the *Réminiscence* series. The more compact central structure, flat integrated forms, controlled palette and stippled impasto technique point to a later date than the pictures reviewed thus far. It was exhibited at la Boétie in its present state in 1924; one would be tempted to identify it as cat. no. 43: *Panneau décoratif (à deux plans)*, dated (approximatively) 1921-23.

Earlier motifs from nature (snow flurries, clouds) are here transformed into flat decorative panels. The architectonic central image and the panels themselves evoke the modern cathedral or skyscraper rather than the cathedral of medieval times. Although one cannot speak of skyscrapers in Paris, the small figured moldings on the left imitate the relief panels beginning to appear on modern Parisian façades (Auguste Perret's 1913 Théâtre des Champs-Elysées, for example).

Kupka's interest in modern architecture can only be conjectured. Yet in view of his unbounded curiosity concerning his environment, his interest in all other periods of architecture and his preoccupation with modernity—its science and techniques—this conjecture does not seem unfounded. By 1923, he was teaching Czech scholarship students in Paris; some young architects were among them. Many sketches based on building façades are in The Museum of Modern Art Study Collection. Visibly they are the source of many of his vertical and diagonal plane compositions, both earlier and later than this one. For Kupka, the vertical plane was fundamentally architectural, either in real or visionary terms.

146 *Lines, Planes, Spaces* or *Attempt at Depth (Traits, plans, espaces* or *Essai pour le profondeur).*
1913-22

Oil on canvas, 31¾ x 25⅝"
(80.5 x 65 cm.)

Signed lr "Kupka"

Private Collection

PROVENANCE:

the artist
to present owner

EXHIBITION:

*Prague, 1946, Mánes, no. 137 (as *Pokus o hloubku I [Attempt at Depth]* 1913-22)

According to Fédit, the first studies on this theme were done as early as 1913, and this painting, although reworked later, was started at that time. One can indeed see analogies with *Amorpha, Fugue* of 1912: in the predominantly red and blue palette, the fluid elliptical shapes and the idea of interlocking abstract patterns of pure color or pure sound. However, in contrast to *Amorpha, Fugue,* in which the visual ambiguity and revolutionary character derive from the painting's radical flatness, this picture shows a complex interplay between surface and depth. Kupka's pictorial goals are confirmed by the title he gave this painting in 1946: *Attempt at Depth.*

A passage from Kupka's 1912-13 manuscript describes an image which is strikingly close to the configurations seen here, although the analogy may be purely coincidental. In discussing the effect of red on blue, a combination Kupka favored, he said: "Have you never stopped to observe the horses which pull the wagons full of building materials? One can see a thin line of carmine red on their ultramarine blue collars. This thread of color is enough to make the blue vibrate with purple."[1]

1 Manuscript II, p. 19.

147 *Lines, Planes, Spaces III (Traits, plans, espaces III).* c. 1923 [reworked 1934]

Oil on canvas, 70⅞ x 50⅜″ (180 x 128 cm.)
Signed ll "Kupka"
Fédit, no. 99, repr.
Vachtová, no. 230, repr. p. 176
Musée National d'Art Moderne, Paris (AM 4183-P)

PROVENANCE:

the artist
Eugénie Kupka
to present owner, gift, 1963

EXHIBITIONS:

*Paris, 1924, la Boétie, no. 41 (first version, dated 1921, as *Formes en repoussoir*)
Lille, 1925, no. 2 (as *Traits, plans, clarté*)
*Paris, 1936, Jeu de Paume, no. 35
*Prague, 1946, Mánes, no. 136 (dated 1913-22)
Paris, 1949, *Salon des Réalités Nouvelles*, no. 283
*Paris, 1953, *Salon des Réalités Nouvelles*, no. XLVI
*New York, 1953, Rose Fried, no. 7 (dated 1913)
*Paris, 1958, MNAM, no. 43, pl. XVI
*Cologne, 1967, no. 34, repr.; Munich, 1967, no. 34, repr.; Amsterdam, 1968, no. 70; Prague, 1968, no. 87, repr.
Strasbourg, 1972, no. 62, fig. 19

1 According to Fédit (in conversation with the author), "destroyed" means sanded down.

2 See Fédit, p. 112, for photograph of original version.

On February 12, 1934, Eugénie Kupka wrote to Waldes, saying that over the past three days Kupka had "destroyed" this painting "begun in 1923."[1] A small canvas (cat. no. 146) which had served as a study remained. However before the end of the month Kupka had reworked the painting and given it its present form.

The initial state of this painting showed a more intricate pattern of loops recoiling into space similar to those seen in cat. no. 146.[2] In that state, the painting was exhibited at la Boétie as *Formes en repoussoir, 1921 (Forms against a Foil).* The present rendering is more open, more loosely articulated and more two-dimensional. The infinite arabesques meandering into undetermined depth are transformed into curved and severed abstract planes.

148 *Moving Blues* (II?) (*Bleus mouvants* [II?]). 1923-24

Oil on canvas, 43⅜ x 42½"
(110 x 108 cm.)

Signed lr "Kupka"

Fédit, no. 93, repr.

Vachtová, no. 254, repr. p. 310

Musée National d'Art Moderne,
Paris (AM 4186-P)

PROVENANCE:

the artist
Eugénie Kupka
to present owner, gift, 1963

EXHIBITIONS:

*Prague, 1946, Mánes, no. 154 (dated
    1923)
*Paris, 1953, *Salon des Réalités Nou-
    velles* (hors catalogue)
Lille, 1956
*Cologne, 1967, no. 31, repr.;
    Munich, 1967, no. 31, repr.;
    Vienna, 1967, no. 37; Amsterdam,
    1968, no. 61, repr.; Prague, 1968,
    no. 85, repr.

1 As proposed by Vachtová, p. 190. The
    illustration is the cul de lampe for Vol.
    I, Book I, Chapter VI, "Divisions and
    Rhythm of History," published in
    1905. Thus Vachtová's 1907 date is
    incorrect. See fig. 2a, p. 42 here.

2 Volume I, Book II, Chapter III,
    "Potamia," p. 530.

Three variations on this theme exist today. A fourth, probably the first version (destroyed by the artist) was exhibited at la Boétie in 1924 as *Bleus mouvants (réminiscence d'Estérel)* 1922-24, cat. no. 47. The subtitle provides a key to the iconography of the series, Estérel being a seaside resort on the Riviera. As Fédit points out, Kupka was attempting to depict the universal cosmic rhythm which rules the tides and the constellations in this image, where waves and sky meet in two distinctive arabesques.

An illustration from *L'Homme et la terre* in which one sees bodies borne by waves in a rhythmic flow may have been a distant source for this series.[1] A typically Art Nouveau interpretation, this type of imagery is found not only in Klimt (*Fishes Blood*, as Vachtová notes) but in a 1902 picture by the Czech artist Švabinský (*Rodin's Inspiration*) which shows intertwined figures floating in the sky.

If one looks back as far as *L'Homme et la terre*, a book which marked Kupka's thinking decisively, another of its pictures may have engendered Kupka's pictorial idea. A diagram with the inscription "How men of antiquity understood the world" shows two vaulted forms, one above the other, labeled respectively "the starry vault" and "the earth." These two shapes are surrounded by emblematic waves which signify "the celestial ocean" and "the inferior ocean: chaos."[2]

The third version (cat. no. 149), according to Vachotvá (p. 279), was reworked between 1928 and 1936. It is difficult to say whether it was done earlier or later than this painting. When exhibited in Kupka's 1936 retrospective, the artist dated it 1923, which seems a bit early in view of the la Boétie dates which presumably would be more exact. The artist dated the present painting 1923 (Prague, 1946) and 1923-24 on his personal label on the back.

149 *Moving Blues (Bleus mouvants).*
1923; reworked 1928-36

Oil on canvas, 46½ x 44⅛"
(118 x 112 cm.)
Signed lr "Kupka"
Vachtová, no. 255, color pl. XXI
Collection Národní Galerie, Prague
(O 5943)

PROVENANCE:

the artist
Prague Castle
to present owner, 1951

EXHIBITIONS:

*Paris, 1936, Jeu de Paume, no. 39,
  repr.
*Prague, 1946, Mánes, no. 153 (dated
  1923)
*Paris, 1958, MNAM, no. 49
*Prague, 1965, no. 9 (dated 1922-36)
*Ústí nad Orlicí, 1965
*Cologne, 1967, no. 75, repr.;
  Munich, 1967, no. 75, repr.; Vienna,
  1967, no. 35; Amsterdam, 1968, no.
  60, repr.; Prague, 1968, no. 84, repr.
Stockholm-Göteborg, 1973, no. 96
(dated 1922-36)

150 *Moving Blues (Bleus mouvants)*.
c. 1925-27

Oil on canvas, 44½ x 44½"
(113 x 113 cm.)
Signed and dated ll "Kupka//33"
Vachtová, cat. no. 256 (incorrect
entry), repr. p. 193
Collection P. P., Paris

PROVENANCE:

the artist
to present owner

EXHIBITIONS:

*Paris, 1936, Jeu de Paume, no. 34
  (as *Plans en mouvement*)
Paris, 1949, *Salon des Réalités Nou-
velles,* no. 284, (as *Bleus par plans*)
*Paris, 1953, *Salon des Réalités
  Nouvelles*
*Paris, 1958, MNAM, no. 64,
  pl. XXIII

In this late version of *Moving Blues*—the last of the series and probably painted c. 1925-27 despite the fact that it is dated 1933 on the canvas—the upper and lower arabesques are virtually identical in formal structure. This is in keeping with Kupka's theory of the unique cosmic rhythm that regulates both stars and oceans. It is also consistent with his more purely philosophical belief that what is above is also below (see cat. no. 96).

In his 1910-11 notebook he wrote (in Greek and then in German): "Table of Memphis: Heaven above heaven below//Stars above stars below//Everything above is also below//Accept it thus and be content."[1]

1 Manuscript I, p. 19.

151 *Equation of Moving Blues (Equation des bleus en mouvement).*
1929-31

Oil on canvas, 35½ x 35½"
(90 x 90 cm.)

Signed lr "Kupka"

Vachtová, no. 282, repr. p. 209

Collection P. P., Paris

PROVENANCE:

the artist
to present owner

EXHIBITIONS:

*Paris, 1936, Jeu de Paume, no. 65
  (as *Equation des bleus mouvants,*
  dated 1929)
*Prague, 1946, Mánes, no. 155 (dated
  1929)
São Paulo-Buenos Aires, 1949, no. 47
(as *Equação de planos mouventes
III*), repr. 14
Paris, 1953, *Salon des Réalités
Nouvelles*
*Paris, 1958, MNAM, no. 62 (as
  Equation des plans mouvants III,
  dated 1931)

This painting shows a more abstract interpretation of the theme illustrated in *Moving Blues* (cat. nos. 148-150). The arithmetic terminology in the title and the geometric forms suggest that Kupka was referring to Plato's cosmology as presented in the *Timoeus*.[1] According to Plato, arithmetic and geometric terms are the mean between the phenomenon and the idea, or a way of translating the undifferentiated mass of the material world into the realm of ideas. Furthermore, within this system, each element of the world corresponds to a precise geometric figure which is a triangle. In the present painting, Kupka's earlier emblematic imagery is translated into an equation of geometric figures.

Kupka dated this painting 1929 for his 1946 exhibition. It was reproduced in *Abstraction-Création,* no. 1, 1932, p. 23, dated 1931. Its obvious derivation from *Moving Blues* of 1925-27 (cat. no. 150), yet its more systematic and visible brushwork which forecasts that seen in *Untitled,* 1931 (cat. no. 169), obviously a more advanced variation on the same theme, makes it difficult to date this picture precisely.

1 Apparently *Timoeus* and *Philebus* were
Kupka's favorite Platonic writings.

152   Study for *Around a Point*. (Etude
       pour *Autour d'un point*). 1911-12

       Gouache, watercolor and pencil on
       paper, 7½ x 8½″ (19 x 21.6 cm.)
       Signed lr "Kupka"
       Private Collection

       PROVENANCE:
       the artist
       to present owner

153   Study for *Around a Point* (Etude
       pour *Autour d'un point*). c. 1919

       Gouache, watercolor and pencil on
       paper, 8 x 9″ (20.3 x 22.9 cm.)
       Signed ll "Kupka"
       Private Collection

       PROVENANCE:
       the artist
       to present owner

54 Study for *Around a Point* (Etude pour *Autour d'un Point*). 1920-25

Gouache and pencil on paper, 7¾ x 8″ (19.7 x 20.3 cm.)
Signed ll "Kupka"
Private Collection

PROVENANCE:
the artist
to present owner

55 Study for *Around a Point* (Etude pour *Autour d'un point*). 1920-25

Gouache on paper, 14½ x 16¼″ (36.8 x 41.3 cm.)
Signed ll "Kupka"
Private Collection

PROVENANCE:
the artist
to present owner

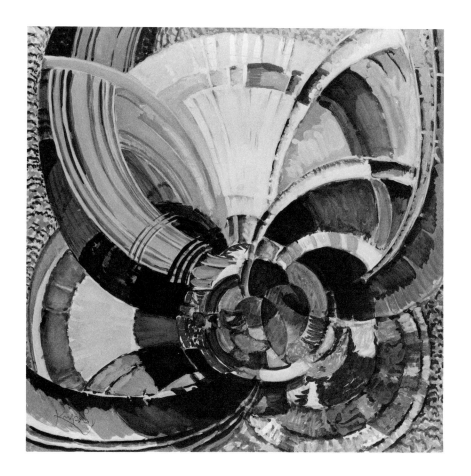

156　Study for *Around a Point* (Etude
pour *Autour d'un point*). 1920-25

Pencil on paper, 5⅞ x 5⅛"
(15 x 13 cm.)
Stamped ll "Kupka"
Fédit, no. 109, repr.
Musée National d'Art Moderne,
Paris (AM 2718-D)

PROVENANCE:
the artist
Eugénie Kupka
to present owner, gift, 1963

157　Study for *Around a Point* (Etude
pour *Autour d'un point*). 1920-25

Pencil on paper, 7¾ x 7¾"
(19.7 x 19.7 cm.)
Stamped ll "Kupka"
Collection Theodoros Stamos

PROVENANCE:
the artist
Estate of the artist
Karl Flinker
Spencer A. Samuels and Company,
Ltd.
to present owner

58 Study for *Around a Point* (Etude
   pour *Autour d'un point*). 1920-25

   Gouache on paper, 16⅞ x 17½″
   (42.9 x 44.5 cm.)
   Signed ll "Kupka"
   Private Collection

   PROVENANCE:
   the artist
   to present owner

59 Study for *Around a Point* (Etude
   pour *Autour d'un point*). 1920-25

   Gouache and gray chalk on light gray
   paper: mat window, 14 x 14¾″
   (35.6 x 37.5 cm.)
   Signed lr "Kupka"
   Private Collection

   PROVENANCE:
   the artist
   to present owner

160 *Around a Point (Autour d'un point).* c. 1925-30; reworked c. 1934

Oil on canvas, 76⅜ x 78¾"
(194 x 200 cm.)

Signed and dated lr "Kupka//11-30;" inscribed ll "AUTOUR//D'UN POINT"

Fédit, no. 111, repr.

Musée National d'Art Moderne, Paris (AM 3213-P)

PROVENANCE:

the artist
purchased by the French government, 1947
to present owner, transferred, 1953

EXHIBITIONS:

*Paris, 1936, Jeu de Paume, no. 36
*Prague, 1946, Mánes, no. 135
*Paris, 1953, *Salon des Réalités Nouvelles,* unnumbered
Saint Etienne, 1957, no. 19, fig. 8
London, 1957, no. 73
*Paris, MNAM, no. 13, pl. VI
*Cologne, 1967, no. 40, repr.; Munich, 1967, no. 40, repr.; Vienna, 1967, no. 17, repr.; Amsterdam, 1968, no. 80, repr. black and white, color; Prague, 1968, no. 88, repr. (upside down)

Kupka dated this painting 1911-30 because the first tentative studies on the theme dated from c. 1911-12. Most of the final studies and the painting itself were executed in 1920-30. Curiously, although Kupka did literally dozens of studies on paper on this theme, no other canvases are recorded.

The earliest studies show the genesis of the idea: a mixture of the lotus flower (with its symbolism of mystical evolution; see cat. no. 4), cosmic space, and the *Disks of Newton* (cat. nos. 73, 75). As the image evolved, it became increasingly legible as the unfurled petals of a flower. Thus symbolic, cosmic and biological significance are combined.

In the present painting these three dimensions are sublimated into a supremely abstract pictorial idea. The centrifugal/centripetal spiraling motion is of course one of Kupka's central themes.

According to Fédit, a first state was probably achieved c. 1927 (see fig. 12, p. 314), and was reworked c. 1934. This reworking, similar to that carried out on cat. no. 147 (and even cat. no. 146 at an unknown date), consisted of painting out many of the original colored motifs with white and opening up the composition.

161 *Planes by Curves (Plans par courbes).* c. 1926

Oil on canvas, 33⅛ x 35⅞″
(84 x 91 cm.)
Signed lr "Kupka"
Vachtová, no. 306, repr. p. 230
Private Collection

PROVENANCE:

the artist
Eugénie Kupka
to present owner

EXHIBITIONS:

Paris, 1958, *Salon des Comparaisons,*
no. 204
*Paris, 1958, MNAM, no. 55, pl. XIX

The flat curved planes in this composition and in cat. no. 162 evolved from a group of pictures of 1919-22 (see discussion cat. no. 134). Vachtová identifies this canvas as *Curved Planes II* and dates it 1926-32. Because the title may have changed since the work was executed, and much of the surface has been repainted, it is difficult to document these dates exactly. However the evenly shifting curving planes (seen in both versions of *Around a Point*) situate this work at around that time.

Planes by Curves (Plans par courbes). c. 1926-30

Oil on canvas, 26¾ x 26¾"
(68 x 68 cm.)
Signed lr "Kupka"
Private Collection

PROVENANCE:

the artist
to present owner

A watercolor for this painting exists in the collection of the Musée National d'Art Moderne, Paris (Fédit, cat. no. 103, p. 115). In her discussion of the study, Fédit identifies the present picture as *Planes by Curves II* and dates it c. 1926. This is plausible but hard to document. Whether this painting or cat. no. 161 is really *Planes by Curves II* remains to be established. However this picture appears to have been conceived and executed later than cat. no. 161 in that the central imagery is more autonomous and clearly defined, and less dependent on earlier themes and motifs. Furthermore, the horizontal-vertical framework of the composition and the predominantly blue ground with an accent of red relate this painting to *The Form of Blue,* 1930-31 (cat. no. 168).

163 *Arabesque II (Arabesque II).*
1925-26

Oil on canvas, 39⅜ x 31⅞″
(100 x 81 cm.)
Signed ll "Kupka"
Collection Margit Chanin, Ltd.

PROVENANCE:

the artist
Galerie Louis Carré, Paris
to present owner

EXHIBITIONS:

*Prague, 1946, Mánes, no. 124 (as
  Arabesque II, dated 1925-26)
São Paulo-Buenos Aires, 1949, no. 45
(dated 1925)
Vienna, 1953 (cat. not located)

The arabesque was a motif which intrigued Kupka from a very early date. He referred to it often in his written texts, expressing his admiration for Islamic ornament. This formal idiom which does not copy nature, said Kupka, "appears to us
as a harmony of pure forms of noble distinction; it is a world superior to our own.
There is more there than just a simple arabesque. There is much intelligence *[esprit]*,
an intelligence which sings eurythmy in its distribution of formal components."[1]
    An unpublished text of c. 1919, in which Kupka discussed the illustrations for
The Song of Roland,[2] includes a long passage on the arabesque. Here Kupka refers
to the eighth to eleventh century illuminated manuscripts he studied in preparation
for his book: Celtic, Carolingian, Mozarabic, French and Spanish Romanesque,
and describes the distinctive characteristics of each. The reader feels that he would
have preferred to do abstract motifs for this early medieval text than the academic
illustrations required of him.
    In 1925-26, Kupka did a series of paintings on the arabesque theme: *Arabesque
I, II, III; Closed Motif, Verticals and Diagonals in Green* (MNAM, Paris). He also
used this motif in the fourth section of his album of woodcuts devoted to vertical
and diagonal planes (see cat. no. 165).

1 Manuscript IV, Chapter I, p. 15.

2 Executed 1917-18. Text courtesy of
  Andrée Martinel-Kupka.

Oil on mattress ticking, 33½ x 55⅛"
(85 x 140 cm.)

Signed ll "Kupka"

Vachtová, no. 269, color pl. XXIII

Collection Národní Galerie, Prague
(O 3823)

PROVENANCE:

the artist
to present owner, 1946

EXHIBITIONS:

Paris, 1926, *Salon des Indépendants*,
no. 1954
*Paris, 1936, Jeu de Paume, no. 68
*Prague, 1946, Mánes, no. 108
*Paris, 1958, MNAM, no. 52
*Písek—České Budějovice, 1961,
no. 20, repr.

*Cologne, 1967, no. 76, repr.;
Munich, 1967, no. 76, repr.;
Vienna, 1967, no. 44, repr.; Amster-
dam, 1968, no. 71, repr.; Prague,
1968, no. 83, repr.
Stockholm—Göteborg, 1973, no. 98

The dulled palette, impastoed surface and jagged forms in this picture are characteristic of a small series of paintings and many studies on paper which Kupka executed in c. 1926. The series included *Energetics I* (Vachtová, cat. no. 268) *Energetic
on Violet* (MNAM, Paris).

Both the dynamic deployment of energy seen in these autonomous lines and
forms and the horizontal format echo *Solo of a Brown Line* of 1912-13 (cat. no.
108). The interlacing of lines and planes evokes the idea of a fugue. Kupka may
have been thinking in musical terms; a photograph found among his personal
papers shows a 1925 painting, *Orgue sur fond vert (Organ on a Green Ground)*,
which seems to be transitional between the *Arabesque* subjects and the *Energetics*.

One of the four themes of Kupka's 1926 album of woodcuts was based on these
dynamic and asymmetrical motifs.

165 *Four Stories in Black and White*
(Quatre histoires de blanc et noir).
Paris, 1926

Portfolio of 26 woodcuts
Sheet: 13⅛ x 9⅞" (33.3 x 25.1 cm.);
Block: 8 x 6⅛" (20.3 x 15.5 cm.)
No. 149 of limited edition of 300
Pages 4, 11, 17, 23
Private Collection

As the title suggests, this album of woodcuts is based on four formal themes which can be freely described as the following (in order):

1) Organic/decorative
2) Angular
3) Undulating/cosmic
4) Vertical and diagonal planes

Almost all these themes and variations are found in Kupka's paintings throughout the decade of the twenties.

Each theme was illustrated in six variations. One of each series is shown here. The album included a title page and a written introduction by Kupka in which he explained the independent life and significance of abstract formal motifs. This book, far removed in time from the artist's pre-1900 Central European training (see pp. 17-23 here), nonetheless shows its enduring imprint.

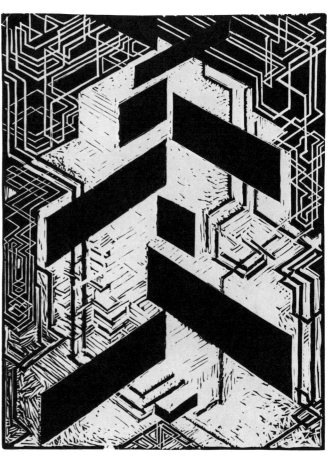

166 *Drinking Steel (L'Acier boit).*
    1927-30

Oil on canvas, 17¾ x 20⅞"
(45 x 53 cm.)
Signed lr "Kupka"
Collection Karl Flinker

PROVENANCE:

the artist
Eugénie Kupka
to present owner

EXHIBITION:

*Paris, 1960, Karl Flinker, repr. color

Between 1927 and 1930, Kupka suffered a period of crisis in his art. Aside from his ill health which is abundantly noted in the correspondence between Eugénie Kupka and Iča Waldes, the critical failure and financial disaster of his 1926 woodcut album may have contributed to his acute anxiety. The fact that he did not exhibit at the *Salon des Indépendants* between 1926 and 1933 offers further evidence of his disarray.

It was during this period that Kupka began a series of pictures on the subject of machines. Apparently he looked toward the world of machines to enrich his formal vocabulary. The contrast of circular and rectilinear elements emphasized in the machine paintings will be found, distilled into pure abstract components, in many paintings of the 1930s.

Despite the fact that many of the machine pictures are quite successful in terms of formal composition, Kupka seems to have considered them marginal and chose not to include them in exhibitions of his work.

There are three virtually identical paintings of *Drinking Steel*. The other two are in the Národní Galerie, Prague, and the Musée National d'Art Moderne, Paris.

67　*Machines.* 1929-32

Oil on canvas, 41¾ x 42¾″
(106 x 108.5 cm.)
Signed ll "Kupka"
Vachtová, no. 288, color pl. XXV
Collection Národní Galerie, Prague
(O 2265)

PROVENANCE:

the artist
Jindřich Waldes
to present owner, 1940

EXHIBITIONS:

*Písek—České Budějovice, 1961, no.
  25, repr.
*Prague, 1968, no. 95, repr.
*Belgrade, 1969, no. 18, repr.

168 *Untitled; The Form of Blue (?) (La Forme du bleu [?]). 1929-31*

Oil on canvas, 26¾ x 26¾″
(68 x 68 cm.)

Signed lr "Kupka"

Private Collection

PROVENANCE:

the artist
Rose Fried Gallery, New York
to present owner

EXHIBITIONS:

Paris, 1929 (as *La Forme du bleu*)?
*Prague, 1946, Mánes, no. 164 (as [*The Form of Blue*], 1931, 70 x 70 cm.)?
*New York, 1953, Rose Fried, no. 9 or 10
*New York, 1964, Royal S. Marks, no. 6 or 7
London-Austin, 1973, no. 73, repr.

1 Manuscript II, pp. 19-20.

For Kupka, the physiological properties of color (number, length, speed of wave lengths) dictate an ideal shape. The ideal form for red is round, orange is oval, green is undulating, etc. Although individual paintings illustrating these ideas were executed starting in 1919-23, the theory was formulated prior to World War I.

The ideal form of blue is vertical and rectilinear: "Blue, like its closest neighbors on the spectrum, because it seems to recede in space, or at least draw back into itself, should be motivated or enclosed by tapered, rectilinear forms.[1]

Most of the paintings called *The Form of Blue* (NG, Prague; Collection Mr. and Mrs. Andrew P. Fuller, New York), remain strictly within the range of the blue palette and are rendered in a hatched almost woven impasto, in which the direction of the brushstrokes seems to duplicate the color's wave lengths as Kupka understood them. The present painting appears to be a later version: the surface texture is more even; the brushstroke relatively invisible. The red line pushes the blues toward violet, just as in *Family Portrait* (cat. no. 44) and *Amorpha, Fugue* (cat. no. 92).

All the paintings on the theme of blue are equivocal in their connotations of ascent/descent. As seen elsewhere (see discussion, cat. no. 96), the two movements are equivalent, not contradictory, in Kupka's mind. The diamond-shaped forms used in other paintings on this theme and the tapered diagonal planes pointing upward/downward here unite both directions in a single form.

69   *Untitled.* 1931

Oil on canvas, 26¾ x 26¾"
(68 x 68 cm.)

Signed ll "Kupka"

Private Collection

PROVENANCE:

the artist
Rose Fried Gallery, New York
to present owner

EXHIBITIONS:

*New York, 1953, Rose Fried, no. 9
  (as *Triangles,* dated 1934)
New York, 1960, Chalette; Cincinnati, 1960; Chicago, 1960; Minneapolis, 1961, no. 16 (as *Triangles,*
dated 1934)
*New York, 1964, Royal S. Marks,
  no. 6 or 7
Dallas, 1972, no. 33 (as *Triangles,*
dated 1934), repr.

Since the exact title of this painting is unknown, it is impossible to find any clues to its dating through early exhibition histories. Furthermore the image is unique and the technique of threaded color is unusual. The triangles, their interrelationships, and the diagonally articulated ground, relate this painting to *Equation of Moving Blues* (cat. no. 151). Yet the rhythm which was so important to Kupka is entirely different here. The strictly parallel alignments in the present picture are far removed from the free-flowing natural rhythms seen in the earlier painting. The tighter more symmetrical arrangement will be characteristic of Kupka's work in the 1930s. The square format is also more frequent during that decade.

170 *Abstractions drawn by František Kupka (Abstrakce Kreslil František Kupka).* 1928-32; 1945-46

Book of 16 pages, 8¼ x 6″
(21 x 15.3 cm.) each
Private Collection

According to Fédit (p. 137), these drawings were probably worked on in the period 1928-32, at a time when Kupka was attempting to purify his forms. The first twelve of the total of sixteen were originally published on a single page in *Abstraction-Création,* no. 2, 1933, p. 26. This repertory of forms will be found developed in diverse manners throughout the 1930s. Many of the original gouaches and related studies are in the Musée National d'Art Moderne, Paris.

In 1948, the entire sixteen were published on separate sheets in the small book exhibited here.

*Diagonal Planes II (Plans diago-
naux II).* 1931

Oil on canvas, 35½ x 43¼"
(90 x 110 cm.)

Signed lr "Kupka"

Vachtová, no. 302, repr. p. 225;
color pl. XXVII

Collection Národní Galerie, Prague
(O 3824)

PROVENANCE:

the artist
to present owner, 1946

EXHIBITIONS:

*Paris, 1936, Jeu de Paume, no. 67

*Prague, 1946, Mánes, no. 114

*Písek—České Budějovice, 1961, no.
  27, repr.

*Ustí nad Orlicí, 1965, no. 17

*Cologne, 1967, no. 79, repr.;
  Munich, 1967, no. 79, repr.; Vienna,
  1967, no. 53; Amsterdam, 1968, no.
  93, repr.; Prague, 1968, no. 101,
  repr.

Geneva, 1970, no. 72; Zurich, 1970,
no. 72

172 Reduced replica of *Diagonal Planes V (Plans diagonaux V)*.
1931-33

Gouache, 6¼ x 6⅞″ (16 x 17.5 cm.)
Signed lr "Kupka"
Collection Karl Flinker

PROVENANCE:

the artist
Eugénie Kupka
to present owner

This is a small scale replica of an oil painting of 1931-33.[1] The number of the painting in the series of *Diagonal Planes* remains unclear. Kupka has identified the gouache as *Diagonal Planes V;* the dimensions for it in the Carré 1951 exhibition catalogue correspond to those of *Diagonal Planes I,* Prague 1946, cat. no. 113. Vachtová identifies this composition as *Diagonal Planes III.*

1 Collection Louis Carré, Paris.

173 *Abstract Painting (Peinture abstraite).* 1930-32

Oil on canvas, 49¼ x 33½″
(125 x 85 cm.)

Signed l of c "Kupka"

Vachtová, no. 301, color pl. XXIX

Collection Národní Galerie, Prague
(O 3827)

PROVENANCE:

the artist
to present owner, 1946

EXHIBITIONS:

Paris, 1936, *Salon des Indépendants,*
no. 1810

*Paris, 1936, Jeu de Paume, no. 58,
repr.

*Prague, 1946, Mánes, no. 82

*Paris, 1958, MNAM, no. 60

*Písek—České Budějovice, 1961,
no. 26

*Prague, 1965, Galerie Karlovo
Náměstí, no. 13

*Ústí nad Orlicí, 1965, no. 16

*Cologne, 1967, no. 78, repr.;
Munich, 1967, no. 78, repr.; Vienna,
1967, no. 51, repr.; Amsterdam,
1968, no. 81, repr.; Prague, 1968,
no. 99, repr.

Geneva, 1970, no. 71; Zurich, 1970,
no. 71

Stockholm-Göteborg, 1973, no. 110

This painting is one of Kupka's earliest and purest neo-plastic statements. Obviously inspired by the black and white gouaches of 1928-32, it can be specifically related to the third and sixth drawings in that series. In drawing no. 3 of the 1933 publication, a vertical line extends from the top edge of the study, a horizontal from the right side. The position of the off-center rectangle is determined by their intersection at its upper left corner. A third vector, from the lower edge and longer than the other two, is not drawn, but is implicit. Similarly, the three lines in *Abstract Painting,* if extended, would intersect and bound the three sides of a rectangle.

In 1912-13, Kupka wrote: "The straight line represents the abstract world. It is absolute . . . the optical sense grasps it in its entirety and easily imagines its extension in space. Since the line starts from a point, the eye merely records it as a direction."[1]

This painting is generally dated 1930. Supposedly in that year, Kupka did little painting (see Chronology) and there are no paintings showing such a pure conception and consummate control before 1931-32. Apparently the founding of the *Abstraction-Création* group in February 1931 encouraged him to pursue his objective of "pure painting." In 1932, he wrote to Waldes: "I have abandoned machines and am back to pure abstraction."[2] Since the black and white gouaches were not published until 1933, and this painting was not exhibited before 1936, one is tempted to question the 1930 date.

1 Manuscript II, p. 35.

2 Vachtová, p. 222.

174 *Planes II (Plans II). 1932*

Watercolor on paper, 10⅝ x 14″
(27 x 35.5 cm.)
Signed ll "Kupka"
Courtesy Galerie Denise René, Paris

PROVENANCE:

the artist
Eugénie Kupka
Karl Flinker
to present owner

5   *Eudia (Eudia).* 1933

Oil on canvas, 26 x 26″ (66 x 66 cm.)

Signed ll "Kupka"

Vachtová, no. 308, repr. p. 227; color
pl. XXVIII

Collection Národní Galerie, Prague
(O 3832)

PROVENANCE:

the artist
to present owner, 1946

EXHIBITIONS:

*Paris, 1936, Jeu de Paume, no. 53
*Prague, 1946, Mánes, no. 85
*Písek—České Budějovice, 1961, no.
  28, repr.
*Ústí nad Orlicí, 1965, no. 18
London, 1967, no. 82, repr.
Brussels-Rotterdam, 1967, no. 82
*Prague, 1968, no. 102, repr. (on its
  side)

1 Manuscript I, p. 9.
2 Ibid., p. 26.

The term *"Eudia"* was one which Kupka referred to throughout his lifetime. It was fundamental to his aesthetic. The first written reference to the term is in the 1910-11 notebook: "Greece gave us *Eudia*, measure, a sense of proportions and rhythms; [Greece] gave us rational knowledge, but could not and never will transform our tendencies toward intuitions, sentimentality, dreams."[1] A few pages later he noted: "The spontaneous rhythm [created] by the repetition of proportions represented by lines or planes is like the assemblage of motifs on a printed fabric. The conscious and desired rhythm, harmony, *Eudia* of all components."[2]

176 *Syncopated Black Disks (Disques noirs syncopés).* 1930-33

Gouache and pencil on paper,
9⅞ x 7⅞" (25 x 20 cm.)

Signed lr "Kupka"

Lent by the Metropolitan Museum of Art, Purchase, Rogers Fund, 1968 (68.108)

PROVENANCE:

the artist
Estate of the artist
Galerie Karl Flinker, Paris
Private Collection, New York
Spencer A. Samuels and Company, Ltd.
to present owner

This watercolor is one of the earlier of Kupka's 1928-32 abstractions, revealed by the fluidity of its forms. The composition is obviously inspired by *Etalage jaune et violet (Display of Yellow and Purple),* dated 1921-29 by Kupka (Vachtová cat. no. 219, repr. p. 304; dated 1921). In a 1933 photograph of Kupka in his studio, one can see this painting on the upper left wall (fig. 12, p. 314). *Syncopated Black Disks* also draws on the formal invention of *The Horesmen* (cat. no. 9) and shows a point of departure for the disarticulated circles seen throughout the 1930s.

7 *Dynamic Disks? (Disques dynamiques?)*. 1931-33

Gouache on paper, 11 x 11″
(28 x 28 cm.)
Signed ll "Kupka"
Collection Richard S. Zeisler,
New York

PROVENANCE:
the artist
Rose Fried Gallery, New York
to present owner

This gouache is a study for the painting on the left in fig. 12, p. 314, a work which was obviously derived from the circular forms and rectilinear background seen in the machine painting, *Synthèse (Synthesis,* NG, Prague) visible to the right of it. The juxtaposition of these two paintings shows how the abstract imagery of the 1930s and 1940s developed from the machine series.

The painting *Around a Point,* visible on Kupka's easel in this photograph, is seen in its first state, prior to c. 1934. *Synthesis* is seen here in its final state, probably 1933, which confirms a 1933 dating of the photograph, and helps establish the dating of this gouache.

178 Study for *Circulars and Recti-*
    linears. 1931-35

Gouache on paper, 12¼ x 11¾"
(31.1 x 29.9 cm.)
Signed lr "Kupka"
Collection Mr. and Mrs. G. E. S.,
New York

PROVENANCE:

the artist
to present owner, 1955

The collage technique used in this study (an assemblage of three separate pieces
of paper) provides an insight into Kupka's way of preparing some of his compositions during this period. In view of the fairly classic closed forms, this must be a
rather early study for the 1937 painting *Circulars and Rectilinears.*

179 *Circulars and Rectilinears (Circu-*
    laires et rectilignes). 1937

Oil on wood, 40⅛ x 40⅛"
(102 x 102 cm.)
Signed lr "Kupka"
Vachtová, no. 316, color pl. XXVI
Collection Národní Galerie, Prague
(O 3826)

PROVENANCE:

the artist
to present owner, 1946

EXHIBITIONS:
*Prague, 1946, Mánes, no. 147
*Písek–České Budějovice, 1961,
  no. 30
*Prague, 1965, Galerie Karlovo
  Náměstí, no. 12
*Ústí nad Orlicí, 1965, no. 19
London, 1967, no. 83
Brussels-Rotterdam, 1967, no. 83,
repr.
*Prague, 1968, no. 103, repr.
*Belgrade, 1969, no. 19, repr.
Stockholm-Göteborg, 1973, no. 112

The overlapping and segmented circular forms in this painting are distinctly reminiscent of Lissitsky's revolutionary *Proun* paintings executed prior to 1924. In Kupka's case, it is generally assumed and visually logical that he developed these configurations autonomously, as an abstract extension of his studies of machines. Nonetheless the question of whether Lissitsky's *Prouns* exerted some influence remains unanswered. The latter works were surely known to Kupka, through his involvement with the *Abstraction-Création* group.

180   *Divertimento I (Divertissement I).*
      1938

Oil on canvas, 23⅝ x 36¼"
(60 x 92 cm.)

Signed lr "Kupka"

Vachtová, no. 315

Collection Mr. and Mrs. Andrew P.
Fuller

PROVENANCE:

the artist
Galerie Louis Carré, Paris
to present owner

EXHIBITIONS:

*Prague, 1946, Mánes, no. 148
Lausanne, 1955, no. 47

81 *Divertimento II (Divertissement II).* 1938

Oil on canvas, 24 x 35″ (62 x 90 cm.)

Signed lr "Kupka"

Collection Mr. and Mrs. G. E. S., New York

PROVENANCE:

the artist
to present owner, c. 1955

EXHIBITIONS:

*Prague, 1946, Mánes, no. 149
*New York, 1953, Rose Fried, no. 4
New York, 1960, Chalette; Cincinnati, 1960; Chicago, 1960; Minneapolis, 1961, no. 14, repr.
New York, 1964, Sidney Janis, no. 9, repr.

1 A good selection of these paintings is in the MNAM, Paris.

Divertimento I and *II* show the complex circular forms seen in *Circulars and Rectilinears*. They owe their horizontal format, intricate rhythms and deviation from the primary color scale to a group of pictures on the theme of Jazz which, as looser variations on the machine theme, were executed in 1935-37.[1] The title *Divertimento* may contain an allusion to music and thereby be a conscious extension of the Jazz concept and formal themes.

182   *Untitled.* 1933?

Gouache on paper, 10¾ x 11″
(27.3 x 28 cm.)

Inscribed, signed and dated lr "A
mon cher ami//Lieberman [sic]//
Kupka//33"

Collection Mr. and Mrs. Alexander
Liberman

PROVENANCE:

the artist
to present owner, 1950's

83 *Orange Circle (Cercle orangé)*.
1945-46

Gouache on paper, 16½ x 16½"
(42 x 42 cm.)
Signed lr "Kupka"
Collection Richard S. Zeisler,
New York

PROVENANCE:
the artist
Eugénie Kupka
Galerie Karl Flinker, Paris
to present owner

This is a study for the painting *Orange Circle* (Private Collection, New York)
exhibited in Prague, 1946, cat. no. 150, dated 1946. The motif is seen in the late
abstract drawings of 1945-46 (see cat. no. 170, no. 14). Once again the source of
inspiration was probably a mechanical apparatus, such as the one in the upper
left of fig. 16, p. 317, which may be a strobe light.

184 Reduced replica of *Contrasts Series C III, Elevation (Série Contrastes III, Elévation)*. 1932-38

Gouache on cream paper, 9⅞ x 13″ (25 x 33 cm.)

Signed lr "Kupka;" inscribed r margin "Elévation,//Exp. New York//1932-38//chez L. Carré."

Fédit, no. 153, repr.

Musée National d'Art Moderne, Paris (AM 2791-D)

PROVENANCE:

the artist
Eugénie Kupka
to present owner, gift, 1963

1 Listed by Fédit as a study for the painting, this author believes this work to be a reduced replica done after the finished work.

This gouache is a replica of *Contrasts Series III*.[1] The painting (Prague, 1946, cat. no. 96, dated 1935-46) is in the Collection Louis Carré, Paris. Carré dated it 1938 in his 1951 exhibition of the artist's work. The title betrays the work's architectural inspiration. The formal components derive from the 1928-32 gouaches.

Kupka, *Contrasts Series VI*, 1935-46, oil, NG, Prague.

85 *Contrasts Series (IV?) (Série contrastes [IV?]).* 1935-46

Oil on canvas, 26 x 28⅜″
(66 x 72 cm.)

Signed lr "Kupka"

Collection Mr. and Mrs. Andrew P. Fuller

PROVENANCE:

the artist
Galerie Louis Carré, Paris
to present owner

EXHIBITION:

*Prague, 1946, Mánes, no. 97 (as *Série C IV*)

1 See chronology. Fédit maintains that Kupka did no painting in Beaugency (in conversation with the author).

2 See fig., p. 298. This painting shows surprising similarities to Sophie Taeuber-Arp's 1926 architectural drawings for *L'Aubette* in Strasbourg, drawings which include, in an architectural framework, her designs for floor tiles. (See cat. for exhibition *Art abstrait constructif international,* December 1961, Galerie Denise René, Paris, n.p., repr.) A reminiscence (?) of the tile pattern is seen in the central portion of this painting.

3 For example, van Doesburg's *Destructive Composition,* 1918 (watercolor), *The Non-Objective World, 1914-1955,* University Art Museum, University of Texas at Austin, 1973, repr. p. 63.

This work, like cat. nos. 184, 186, 187, belongs to a series which Kupka worked on primarily between 1935 and 1946. It is unclear whether he worked on them during the war years, or started them before going to Beaugency and finished them afterwards.[1] Ten paintings called *Série C,* numbered I through X, all dated 1935-46, were exhibited in Prague, 1946 (cat. nos. 94-103).

All of these paintings show a definite architectural inspiration. The most obvious is seen in *Série C VI,* Národní Galerie, Prague.[2] Some of the studies (ex. cat. no. 186; also Fédit, cat. no. 154, p. 152) suggest a debt to van Doesburg.[3] The early works in the series contained complex patterns and vivid colors. Gradually the compositions became simpler, the colors more monochromatic (see cat. nos. 186, 187).

The dimensions of this painting suggest that it was *Série C IV* (Prague, 1946, no. 97).

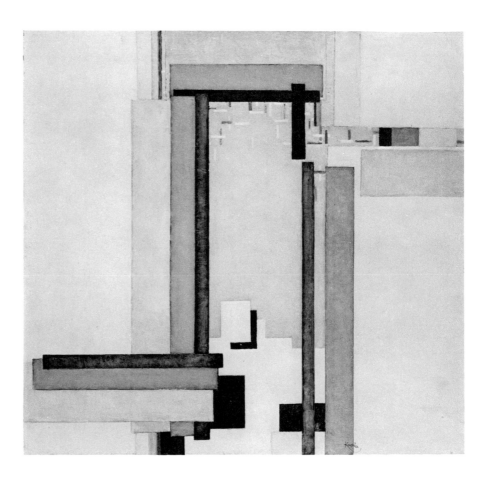

186 Study for *Series C* (Etude pour
Série C). 1935-46

Gouache on paper, 10⅞ x 11½″
(27.4 x 29.2 cm.)
Signed lr "Kupka"
Private Collection

PROVENANCE:
the artist
Eugénie Kupka
Karl Flinker
Gimpel Fils, London
to present owner, 1964

7 *Contrasts Series XI (Série con-trastes XI).* 1947

Oil on composition board, 28⅜ x 23⅝″ (72 x 60 cm.)

Signed lr "Kupka"

Fédit, no. 155, repr.
Vachtová, no. 328, repr. p. 245

Musée National d'Art Moderne, Paris (AM 4201-P)

PROVENANCE:

the artist
Eugénie Kupka
to present owner, gift, 1963

EXHIBITIONS:

Paris, 1947, *Salon des Réalités Nouvelles*, no. 184 (hors catalogue)
*Paris, 1953, *Salon des Réalités Nouvelles*, no. XLVIII
Saint Etienne, 1957, no. 23, repr. no. 9
*Cologne, 1967, no. 62, repr.; Munich, 1967, no. 62, repr.; Vienna, 1967, no. 57; Amsterdam, 1968, no. 102, repr.; Prague, 1968, no. 105, repr.

The artist's label on the stretcher identifies this painting as *Série contrastes X*, 1947. Since the 1946 Prague catalogue gives very different dimensions for no. X in this series (Prague, 1946, cat. no. 103, 38 x 46 cm.), this painting, presumably done after the exhibition, must be no. XI. The last painting in the series, according to Fédit, no. XII, dated 1954 by Kupka, is also in the Musée National d'Art Moderne, Paris (Fédit, cat. no. 158, p. 156).

188 *Vibration through Lines (Vibrants par traits).* 1948

Oil on canvas, 43⅜ x 35½"
(109.9 x 90.2 cm.)
Signed and dated lc "Kupka//$\overline{48}$"
Collection Margit Chanin, Ltd.

PROVENANCE:

the artist
Galerie Louis Carré, Paris
to present owner

EXHIBITIONS:

Paris, 1949, Maeght, no. 100
*New York, 1951, Louis Carré, no. 16
Paris, 1955, no. 52
Vienna, 1953, no. 53? (cat. not
located)

Autonomous White (Blanc autonome). 1952

Oil on canvas, 27½ x 27½"
(70 x 70 cm.)

Signed and dated lr "Kupka//52"

Fédit, no. 157, repr.
Vachtová, no. 347, repr. p. 244

Musée National d'Art Moderne,
Paris (AM 4202-P)

PROVENANCE:

the artist
Eugénie Kupka
to present owner, gift, 1963

EXHIBITIONS:

*Paris, 1953, *Salon des Réalités
Nouvelles,* no. LV (as *Blanc
automne*)
*Cologne, 1967, no. 63, repr.;
Munich, 1967, no. 63, repr.; Vienna,
1967, no. 58, repr.; Amsterdam,
1968, no. 103, repr. twice; Prague,
1968, no. 106, repr.

190 *Two Blues II (Deux Bleus II)*. 1956

Oil on canvas, 38¼ x 33⅜″
(97.2 x 84.6 cm.)

Signed and dated lr "Kupka//1956"

Collection The Solomon R.
Guggenheim Museum, New York,
Gift, Mme. Eugénie Kupka,
Courbevoie, France, 1962 (1618)

PROVENANCE:

the artist
Eugénie Kupka
to present owner, gift

EXHIBITIONS:

São Paulo, 1957, no. 43
New York, 1967, SRGM
New York, 1970, SRGM

During his last years, once again Kupka returned to the theme of the *Form of Blue* (see cat. no. 168). In 1955, he executed *Two Blues I* (MNAM, Paris), a slightly more elaborate and dynamic painting, followed by *Two Blues II* in 1956. The form of the vertical lozenge is the ideal shape of blue. Usually Kupka used a single form in his paintings on this theme. However the double motif as seen here was used in an earlier version of 1919-24 (Collection Mr. and Mrs. Andrew P. Fuller, New York).

CHRONOLOGY[1]

Meda Mladek and Margit Rowell

[1] The documentation for this chronology has been compiled from many sources. Whenever possible, primary source material has been consulted, most of which is unpublished. These sources include:

Unpublished correspondence: Kupka/ J. S. Machar (1900-1911), Collection Strahov Library, Prague; Kupka/ Arthur Roessler (1894-1914), Collection Wiener Stadtbibliothek, Vienna; Eugénie Kupka/Iča Waldes (1919-1936), Collection Národní Galerie, Prague; Kupka/Jindřich Waldes (1919-1936), Collection Národní Galerie, Prague; Kupka/A. P. Gallien (particularly 1921-1927), Collection Gallien; Kupka/Theo van Doesburg (1926-1931), Collection Nelly van Doesburg; Kupka/Georges Vantongerloo (1934-1951), Collection Max Bill; Kupka/ Max Bill (1945), Collection Max Bill; and unpublished personal notes of the artist.

Since it would be impossible to footnote every item, only the most essential or problematic references have been footnoted here.

[2] In much of his autobiographical material, Kupka gives September 23 as his birth date. The birth certificate of the Opočno parish also indicates September 23. However the Dobruška archives record the date of birth as September 22 and the date of baptism as September 23. The family tree established by Kupka's sister also gives the date September 22. Therefore despite the error which Kupka perpetrated by giving the September 23 date to all of his biographers, September 22 seems to be correct.

[3] An exceptional teacher for his time, Studnička oriented his students toward the abstract symbolism and expressive values of color, shape and line. He wrote a grammar of ornament which was published in installments in the 1880's, upon which many of Kupka's ideas, expressed much later, are based.

1871

Born September 22[2] in Opočno, a small city in Eastern Bohemia to Václav Kupka, a notarial clerk, and his wife Josefa Špačková. Eldest of five children.

1872

Family moves to Dobruška, where father appointed district secretary. Father carves toys for František and teaches him to draw.

1879

Falls dangerously ill with smallpox which scars his face for life.

1881

July 26: death of his mother.

1883

Sent to live with Vogel, a miller, in a small village in Orlické Hory, Olešnice, where he learns German and completes his compulsory education requirements.

1884

Registers as apprentice with master saddler Šiška who initiates him to spiritism. Runs away several times, visiting nearby cities where he admires Baroque painting and sculpture.

1887

Travels to southern Bohemia in search of employment. Fills diary with sketches of regional costumes. Spends several months in Domažlice, where he learns to mix colors and paints saints and trade signs in an artist's studio.

1888

Returns to Dobruška. Receives first commission, for a painting of St. Joseph, from Archleb, mayor of Dobruška. Archleb introduces him to Studnička,[3] director of Crafts School at Jaroměř, who accepts him as a private student and prepares him for Prague Academy. Highly recommended by Studnička, enters preparatory class at Prague Academy in September.

1889

Enrolls in Prague Academy's Department of Historical and Religious painting. Studies with Sequens, a Nazarene painter. Activity as a medium helps him earn a living, but contributes to emotional instability. Summer in Dobruška where he rents a studio in the house of Alois Beer, a folk painter and chronicler. Paints a large view of Dobruška for Archleb.

1890

Manifests strong patriotic sentiment, painting figures in folk costume in the style of Josef Mánes, signing them Dubroš and later D. Kupka to give his name a more Slavonic ring. He longs to go abroad, feeling that his future lies elsewhere.

1891

Admitted to Sequens' master class. Continues to paint historical patriotic themes. Summer in Valašsko, Moravia, a region rich in folklore, where he paints figures in local costume. Continues activity as a medium.

1892

August 22: receives diploma from Prague Academy. Summer in Žiletice near Znojmo.
October 10: enrolls at Vienna Academy where he is admitted directly to master class of Eisenmenger, another

fig. 1.
Kupka, *The Bibliomane*, 1897, oil.

Nazarene. Shares apartment with Milos Meixner, a fellow student from Prague, at Pilgramgasse 13. Under Eisenmenger's influence, paints symbolic allegorical subjects, hoping in vain to win a Rome Prize and a year in Rome.
Extreme poverty forces him to withdraw from Academy.

1893

Reinstated at Academy as scholarship student. Reads avidly; particularly Greek and German philosophers: Plato, Aristotle, Paracelsus, Kant, Schopenhauer, Nietzsche and German Romantics. Also reads extensively on astronomy, chemistry, natural history and sciences, anatomy, astrology, Theosophy, eastern religions, witchcraft and occult sciences. Apartment with Meixner becomes meeting place for members of a Theosophical(?) group who call themselves "Brothers," indulge in philosophical discussions and sign their correspondence with a "W." Commissioned by the Kunstverein to paint a monumental work, *The Last Dream of the Dying Heine*. Rents a studio on Porcelangasse and withdraws from Academy.

1894

With exhibition of *The Last Dream of the Dying Heine* at Kunstverein, becomes overnight celebrity. Receives portrait commissions from Viennese aristocracy. Paints patriotic subjects for Czech organizations in Vienna. Through Meixner, meets Karl Diefenbach, the "Kohlrabi Apostle," a German painter-philosopher living near Vienna since 1892. Becomes devoted disciple: vegetarian and physical culture enthusiast. Meets Maria Bruhn, a Danish dress designer, who offers him work as a fashion illustrator. Intense and stormy relationship develops.
Summer: travels to Denmark with Maria Bruhn. Leaves her to visit Norway, returns to Denmark to accompany her back to Vienna. Meets Austrian university student and art critic Arthur Roessler with whom he discusses philosophy and art and engages in a long correspondence. Involved in Theosophy and Oriental philosophy.

1896

Spring: settles permanently in Paris, taking small sunny attic room in Montmartre.[4] Despite extreme poverty, is very happy, overwhelmed by new impressions. Finds Paris a healthier atmosphere for painting, free from Vienna's mysticism and esoterism. Visits Alphonse Mucha, his compatriot, living in Paris, on rue

4 Almost all of Kupka's biographical and autobiographical material states that he settled in Paris in 1895. However his letters to Roessler indicate that he did not settle there permanently until the Spring of 1896.

fig. 2.
Kupka, *Monkey King,* 1899, watercolor
and pastel, Národní Galerie, Prague.

fig. 3.
Kupka, *Les Fous,* 1899, lithograph.

de la Grand Chaumière. Will see him often in ensuing years.

1897

Maria Bruhn arrives in Paris, helps him financially. Takes short trip alone to London. Attends the Académie Julian briefly; leaves to study with J. P. Laurens, an historical and allegorical painter at the Ecole des Beaux-Arts. Abandons painting temporarily for fashion illustration. Moves with Maria to country house in La Bretèche near Paris. Paints *The Bibliomane,* an attempted rejection of mysticism and return to nature, as well as return to painting. Maria falls seriously ill.

1898

Follows Maria to Vienna where she dies of cancer. Returns to Paris via Strasbourg. With small inheritance from Maria, rents a large studio and apartment at 10, rue Fromentin. Visits Jardin des Plantes to draw monkeys, in reaction against the superficial prettiness of fashion illustration. Dissolute nights in Montmartre until money runs out. Meets Gabrielle whom he will immortalize in *Money* (cat. no. 1) the following year.

1899

Rents small studio at 84, boulevard Rochechouart, almost next door to Bruant's cabaret. Decides to become professional illustrator to earn a living. Illustrations for *Cocorico;* lithographs reproduced in *La Plume* and exhibited at the same gallery; posters for neighboring cabarets (*L'Ane rouge, L'Auberge du clou, Le Chat noir.*) Exhibits for the first time in Paris at the *Salon de la Société Nationale des Beaux-Arts.*

1900

Exhibits at Paris World's Fair in section reserved for Austrian artists— *The Bibliomane, The Fools (Les Fous)* and drawings. Visits World's Fair, is particularly impressed by "Cinéorama," a cinematographic voyage to foreign countries in a balloon, projected on a circular screen. Continues illustrations for *Der Tag* in Berlin; *L'Illustration* in Paris. Illustrations for tales of Edgar Allen Poe (never published). Also a few portraits. Czech poet Machar asks Kupka to illustrate his book covers.

1901

Moves to 57, rue Caulaincourt where he is Jacques Villon's neighbor. Marcel Duchamp will live here with his brother Villon in 1904-05. August: visits Machar in Vienna for four weeks. Enroute to Vienna pauses briefly in Munich to see Roessler.

LES PRÉCÉDENTS, KLYTAIMNESTRA

Sojourn with Gabrielle in Croatian mountains. Returning to Paris, works on cycle of satirical drawings "Money" (cat. no. 11) for anarchist magazine *L'Assiette au beurre*. Furious for having wasted time on sentimental or symbolic subjects; nonetheless he continues to produce them. Fascinated by newly invented electric lights; visits electrical laboratories and workshops to observe light and color.

1902

Exhibits at the *Salon de la Société Nationale des Beaux-Arts,* Paris. Sends twenty-eight drawings and color lithographs to first Workers' Exhibition in Prague. Series "Money" is great success.

1903

Continues satirical drawings for French newspapers including *Le Canard sauvage* and *Les Temps nouveaux*. Travels to Rome for *l'Illustration*. Traumatic break with Gabrielle. Visits Parisian studios with Czech critic; disappointed by what he sees. Calls the painters "comedians," more interested in success than art. Admires Villon however. "He suffers from Japonism and finds my painting

old fashioned." Reads French authors, likes Baudelaire, Villiers de l'Isle-Adam; rejects Dumas and Victor Hugo.

1904

Exhibits *Ballad-Joys* (cat. no. 8) and lithographs at St. Louis World's Fair. Works on several new satirical cycles for *L'Assiette au beurre:* "Religion," "Civilization," "Freedom," "Peace." Learns some English. Meets Eugénie (Nini) Straub, wife of Alsatian army officer, mother of three-year old Andrée. By year's end they are living together. Accepts offer to illustrate *L'Homme et la terre* by anarchist writer Elisée Reclus. Book and its thesis "Man is nature becoming aware of itself" appeals to him.

1905

L'Assiette au beurre sold; Kupka's contract cancelled. Extensive study and work on Reclus' illustrations— studies Chaldaic and Phoenician excavation material exhibited in Paris by Renan, Layard, Dienlafoi. Reads books on antiquity, the Bible. Also attends lectures on physics, biology, physiology at the Sorbonne. Writes Machar "It seems unnecessary to

fig. 4.
Kupka, Illustration for Elisée Reclus, *L'Homme et la terre,* 1905, Vol. I, Book 1, title page.

fig. 5.
Kupka, Illustration for *Les Erinnyes,* 1906-08.

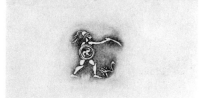

fig. 6.
Kupka in his garden at Puteaux, c. 1906.

fig. 7.
Kupka, Illustration for *Prometheus*,
1908-09, etching.

5 In a letter to Machar dated March 12,
1906, Kupka announces his intention
to move to Puteaux and gives his new
address.

paint trees when people see more
beautiful ones on the way to the
exhibition. I paint only concepts,
syntheses, chords. . . . But this I do . . .
only for myself. I am not anxious to
show it . . . ." (April 24)
August: holiday in St. Prix where he
makes studies, erotic drawings,
watercolors. Some will be used for
second edition of *The Song of Songs*
(cat. no. 15). First one-man exhibition
organized in Bohemia—about fifty
oils, one hundred drawings, pastels,
prints—will travel for two years.
Great popular success but poor
critical response.
July: death of Elisée Reclus. October:
publication of first five volumes of
L'Homme et la terre.

1906

Continues work for last volume of
L'Homme et la terre (to be published
1908) and begins work on illustrations for Leconte de Lisle's *Les
Erinnyes*. Spring: moves with Nini to
small house with garden at 7, rue
Lemaître in Puteaux, a suburb of
Paris.[5] Villon and Raymond Duchamp-Villon will be his next door
neighbors. Summer in Théoule in
south of France with Nini and

Andrée. Exhibits for first time at Paris
Salon d'Automne showing *Autumn
Sun* (cat. no. 17).

1907

January: visits Louny, Czechoslovakia, with Nini for final showing
of traveling exhibition. Pleased by
exhibition's popular success. Spring:
trip to Prague. Becomes member of
Salon d'Automne and shows *Project
for Mural Painting* (see fig. p. 46)

1908

Begins work on illustrations for
Aeschylus' *Prometheus* and Aristo-
phanes' *Lysistrata*. Begins series of
"Gigolettes."

1909

Stops working for newspapers to
concentrate on illustrated books—
new edition of *The Song of Songs;*
Lysistrata and Kropotkin's *La
Grande révolution* (the latter never
published). Inspired by Mallarmé's
poetry, starts working on illustrations
for a selection of his poems. Writes
Machar "Here I have only chords and
this corresponds to my feelings; for
the other books I need a great deal
of documentation." (February 5)

fig. 8.
French newspaper *Excelsior,* October 2, 1912, p. 5.

However Mallarmé's daughter will refuse permission to publish them. February 20: First *Futurist Manifesto,* published in *Le Figaro* in Paris, makes lasting impression on Kupka. Prize from Prague Academy provides financial aid and allows him to devote more time to painting. Visits Onésime Reclus, Elisée's brother, in Uccle, Belgium, where he may have seen large-scale model of the moon.

1910

March: finally marries Eugénie. Studies biology, physiology, neurology.
May 18: *Technical Manifesto of Futurist Painting* published in French in *Comoedia* IV, no. 961.
Lives and works in feverish excitement, destroying much as he progresses. Writes to Roessler "Finally . . . I have achieved awareness and I stand healthy before myself. The moment has come for me to write my CREDO (paint, draw)." (October 6)

Exhibits *The Yellow Scale* (cat. no. 29), *Peonies,* and two works on paper at *Salon d'Automne.* Begins making notes for a treatise on painting.

1911

Participates in meetings of Puteaux group: includes Duchamp-Villon, Villon, Gleizes, Metzinger, Picabia, Tobeen, La Fresnaye, Le Fauconnier, André Mare, Léger and sporadically Duchamp and Gris. Also Apollinaire and critics Allard, Roinard, Olivier-Hourcade, Salmon and Raynal; mathematician Maurice Princet, philosopher Henri-Martin Barzun and Georges Ribemont-Dessaignes. Meetings on Sundays at Villon's; on Mondays at Gleizes' in nearby Courbevoie. Discussions about Leonardo, Cézanne and Seurat, divine proportions and the golden section, mathematics, non-Euclidean geometry, Bergson, "correspondences" between music and painting, the concept and

6 Despite extensive research, it remains impossible to determine whether Kupka participated in the *Salon de la Section d'Or.* Although Kupka's name does not appear in the catalogue, or in any reviews of this exhibition there is reason to believe that he may have been included in the show.

The most compelling evidence in support of this belief is Nicolas Bauduin's article of 1956 (see bibliography), in which the author gives a vivid eyewitness account of the exhibition. He describes Apollinaire's lecture and the clothes he was wearing, the walls of the rooms, hung with purple silk, and says that it was in front of Kupka's three paintings that Apollinaire expounded his Orphic theory of abstraction. It seems improbable that Bauduin would have concocted this, even after forty-four years. Bauduin also notes that Kupka made up his mind to exhibit only at the last minute, when it was too late to include him in the catalogue. This is not only consistent with Kupka's character but reflects his reluctance to be identified with "Cubists" of any sort. A second piece of evidence arguing for his participation is a letter from Eugénie Kupka to Alfred Barr (December 22, 1955), in which she refers to an unidentified painting which had been exhibited at the *Section d'Or* many years before. However, one cannot consider this vague recollection entirely reliable. Finally in Turpin's 1931 biography of the artist (in Edouard-Joseph's *Dictionnaire biographique*, see bibliography) the author alludes to Apollinaire's comments before Kupka's paintings at the *Section d'Or*. Again, the accuracy of this account is somewhat questionable since in Kupka's handwritten notes for this article (which Turpin used almost verbatim) there is no mention of the *Section d'Or*.

The arguments against Kupka's participation are equally inconclusive. Fédit, who owns Kupka's personal copy of the catalogue, says that among the copious annotations, there is no mention of his own inclusion. Marcel Duchamp, in a 1961 interview with William Camfield on the subject of the *Section d'Or* said that the catalogue was correct, as far as he could remember, and no exhibitors were excluded. However, once again, memories spanning almost fifty years are involved. Finally Kupka's personal notes and his own autobiographical essays which contain precise references to his most important early exhibitions include no mention of the *Section d'Or*. Again, however, there is room for question, as Kupka may not have considered the paintings sent to the *Section d'Or* important enough to mention. (Because of Kupka's habit of changing titles, none of these paintings have been precisely identified.)

depiction of motion, color theory and the fourth dimension.
Signac's *D'Eugène Delacroix au néo-impressionnisme* of 1899 republished in August. Apollinaire speaks highly of it and Kupka probably read it at this time. Concert of Bach fugues crystallizes Kupka's thinking that painting may be as abstract as music; that nature is better rendered by cinematography; that painting is specifically concerned with lines, planes, colors, light and shadow. Begins studies for *Amorpha, Fugue* (cat. no. 92). Continues making notes for his book on his concept of the function of painting. Exhibits three works from *"Gigolettes"* series at the *Salon des Indépendants* in Spring where Cubist painters first show as a group, and *Planes by Colors* (cat. no. 42) and *Family Portrait* (cat. no. 44) at *Salon d'Automne* in the Fall.

1912

February: First Futurist exhibition in Paris, Galerie Bernheim Jeune. Continues to work feverishly according to his new ideals. Continues notes for his book. Exhibits three paintings all called *Planes by Colors* (cat. nos. 53, 55, 59) in the Cubist room at the *Salon des Indépendants* where Duchamp first exhibits *Nude Descending a Staircase*. Displeased at being identified with Cubists. Finally at the *Salon d'Automne,* exhibits *Amorpha, Fugue in Two Colors* (cat. no. 92) and *Amorpha, Warm Chromatics* (cat. no. 86). Critics are disconcerted. Gaumont newsreels film the paintings and show them all over Europe and America; ask Kupka to defend his art and "initiate the public" by painting a picture before the camera. Kupka declines. Withdraws from Puteaux group to lead a solitary existence. However will remain friendly with his neighbors Villon and Duchamp-Villon. October 10-30, Galerie la Boétie, *Salon de la Section l'Or.* It is unclear whether Kupka exhibited.[6]

1913

Continues to develop ideas on non-objective art. Does not exhibit at

Armory Show. Exhibits *Vertical Planes III* (cat. no. 97) at *Salon des Indépendants* in spring; *Organization of Graphic Motifs I* and *II* (cat. nos. 105, 106) at *Salon d'Automne*. Between these two exhibitions, in July—according to Kupka's personal notes—discovers Kandinsky's *Über das Geistige in der Kunst* through his friend the musician Morse-Rummel. October 19: *The New York Times* publishes article " 'Orpheism' Latest of Painting Cults" emphasizing Kupka's role in the development of abstract art. "I am still groping in the dark," Kupka tells the interviewer Warshawsky, "but I believe I can find something between sight and hearing and I can produce a fugue in colors as Bach has done in music."

1914

At outbreak of World War I, enlists as volunteer and fights alongside Blaise Cendrars at front at La Somme.

1915-18

Evacuated because of illness, participates in organization of Czech resistance in Paris. Appointed President of Czech colony; produces Czech propaganda posters under pseudonym Dalny which he uses throughout the war. Gives lectures, designs uniforms, medals, postcards, stamps, banners; illustrations for Czech newspapers. 1917-18 works on illustrations for *The Song of Roland*.
Organizes Czech infantry force which will become a regular French army regiment. 1918: returns to combat under Maréchal Foch with rank of Lieutenant.

1919

February: made honorary member of Mánes Fine Arts Society in Prague. April: visit to Prague; discharged from army with rank of Captain. Meets Jindřich Waldes who will be his benefactor and friend until 1936. Returns to Paris in September where he works a great deal "to make up for time lost during the war." (Kupka to Waldes, December 9, 1919). Arrangements made to translate and

publish manuscript written in French before the war. Exhibits *A Tale of Pistils and Stamens* (cat. no. 120) and *Blue Scaffolding* (cat. no. 125) at *Salon d'Automne*.

1920

Corrects Czech translation of his book *La Création dans les arts plastiques*. Visits Chartres often and Brittany where he studies Celtic art. Works in relative solitude in Puteaux, going to Paris infrequently. Waldes visits Paris and offers Kupka badly needed financial aid. Exhibits *Animated Lines* (cat. no. 135) at *Salon d'Automne*. Meets Félix Del Marle and A. P. Gallien around this time.

1921

Continuing financial difficulties. June: first one-man exhibition in Paris at Galerie Povolozky. Exhibition, which includes much recent work, and in particular, a series in black and white, is well received.

July: *La Vie des lettres* publishes an article by Kupka in which he explains his reasons for abandoning the object in painting.

1922

Publication of first monograph on Kupka, by L. Arnould-Grémilly, in France. Summer in Théoule. October: invited to Prague by Prague Academy to give series of lectures on the psychology of the artist. In first lecture, attacks all academic training upon which contract cancelled. Remains in Prague until December. December: Prague Academy appoints him Professor in Paris with full professor's salary. Must introduce Czech students in Paris to French culture.

1923

Begins preparing courses which will start in March: weekly lectures on French art and culture, and excursions to French museums and monu-

fig. 9.
Kupka, Illustration for *The Song of Roland* (signed P. Regnard), 1917-18; published 1919.

fig. 10.
Kupka in his garden, Puteaux, c. 1920?

fig. 11.
Partial installation photograph, Galerie
la Boétie, Paris, October 16-31, 1924.

ments (Notre Dame, Chartres,
Versailles, Fontainebleau, etc.). Experiments, begun at unknown date,
with kaleidoscope and microscope.
Exhibits *Lines, Planes, Depths* (see
cat. no. 136) and *Gradations* at *Salon
des Indépendants*. The museum in
Grenoble, the most avant-garde in
France, expresses interest in his work.
Summer in Théoule and extensive
traveling in south of France (Nîmes,
Arles, Avignon). *La Création dans les
arts plastiques* published in Prague.

1924

In an interview (*Paris-Journal,* May
9, 1924) Picabia says that "Kupka,
Marcel Duchamp . . . Man Ray" are
among the painters he most esteems.
With help of friends, rents Galerie la
Boétie to mount a retrospective of his
work held October 16-31. Widely reviewed, both favorably and unfavor-
ably, in international press. Attends
lectures at Sorbonne. Mánes Society

in Prague offers Kupka retrospective
but he feels the space is not appropriate. "These paintings need space
and much light" writes Nini to
Waldes (January 31, 1925). December: visits Bordeaux, the Pyrenees,
Toulouse.

1925

Kupka's friends Del Marle and Gallien discuss translating Kandinsky's
Uber das Geistige in der Kunst into
French; also envisage French edition
of Kupka's book. Close friendship
with Gallien during this period. Summer in Théoule. Begins preparatory
gouaches for album of woodcuts,
many based on motifs developed during preceding years. December: exhibits with group *Vouloir* in Lille.

1926

March: first personal contact with
van Doesburg. Receives the *Croix de
la Légion d'Honneur.* Summer in
Brittany. At year's end, publishes

fig. 12.
Kupka in his studio, Puteaux, c. 1933.

woodcut album *Quatre histoires de blanc et noir* (cat. no. 165) at own expense. Aided in technical aspects and formulation of introductory text by Gallien. Publication generally ignored and financially disastrous for Kupka.

1927-28

Reputation continues to grow slowly in Prague. Continuing financial difficulties and help from Waldes. Biography published by Siblík in Prague in 1928 (French edition, 1929). Begins a bust of Nini for Waldes, the only sculpture he will ever do.

1929

January: visits Kandinsky exhibition in Paris, finds paintings cold, mechanical; believes that some indication of the artist's process should be visible. Van Doesburg asks him to participate in launching a new art magazine. Finishes bust of Nini.

1930

Spring: visits the Waldes' in Prague where he gives lectures and interviews. Visit inspires interest among critics, artists. Returns to south of France for Summer and Fall. Poor health sends him to Corsica until mid-December. Stops all painting. Extremely nervous and depressed.

1931

February 15: founding of *Abstraction-Création* group. Founding members include van Doesburg, Herbin, Vantongerloo, Hélion, Arp, Gleizes, Kupka, Tutundjian, Valmier. Encouraged by confirmation of his ideas on abstraction, begins to paint again.

1931-33

Turns from machine series to pure abstractions. Poor health obliges him to spend much time in south of France and in Savoie.

1934

Repaints interior of his house with decorative panels in folk-art style (see fig. 15). Trip to London with Nini, Waldes and his wife. Shows with Czech artists at the Jeu de Paume and in the *Salon des Indépendants* fiftieth anniversary exhibition (*Vertical Planes* and *The Form of Vermilion*). Resigns from *Abstraction-Création,* but remains in cordial contact with group and particularly

fig. 13.
Prague, 1935?, Standing l to r: Kupka,
Iča Waldes, Jindřich Waldes; Seated:
Eugénie Kupka.

fig. 14.
Kupka at Beaugency, 1944.

friendly with Herbin and Vantongerloo until the end of his life.

1935

Improved health. July: visit from
Alfred Barr in preparation for 1936
The Museum of Modern Art exhibition *Cubism and Abstract Art*. Encouraged by this visit, Kupka begins
working again. Visits prehistoric
caves near Alvignac (Lot) during
summer vacation. Trip to Prague
over Christmas.

1936

Exhibits *Static Ensemble* and *Abstract Painting* (cat. no. 173) at *Salon
des Indépendants*. Exhibits *Disks of
Newton* (cat. no. 75), *Vertical Planes*
(cat. no. 97) and *Elementary Games*
of 1931 in *Cubism and Abstract Art*
in New York.
June: large two-man exhibition with
Alphonse Mucha at Jeu de Paume,
Paris. Health deteriorates.

1940-45

Moves to wife's house in Beaugency
to rest and restore health during war
years. Little painting activity. Returns

to Puteaux in October 1945. Vantongerloo brings Max Bill to visit
him. Bill much impressed by Kupka's
work.

1946

June: Marcel Duchamp notifies
Kupka of Alfred Barr's interest in
buying works for The Museum of
Modern Art, New York.
First *Salon des Réalités Nouvelles* in
Paris, where Kupka will exhibit regularly until his death.
November-December: major retrospective exhibition at Mánes Fine
Arts Society in Prague to celebrate his
seventy-fifth birthday. Long visit to
Prague during which he prepares
catalogue, hangs show. Exhibition of
his graphic work mounted by
Národní Galerie, Prague. Czech government purchases about twenty
major works.

1951

Signs contract with Louis Carré; sells
him large number of paintings from
studio. One-man exhibition at Louis
Carré Gallery, New York.

fig. 15.
Kupka in his dining room, Puteaux,
1952. Note the decorative panels done
by the artist in 1934.

fig. 16.
Kupka in his studio, 1952.

1952
General recognition begins around this time; long articles in French periodicals.

1953
One-man exhibition at Rose Fried Gallery, New York. Special exhibition of twenty-two works (*Jubilé Kupka*) at the *Salon des Réalités Nouvelles,* Paris.

1954
Exhibits for last time at *Salon des Indépendants—Planes by Colors* (cat. no. 42) and *Disks,* 1911.

1956
Alfred Barr purchases group of major works for The Museum of Modern Art, New York. In gratitude, Kupka gives the museum a large collection of studies and sketches.

1957
June 24: death in Puteaux.

1958
Large retrospective exhibition at Musée National d'Art Moderne, Paris (156 works). Creation of a permanent *Salle Kupka.*

1963
Eugénie Kupka makes large donation to Musée National d'Art Moderne, Paris.
May 23: death of Eugénie Kupka.

ONE-MAN EXHIBITIONS

1906

Brno, *František Kupka* (cat. text by
J. V. Stejskal)
Catalogue not located

Prague, Klub "Slavia," April 15-
May 17
*Kupkovy Výstavy [Kupka
Exhibition]*
133 works

1921

Paris, Galerie Povolozky, June 6-20
*François Kupka: Peintures—Blancs et
Noirs* (cat. text by A. Mercereau)
32 works

1924

Paris, Galerie la Boétie, October
16-31
Exposition des oeuvres de F. Kupka
(cat. text by F. Kupka)
101 works

1936

Paris, Musée des Ecoles Etrangères
Contemporaines, Jeu de Paume des
Tuileries, June
F. Kupka-A. Mucha (Kupka cat. text
by G. Kahn)
95 works by Kupka

1946

Prague, Národní Galerie, September
17-November 17
*Kresby A Grafika Františka Kupky
[Drawings and Prints by František
Kupka]* (cat. text by J. Loriš)
77 works

Prague, Galerie S.V.U. Mánes,
November 14-December 8
František Kupka (cat. text by
K[upka])
213 works

1951

New York, Louis Carré Gallery,
May 7-June 2
Kupka (cat. text by J. Cassou)
16 oils

1953

New York, Rose Fried Gallery,
February 23-March 21
Kupka (checklist)
10 oils

Paris, Musée des Beaux Arts de la
Ville de Paris, *VIII Salon des Réalités
Nouvelles: Jubilé Kupka*
22 works
Catalogue not located

1958

Paris, Musée National d'Art
Moderne, May 27-July 13
Kupka (cat. texts by J. Cassou, F.
Kupka)
72 oils, 4 gouaches

1960

Paris, Galerie Karl Flinker, May 24-
June 30
Kupka: Gouaches, Aquarelles, Pastels
(cat. texts by M. Brion, G. Habasque)
5 oils, 49 watercolors and gouaches,
6 pastels

1961

New York, Royal S. Marks Gallery,
January 11-February 18
*Kupka: Paintings, Pastels and
Gouaches 1909-1923* (cat. text by
Y. Hagen)
30 works

Zurich, Galerie Charles Lienhard,
March
Frank Kupka (cat. texts by J. Cassou,
F. Kupka, H. Neuburg)
40 gouaches, 5 pastels, 2 oils

Písek, Czechoslovakia, Vlastivědné
Museum, October-November 1961.

Traveled to České Budějovice, Czech-
oslovakia, Dům umění, January-
February 1962
Kupka 1871-1957 (cat. texts by J.
Kříž, L. Vachtová)
30 oils, 105 works on paper

1962

New York, Saidenberg Gallery,
February 13-March 10
*Kupka: pastels, gouaches, water-
colors* (checklist)
10 gouaches, 11 watercolors, 5 pastels, 4 watercolor and gouaches

1964

Paris, Galerie Louis Carré, May 21-
July 31
Kupka: peintures 1910-1946 (catalogue; checklist)
22 works

Paris, Galerie Karl Flinker, May 26-
June 30
*Kupka: pastels et gouaches 1906-
1945* (cat. text by D. Fédit; checklist)
57 gouaches, 23 pastels, 18 woodcuts,
8 oils

New York, Royal S. Marks Gallery,
September 21-October 24
Kupka (checklist)
13 oils, 3 gouaches, 1 pastel

London, Gimpel Fils, September-
October
Kupka Gouaches 1904-1945 (cat.
texts by D. Fédit, C. Gimpel)
27 gouaches

1965

Prague, Galerie Karlovo Náměstí,
May-June
*František Kupka-obrazy, kresby,
grafika [František Kupka-Paintings,
Drawings, Graphics]* (cat. text by
L. Vachtová)
29 works

Ústí nad Orlicí, *František Kupka*
cat. text by J. Pečírka)
Catalogue not located

Milan and Rome, Galleria del
Levante, April-May
Kupka (cat. text by G. Veronesi)
28 works on paper, 2 oils

London, Gimpel Fils, November 2-27
Kupka: The Centre Period 1899-1908 (cat. text by S. Williams)
35 works on paper

1966

London, Redfern Gallery, March
2-26
Kupka (checklist)
24 works on paper

Paris, Galerie Karl Flinker, March
18-April 23
Kupka avant 1914 (cat. text by D.
Fédit)
9 oils, 44 gouaches, pastels and
drawings

Hanover, Kestner Gesellschaft, July
13-September 18
Frank Kupka (cat. text by W.
Schmied)
53 works on paper

1967

Stockholm, Galerie Aronowitsch,
October 28-November 15
Frank Kupka 1871-1957 (cat. text by
W. Aronowitsch)
17 gouaches, 2 drawings, 1 water-
color

1967-68

Cologne, Kölnischer Kunstverein,
April 15-June 25, 1967
Frank Kupka 1871-1957 (cat. texts
by A. Becker, B. Dorival, T.
Feldenkirchen)
110 oils and works on paper
Traveled to
Munich, Städtische Galerie im Len-
bachhaus, September 23-October
22, 1967 (cat. text by B. Dorival)
110 oils and works on paper

Vienna, Museum des 20. Jahrhunderts, November 4-December 17,
1967 (cat. text by B. Dorival, W.
Hofmann)
107 oils and works on paper

Amsterdam, Stedelijk Museum,
January 11-February 25, 1968
(cat. text unsigned)
104 oils and works on paper

Prague, Národní Galerie, March 20-
April 20, 1968 (cat. texts by L.
Vachtová, J. Kotalík, B. Dorival)
322 oils and works on paper

1968

New York, Spencer A. Samuels and
Company, Ltd., March-April
Frank Kupka (cat. texts by A. H.
Barr, Jr., N. Schwartz)
17 oils, 43 works on paper

1969

New York, Gertrude Stein Gallery

Belgrade, Salon Muzeja savremene
umetnostı, June 12-July 20
František Kupka (cat. texts by J.
Kotalík, M. B. Protić)
107 works

SELECTED GROUP EXHIBITIONS

1902

Paris, Grand Palais, April 20-June 30,
*Société Nationale des Beaux-Arts
XIIe exposition*

Vienna, Hagenbund
Catalogue not located

1904

St. Louis, The Louisiana Purchase
Exposition Company, *Universal
Exposition*

1906

Paris, Grand Palais, October 6-No-
vember 15, *Salon d'Automne: 4me
exposition*

1908

Vienna, Kunstschau, May-October,
Gebäude der Secession

1910

Paris, Grand Palais, October 1-No-
vember 8, *Salon d'Automne: 8me
exposition*

1911

Paris, Grand Palais, October 1-No-
vember 8, *Salon d'Automne: 9me
exposition*

1912

Paris, Quai d'Orsay, March 20-May
16, *Artistes Indépendants 28e exposition: Salon des Indépendants*

Paris, Grand Palais, October 1-No-
vember 8, *Salon d'Automne: 10me
exposition*

Paris, Galerie la Boétie, October
10-30, *Salon de la Section d'Or* (?)

1913

Paris, Quai d'Orsay, March 19-May
18, *Salon des Indépendants (29e
exposition)*

Paris, Grand Palais, November 15,
1913-January 5, 1914, *Salon d'Automne: 11me exposition*

1919

Paris, Grand Palais, November 1-
December 10, *Salon d'Automne*

1920

Paris, Grand Palais, October 15-
December 12, *Salon d'Automne*

1925

Lille, Au Conservatoire, December
19-27, *Vouloir*

1926

Paris, Grand Palais, February 20-
March 21, *Société des Artistes
Indépendants: trente ans d'art indé-
pendant, 1884-1914*

Paris, Quai d'Orsay, March 20-May
2, *Salon des Indépendants (37e
exposition)*

1929

Paris, October, *Expositions sélectes
d'art contemporain (ESAC)*
Catalogue not located

1934

Paris, Quai d'Orsay, February 2-
March 11, *exposition; Salon des
Indépendants*

1936

Paris, Quai d'Orsay, February 7-
March 8, *Salon des Indépendants*

New York, The Museum of Art,
March 2-April 19, *Cubism and Abstract Art*

1937

Paris, Musée du Jeu de Paume, July 30-October 31, *Origines et développement de l'Art international indépendant*

1939

Prague, Galerie SVU Mánes
Catalogue not located

1947

Paris, Musée des Beaux-Arts de la Ville de Paris, July-August, *Salon des Réalités Nouvelles (IIe exposition)*

1948

Paris, Musée des Beaux-Arts de la Ville de Paris, *Salon des Réalités Nouvelles (IIIe exposition)*

1949

São Paulo, Museu de Arte Moderna, March 8-30, *Do Figurativismo ao Abstracionismo.* Traveled to Buenos Aires, Instituto de Arte Moderno
Catalogue not located

Art Institute of Chicago, October 20-December 18, *Arensberg Collection*

Paris, Galerie Maeght, April 29-June 3, *L'Art abstrait: ses origines, ses premiers maîtres,* I, *Les Recherches préliminaires;* II, *L'Epanouissement de l'art abstrait*

Paris, Musée des Beaux-Arts de la Ville de Paris, July 22-August 30, *Salon des Réalités Nouvelles (IVe exposition)*

1950

Prague, The School of Fine Arts, *Výstava professoru a zakú AVU [Exhibition of Professors and Students]*
Catalogue not located

Paris, Musée des Beaux-Arts de la Ville de Paris, June 10-July 15, *Salon des Réalités Nouvelles*

1952

New York, The Museum of Modern Art, May 6-June 8, *Recent Acquisitions*

New York, The Museum of Modern Art, November 25, 1952-September 13, 1954, *Paintings, Sculpture and Graphic Art from the Museum Collection*

1953

Vienna, Galerie Wurthle, May-June, *Léger, Gromaire, Villon, Kupka*
Catalogue not located

Turin, Palazzo Belle Arti, September-October, *Pittori d'oggi Francia-Italia*

1954

Paris, Quai d'Orsay, April 14-May 9, *Salon des Indépendants*

Paris, Musée des Beaux-Arts de la Ville de Paris, July 8-August 8, *Salon des Réalités Nouvelles*

Philadelphia Museum of Art, October 16, *The Louise and Walter Arensberg Collection.* Opening of permanent installation of Arensberg Collection

New York, The Museum of Modern Art, October 19, 1954-February 6, 1955, *XXVth Anniversary Exhibitions: Paintings*

1955

Paris, Musée Galliera, January 21-February 28, *Regards sur la peinture contemporaine*

Lausanne, Musée Cantonal des Beaux-Arts, June 24-September 26, *Le Mouvement dans l'art contemporain*

New York, The Museum of Modern Art, October 5, 1955-November 8, 1957, *Painting, Sculpture and Graphic Arts from the Museum Collection*

1956

Birmingham; London, Tate Gallery, *Autour du Cubism*
Catalogue not located

Lille, Musée des Beaux-Arts de Lille, *Peinture contemporaine*
Catalogue not located

Newark Museum Association, April 2-June 10, *Abstract Art from 1910 to Today*

1957

Saint Etienne, Musée d'Art et d'Industrie, *Art abstrait: les premières générations (1910-1939)*

London, Royal Society of British Artists, Arts Council of Great Britain, April 13-May 18, *An Exhibition of Painting from The Musée National d'Art Moderne*

Amsterdam, Stedelijk Museum, July 8-September 30, *Europa 1907*

São Paulo, Museu de Arte Moderna, September-December, *IV Bienal do Museu de Arte Moderna*

New York, The Museum of Modern Art, November 13, 1957-January 5, 1958, *Recent Acquisitions*

1958

Paris, *Salon des Comparaisons*

New York, The Museum of Modern Art, March 23-April 7, *Paintings, Sculptures and Graphic Arts from the Museum Collection*

New York, The Museum of Modern Art, October 6, 1958-October 25, 1959, second floor galleries

1959

Gottwaldov, Czechoslovakia, traveling exhibition
Catalogue not located

Edinburgh, Royal Scottish Academy, August 21-September 20, *Masterpieces of Czech Art.* Traveled to Leeds, City Art Gallery, October 4-November 1

Liberec, Czechoslovakia, Krajesá galerie Liberec. Traveled to Prague.
Catalogue not located

New York, Rose Fried Gallery, October 26-November 30, *Twenty-four Modern Masters*

1960

New York, Galerie Chalette, March 31-June 4, *Construction and Geometry in Painting: From Malevitch to "Tomorrow."* Traveled to Cincinnati, Contemporary Art Center, July 5-October 9; Arts Club of Chicago, November 11-December 30; Minneapolis, Walker Art Center, January 14-February, 1961

Cleveland Museum of Art, October 5-November 13, *Paths of Abstract Art*

Paris, Musée National d'Art Moderne, November 4, 1960-January

3, 1961, *Les Sources du XXe siècle: les arts en Europe de 1884 à 1914*

New York, Rose Fried Gallery, November 8-December, *Modern Masters*

1961

New York, The Solomon R. Guggenheim Museum, February 7-April 16, *Paintings from the Arensberg and Gallatin Collections of the Philadelphia Museum of Art*

Rennes, Musée des Beaux-Arts, *Mesure*
Catalogue not located

1962

Dobruška, Czechoslovakia, Vlastivedné Muzeum
Catalogue not located

Vienna, Museum des 20. Jahrhunderts, September 21-November 4, *Kunst von 1900 bis heute*

1963

Grenoble, Musée de Peinture et de Sculpture, June 19-August 31, *Albert Gleizes et tempête dans les salons: 1910-14*

New York, Royal S. Marks Gallery, November 25-December 21, *Much has Happened, 1910-1959: Key Transitions*

Washington, D.C., National Gallery of Art, December 16, 1963-March 1, 1964, *Paintings from The Museum of Modern Art, New York*

1964

New York, Sidney Janis Gallery, February 4-29, *The Classic Spirit in the 20th Century*

Florence, Palazzo Strozzi, May-June, *L'Espressionismo: Pittura, Scultura, Architettura*

New York, The Museum of Modern Art, May 27, 1964-September 29, 1965, *Painting and Sculpture from the Museum Collections*

1965

Lisbon, Calouste Gulbenkian Museum, *Un Século de Pintura Francesa 1850-1950*

New York, The Museum of Modern Art, June 8 -December 3, *Painting and Sculpture from the Museum Collections*

New York, M. Knoedler & Co., Inc., October 12-November 6, *Synchronism and Color principles in American Painting: 1910-1930*

Houston, The Museum of Fine Arts, October 20-December 8, *The Heroic Years: Paris 1908-1914*

New York, The Museum of Modern Art, December 3-29, *Painting and Sculpture from the Museum Collections*

New York, The Museum of Modern Art, December 29, 1965-June 6, 1966, *Painting and Sculpture from the Museum Collection*

1966

New York, Public Education Association, shown at M. Knoedler & Co., Inc., April 26-May 21, *Seven Decades of Modern Art*

Hluboké, Czechoslovakia, Alšova Jihočeská Galerie, May-October 1966, *Česká Secese Umění 1900*. Traveled to Brno, Moraveská Galerie, December 1966-January 1967

New York, The Solomon R. Guggenheim Museum, June 23-October 23, *Gauguin and the Decorative Style*

Jerusalem, Israel Museum, Summer 1966, *Paintings from the Collection of Joseph H. Hazen*. Traveled to Cambridge, Fogg Art Museum, Harvard University, October 19-December 1, 1967
Los Angeles, The Art Galleries, University of California at Los Angeles, January-February 1967
Berkeley, University Art Museum, University of California, February 21-March 19, 1967
Museum of Fine Arts at Houston, April-May 1967
Honolulu Academy of Arts, June-August 1967

New York, The Museum of Modern Art, June 6, 1966-April 22, 1969, *Painting and Sculpture from the Museum Collections*

1967

New York, The Solomon R. Guggenheim Museum, May 4-June 25, *Selections from the Museum Collections*

New York, The Solomon R. Guggenheim Museum, June 28-October 1, *Museum Collection; Seven Decades, A Selection*

London, Tate Gallery, September 15-October 27, *Cubist Art from Czechoslovakia*

Brussels, Palais des Beaux-Arts, November 10-December 27, 1967, *Le Cubisme à Prague et la collection Kramář*. Traveled to Rotterdam, Museum Boymans-van Beuningen, January 10-March 3, 1968

1968

New York, The Museum of Modern Art, March 14-May 20, *Painting and Sculpture from the Museum Collections*

1969

New York, The Museum of Modern Art, April 23, 1969-December 14, 1972, *Painting and Sculpture from the Museum Collections*

New York, The Solomon R. Guggenheim Museum, April 25-May 11, *European Paintings from the Museum Collection*

New York, The Museum of Modern Art, May 15-November 4, *Painting and Sculpture from the Museum Collections*

Rome, Galleria Nazionale d'Arte Moderna, May 17-June 15, *Arte Contemporanea in Cecoslovacchia*

New York, The Solomon R. Guggenheim Museum, July 8-September 14, *Selected Sculpture and Works on Paper*

New York, The Solomon R. Guggenheim Museum, September 16-October 12, *Collection: From the Turn of the Century to 1914*

Toronto, Art Gallery of Ontario, November 1-26, *The Sacred and Profane in Symbolist Art*

New York, The Museum of Modern Art, November 5, 1969-November 8,

1972, *Painting and Sculpture from the Museum Collections*

New York, The Solomon R. Guggenheim Museum, December 13, 1969-January 18, 1970, *Collection: From the First to the Second Word War 1915-1939*

Krefeld, Galerie Denise René-Hans Meyer, *Masterpieces of Modern Art* Catalogue not located

1970

The Cleveland Museum of Art, January 28-February 22, *Year in Review for 1969*

Munich, Haus der Kunst, March 7-May 10, *L'Expressionnisme européen.* Traveled to Paris, Musée National d'Art Moderne, May 26-July 27

New York, The Solomon R. Guggenheim Museum, May 1-September 13, *Selections from the Guggenheim Museum Collection: 1900-1970*

Geneva, Musée Rath, May 26-June 28, *Art tchèque du XXe siècle.* Traveled to Kunsthaus Zürich, August 22-September 27, *Tschechische Kunst des 20. Jahrhunderts*

Buffalo, The Albright-Knox Art Gallery, September 15-November 1, 1970, *Color and Field 1890-1970.* Traveled to The Dayton Art Institute, November 20, 1970-January 10, 1971; The Cleveland Museum of Art, February 4-March 28, 1971

1971

Turin, Galleria Civica d'Arte

Moderna, March 18-May 9, *Il Cavaliere Azzurro: Der blaue Reiter*

New York, The Solomon R. Guggenheim Museum, June 11-September 12, *Selections from the Museum Collection and Recent Acquisitions, 1971*

New York, The Museum of Modern Art, July 28-November 1, *Ways of Looking*

New York, The Museum of Modern Art, November 15-December 9, *Painting and Sculpture from the Museum Collections*

San Diego, Fine Arts Gallery, November 20, 1971-January 2, 1972, *Color and Form 1909-1914.* Traveled to The Oakland Museum, January 25-March 5, 1972; Seattle Art Museum, March 24-May 7, 1972

1972

Musée de la Ville de Strasbourg, May 15-September 15, *Occident-Orient: l'art moderne et l'art islamique*

Venice, Museo Civico Correr, Alla Napoleonica, June 11-October 1, "Capolavori della pittura del XX secolo (1900-1945)," *36 Biennale di Venezia: Esposizione internazionale d'arte*

Dallas Museum of Fine Arts, October 7-November 19, *Geometric Abstraction: 1926-1942*

New York, The Museum of Modern Art, October 18, 1972-January 7, 1973, *Philadelphia in New York: 90 Modern Works from the Philadelphia Museum of Art*

New York, The Solomon R. Guggenheim Museum, December 7, 1972-February 22, 1973, *Collection Exhibition*

New York, The Museum of Modern Art, December 15, 1972-March 12, 1973, second floor galleries

1973

London, Annely Juda Fine Art Ltd., July 5-September 22, *The Non-Objective World 1914-1955.* Traveled to University Art Museum, University of Texas at Austin, October 14-December 15

New York, The Solomon R. Guggenheim Museum, August 9-September 3, *Selections from the Guggenheim Museum Collection and Recent Acquisitions*

Stockholm, Liljevalchs Konsthall August 23-September 30, *Tjeckiskt avantgarde 1900-1939.* Traveled to Göteborgs Konstmuseum, October 20-November 18

Milan, Palazzo Reale, December 1973-February 1974, *Boccioni e il suo tempo*

1974

Pittsburgh, Carnegie Institute Museum of Art, October 26, 1974-January 5, 1975, *Celebration*

1975

Los Angeles County Museum of Art, April 12-June 29, *A Decade of Collecting, 1965-1975: Tenth Anniversary Exhibition*

SELECTED BIBLIOGRAPHY

†*works not located*

By the artist

ILLUSTRATIONS

This list includes all bibliophile editions illustrated by Kupka and the monumental work *L'Homme et la terre*. Miscellaneous illustrations for Czech authors are not listed.

Reclus, Elisée, *L'Homme et la terre,* Paris, Librairie Universelle, vols. I-V, 1905; vol. VI, 1908 (prepared c. 1904-08)

Le Cantique des cantiques, French translation and introduction by Jean de Bonnefon, Paris, Librairie Universelle, 1905 (prepared 1903-05); Paris, Librairie Universelle, 1928 (prepared 1905-09); Paris, G. Kadar, 1931

Leconte de Lisle, *Les Erinnyes,* Paris, P. Romagnol, 1908 (prepared 1906-07)

Aristophanes, *Lysistrata,* French translation by Dhuys, Paris, A. Blaizot, 1911 (prepared 1908-10)

Aeschylus, *Prometheus,* French translation by Dhuys, Paris, A. Blaizot, 1924 (prepared 1908-10)

Hérold, Ferdinand, *La Guirlande d'Aphrodite,* Paris, H. Piazza, 1918 (prepared 1917; signed Paul Regnard)

Bédier, *La Chanson de Roland,* Paris, H. Piazza, 1919 (prepared 1917; signed Paul Regnard)

Kupka, František, *Quatre histoires de blanc et noir,* Paris, G. Kadar, 1926 (prepared 1925-26)

Kupka, František, *Abstrakce Kreslil,* introduction by J. Loriš, Prague, Žikeš, 1948 (prepared 1930-32)

BOOKS AND ARTICLES

†["Credo sous un arbre jamais taillé"], *Meister der Farbe,* V, Leipzig, 1913. German translation

†"Initiative officielle," *Bulletin artistique,* July 15, 1920

"Créer! Question de principe dans la peinture," *La Vie des lettres et des arts,* Paris, July 1921, pp. 569-575

Tvoření v umění výtvarném, Prague, 1923

"Raisons de l'évasion," Preface to exhibition catalogue, Galerie la Boétie, *Exposition des Oeuvres de F. Kupka,* Paris, 1924 [Reprinted in *Réalités Nouvelles,* no. 7, July 1953, p. 5]

Untitled preface, M. Baquet ed., *Album "Quatre histoires de blanc et noir,"* 1926

"Réponse à l'enquête sur la stratégie," in Georges Turpin, *La stratégie artistique,* Paris, 1929, pp. 163-164

Untitled text, *Abstraction, création, art non-figuratif,* Paris, vol. 1, 1932 p. 23

Untitled text, *Abstraction, création, art non-figuratif,* Paris, vol. 2, 1933, p. 25

Untitled text, *Abstraction, création, art non-figuratif,* Paris, vol. 3, 1934, p. 28 [reprinted in *Abstraction, création, art non-figuratif,* vols. 1-5, 1932-36, New York, 1968, complete in one volume]

†"Rationnalisme en peinture," *Koh-i-Noor,* Prague, no. 41, May 1933, p. 15

†"František Kupka v Praze" and editor's preface, *Světozor,* Prague, 1934 [Reprinted with French translation as "Kupka o sobě" ("Kupka par luimême"), *Výtvarné Umění,* Prague, no. 7, 1968, p. 352]

Untitled text, *Réalités Nouvelles,* Paris, no. 1, 1947, p. 45

Untitled text, *Réalités Nouvelles,* Paris, no. 4, 1950, p. 7

INTERVIEWS

†Urban, B. S., "Kupkův Orphismus," *Česta,* Prague, no. 16, January 28, 1928

†Sisova, M., "U. Fr. Kupka," *Národní Listy,* Prague, May 2, 1929

Jíra, Jaroslav, "Z hovorůs Františkem Kupkou," [Conversations with František Kupka] *Literární Rozhledy,* Prague, vol. XV, no. 11, October-November, 1931, pp. 354-358

†Massat, René, "Visite d'atelier de Frank Kupka," *Le Progrès,* Paris, August 19, 1950

On the artist

MONOGRAPHS

Arnould-Grémilly, Louis, *Frank Kupka,* Paris, 1922 (First published as: "De l'Orphisme à propos des tentatives de Kupka," *La Vie des lettres,* Paris, 1921)

Cassou, Jean and Fédit, Denise, *Kupka,* Paris, 1964

Fédit, Denise, *L'Oeuvre de Kupka,* Paris, 1966

Siblík, Emmanuel, *František Kupka,* Prague, 1928 (in Czech); Prague, 1929 (in French)

Vachtová, Ludmila, *Frank Kupka, Pioneer of Abstract Art,* New York and Toronto, 1968. (Translated from Czech, *František Kupka,* Prague, 1968, by Zdeněk Lederer.)

ARTICLES

†Machar, J. S., "Kupka," *Rudé květy,* Prague, V, 1905

Dévérin, Edouard, "François Kupka," *L'Art décoratif*, 11e année, 2e semestre, tome XXI, July 1909, pp. 3-14

Weiner, Richard, "Návštěvou u nového Františka Kupky," *Samostatnost*, Prague, August 8, 1912 Reprinted in *Výtvarné Umění*, vol. XV, no. 8, Prague, 1968, pp. 367-371)

Warshawsky, W., "Orpheism, Latest of Painting Cults," *The New York Times*, New York, vol. LXIII, no. 20, 357, part 3, October 19, 1913, p. 4

Gybal, A., "Frank Kupka," *Les Hommes du jour*, June 1921, pp. 14-15

Arnould-Grémilly, Louis, "De l'Orphisme à propos des tentatives de Kupka," *La Vie des lettres*, October 1921, pp. 670-686

†Arnould-Grémilly, Louis, "Orfismus a pokusy Fr. Kupky," *Veraikon*, Prague, IX, 1923

Solari, Emile, "Les Arts," *Le Provençal de Paris*, 11e année, 2e série, no. 511, November 2, 1924, p. 1

Chiselle, Lucien, "Le peintre F. Kupka," *Idées*, deuxième année, no. 12, November-December 1924, n.p.

†Gallien, A. P., "Le Prince du rêve," *Gazette des Alpes*, December 1924

Del Marle, Félix, "Numéro spécial consacré à Franck Kupka," *Vouloir*, Lille, no. 12, June 1925

Bataille, Maurice, "Quatre peintres constructeurs," *Vouloir*, Lille, no. 16, December 1925

†Jíra, Jaroslav, "F. Kupka," *Kulturní Zpravodáj*, Prague, no. 5, 1927

†Arnould-Grémilly, Louis, "A propos de 'Quatre histoires de blanc et noir,' par Frank Kupka," *Signaux*, February-March 1928

van Doesburg, Theo, "Franche Schilderkunst," *De Groesse Amsterdammer*, November 30, 1929

†Siblík, Emmanuel, "Malíř Fr. Kupka," *Aventinum*, Prague, May 8, 1930

†Matějček, Antonín, "Prometheus Františka Kupky," *Umění*, Prague, III, 1930

†Siblík, Emmanuel, "František Kupka," *Hollar*, Prague, vol. 7, no. 2, 1930-1931, pp. 45-56

†Jíra, Jaroslav, ["Frant. Kupka as Artist and as Man,"] *Národní Osvobození*, Prague, no. 261, 1931

†Podešva, E., "František Kupka," *Salón 6*, Prague, 1931

Turpin, Georges, "Kupka," in Edouard-Joseph, René, ed., *Dictionnaire biographique des artistes contemporains, 1910-1930*, Paris, vol. II, 1931, pp. 284-288.

†Matějček, Antonín, K šedesátinám Františka Kupky," *Umění*, Prague, V, 1932

Bill, Max, "Frank Kupka: zum 75. Geburtstag," *Werk*, Winterthur, 33. Jahrgang, Heft 9, September 1946, pp. 106-107

Degand, Léon, "Kupka," *Art d'aujourd'hui*, Paris, série 3, numéro double 3 et 4, February-March 1952, pp. 54-58

Van Gindertael, Roger, "Pour aider à mieux comprendre 'Le Passage de la ligne': Documents réunis par R. V. Gindertael," *Art d'aujourd'hui*, Paris, série 3, numéro 6, August 1952, pp. 18-19

Mellquist, Jerome, "Kupka," *Vogue*, New York, November 15, 1952, pp. 112-113

Massat, René, untitled text, *Réalités nouvelles*, Paris, no. 7, July 1953, p. 4

Sibert, C. H., "Jubilé François Kupka," *Arts, spectacles*, Paris, no. 420, July 17-23, 1953

Bonnefoi, Geneviève, "Frank Kupka: Précurseur et solitaire," *Les Lettres nouvelles*, Paris, April 1954, pp. 591-598

Lassaigne, Jacques, "Kupka," *Revue de la pensée française*, 13 année, no. 6, June 1954

Bauduin, Nicolas, "Les temps héroïques, à propos du Salon de la Section d'Or," *Masques et Visages*, no. 39, June 1956, pp. 6-7 (Reprinted in *Rolet*, May 25, 1957)

Vachtová, Ludmila, "František Kupka," *Tvar*, Prague, no. 6-7, 1956, pp. 216-217

Lonngren, Lillian, "Kupka: Innovator of the Abstract International Style," *Art News*, New York, vol. 56, no. 7, November 1957, pp. 44-47, 54-56

Cassou, Jean, "L'Oeuvre de Kupka," *La Revue des Arts*, Paris, 8e année, no. 6, 1958, pp. 285-287

Chipp, Herschel B., "Orphism and Color Theory," *Art Bulletin*, New York, vol. XL, no. 1, March 1958, pp. 55-63

Descargues, Pierre, "100 Kupka au Musée d'Art Moderne," *Les Lettres françaises*, May 29, 1958, p. 11

†Van Gindertael, Roger, "Kupka," *Les Beaux-Arts*, Brussels, June 6, 1958

†Grenier, Jean, "Kupka et l'art abstrait," *Preuves*, August 1958

†Arnould-Grémilly, Louis, "Kupka, l'orphisme et l'art abstrait," *Combat*, Paris, no. 6, October 1958

Ragon, Michel, "Réhabilitation de Kupka," *Cimaise*, Paris, 6e série, no. 1, October-November 1958

Veronesi, Guilia, "Frank Kupka," *Art actuel international*, Paris, no. 5, 1958, p. 4

Boullier, René, "Frank Kupka," *Chroniques du jour*, Paris, nouvelle série, XXIe année, no. 13, Noël 1959

"L'origine du mot 'tachisme' revient à Franck Kupka," *Art actuel international*, Paris, 1959

Habasque, Guy, "Kupka, trois ans après sa mort, la célébrité," *Connaissance des arts*, Paris, no. 101, July 1960, pp. 30-37

Cassou, Jean, "Kupka: à l'origine de la peinture non-figurative," *La Revue des voyages*, Paris, no. 38, Autumn 1960, pp. 24-28

Vachtová, Ludmila, "František Kupka," *Kulturně politický kalendář*, Prague, 1961, pp. 258-259

†Šmejkal, F., "Výstava Františka Kupky," *Výtvarná práce 14*, Prague, 1931

Petrová, Eva, "Vývojové etapy díla Františka Kupky," *Umění*, Prague, no. 6, année X, November 1962, pp. 597-601

Vachtová, Ludmila, "Kupka," *Dějiny a současnost*, Prague, vol. V, no. 8, 1963, pp. 22-29

Fédit, Denise, "Formation de l'art de Kupka," *La Revue du Louvre*, Paris, 14e année, no. 6, 1964, pp. 333-342

Vachtová, Ludmila, "La Parabola di Kupka," *L'Europa Letteraria*, Rome, vol. V, no. 29, May 1964

Guichard-Meili, Jean, "Kupka se libère dans ses pastels," *Arts, Lettres, Spectacles, Musique*, Paris, no. 966, June 10-16, 1964, p. 11

"Bright Orpheus," *Time*, vol. 84, no. 5, New York, July 31, 1964, pp. 36-37

Fédit, Denise, "Les Gouaches de Kupka," *Quadrum*, Brussels, vol. XVI, 1964, pp. 27-34

Cassou, Jean, "Kupka," *Studio International*, London, vol. 170, no. 868, August 1965, pp. 70-73

Vachtová, Ludmila, "Kupkovy osudy," *Výtvarné umění* Prague, vol. XV, no. 8, 1965, pp. 372-379

†Miler, K., "Kupka v Praze," *Výtvarná práce* Prague, br. 12/XIII, 1965

†Spies, Werner, "Die Büchse der Pandora. Der Maler Frank Kupka in neuer Sicht, *Frankfurter Allgemeine*, May 3, 1966

Czagan, Friedrich, "Frank Kupka und die tschechische Avantgarde," *Werk*, Winterthur, 53. Jg., no. 7, July 1966, pp. 273-280

"Nouvelles de l'A.I.C.A.: le colloque Kupka," *Gazette des Beaux-Arts*, Paris, vol. 72, nos. 1194/95/96, Supplement, July-September 1968, pp. 26-27

Křiž, Jan, "František Kupka a pojem českého umění," *Výtvarné umění*, Prague, vol. XVIII, no. 7, 1968, pp. 354-356. Includes French translation "František Kupka et la notion de l'art tchèque"

Solier, René de, "Prostor a barva u Kupky," *Výtvarné umění*, Prague, vol. XVIII, no. 7, 1968, pp. 348-349. Includes French translation "L'Espace et la couleur chez Kupka"

Vachtová, Ludmila, "Kolokvium o Františku Kupkovi," *Výtvarné umění*, Prague, vol. XVIII, no. 7, 1968, p. 338-339. Includes French translation "Colloque de František Kupka"

Berger, René, "Polarita Kupkovy tvorby," *Výtvarné umění*, Prague, vol. XVIII, no. 7, 1968, pp. 349-350. Includes French translation "Polarité de l'oeuvre de Kupka"

"Trying to see in the abstract," *The Times Literary Supplement*, London, May 8, 1969. [Review of Ludmila Vachtová, *Frank Kupka*]

Henning, Edward B., "Frank Kupka: Amorpha, Fugue for Two Colors II," *The Bulletin of the Cleveland Museum of Art*, Cleveland, vol. LVII, no. 4, April 1970, pp. 106-111

Vachtová, Ludmila, "Kupka 1871-1971," *Art International*, Lugano, vol. XVI, no. 5, May 20, 1972, pp. 17-21; 67

GENERAL BOOKS

Thieme, Ulrich and Becker, Felix, *Das Allgemeine Lexikon der bildenden Kuenstler, XXII*, Leipzig, 1928

Barr, Alfred H., Jr., *Cubism and Abstract Art*, New York, 1936

Nebeský, J. V., *L'Art moderne tchécoslovaque*, Paris, 1937

Seuphor, Michel, *L'Art abstrait, ses origines, ses premiers maîtres*, Paris, 1949 and 1950

Raynal, Maurice; Lassaigne, Jacques; Schmalenbach, Werner; Rüdlinger, Arnold; Bolliger, Hans, *History of Modern Painting, Vol. III, From Picasso to Surrealism*, Geneva, 1949-1950, pp. 90, 121. English translation by Douglas Cooper

Cogniat, Raymond and Maillard, Robert, eds., LA[ssaigne], J[acques], "Kupka," *Dictionnaire de la peinture moderne*, Paris, 1954, pp. 143-144

†*Knaurs Lexikon moderner Malerei*, 1955 and 1957

Vollmer, Hans, ed., *Allgemeines Lexikon der bildenden Künstler des XX. Jahrhunderts*, Vol. III, Leipzig, 1956, p. 141

Dorival, Bernard, *Les peintres du XXᵉ siècle*, Paris, 1957 [*Twentieth Century Painters*, New York, 1958. English translation by W. J. Strachan and A. Rossi]

Seuphor, Michel, *Dictionnaire de la peinture abstraite*, Paris, 1957 [*Dictionary of Abstract Painting*, New York, 1957. English translation by L. Izod, J. Montague, F. Scarfe]

Dorival, Bernard, *L'Ecole de Paris au Musée National d'Art Moderne*, Paris, 1961 [*The School of Paris in The Musée National d'Art Moderne*, New York, 1962. English translation by C. Brookfield and E. Hart]

Cassou, Jean; Langui, Emile; Pevsner, Nikolaus, *Les Sources du vingtième siècle*, Paris, 1961

Cabanne, Pierre, *L'Epopée du cubisme*, Paris, 1963

Maillard, Robert, ed., Lassaigne, Jacques, "Kupka," *Dictionnaire universel de l'art et des artistes, Tome 2*, Paris, 1967, pp. 338-339

Hofmann, Werner, *Turning Points in Twentieth Century Art, 1890-1917*, New York, c. 1969. English translation by C. Kessler

Seuphor, Michel, *L'art abstrait, 1910-1918, Origines et Premiers maîtres, Tome 1*, Paris, 1971

Liberman, Alexander, *The Artist in His Studio*, New York, n.d.

PHOTOGRAPHIC CREDITS

BLACK AND WHITES

Bibliothèque Nationale, Paris: Fig. 2A, p. 38

Bildarchiv der Nationalbibliothek, Vienna: Fig. 11, p. 34

Louis Carré et Cie: Fig. 12, p. 35

Courtesy Cinémathèque française, Paris: Fig. 2, p. 51, fig. 6, p. 56, fig. 8, p. 58, fig. 10, p. 60, fig. 12, p. 62, fig. 13, p. 63

Geoffrey Clements, New York: Cat. nos. 72, 78, 109, 182

Courtesy Cleveland Museum of Art: Cat. no. 63

Courtesy Cliché des Musées Nationaux, France: Cat. nos. 4, 9, 14, 20, 22, 24, 31, 41, 47, 49, 50-52, 57, 65, 66, 69, 74, 83, 96, 120, 135, 147, 148, 156, 184, 187, 189
Fig. 7B, p. 41

Bevan Davies: Cat. no. 101

Courtesy Lucy Delmarle: Fig. 11, p. 313

Jean Dubout, Paris: Cat. nos. 10, 12, 16, 18, 28, 36, 37, 40, 54, 58, 93, 98, 107, 110, 112, 113, 130, 157, 166
Fig. 14, p. 65

eeva-inkeri, New York: Cat. nos. 124, 145, 163, 188

Photo Ellebé, Rouen: Fig. 1, p. 50, fig. 4, p. 53

Thomas Feist: Cat. no. 5

Courtesy Karl Flinker: Figs., pp. 136, 141

Courtesy Gallien Family: Fig., p. 172

Courtesy Lucien Goldschmidt, Inc., New York: Fig., p. 95

Courtesy Mr. and Mrs. M. A. Gribin: Cat. nos. 137, 142

Peter A. Juley and Son, New York: Cat. nos. 180, 185

Courtesy Lilli Lonngren: Fig., p. 132

Courtesy Los Angeles County Museum of Art: Cat. no. 79

Studio Lourmel 77, Paris: Cat. no. 136

Courtesy Andrée Martinel-Kupka: Frontispiece, fig. 1, p. 306, figs. 2, 3, p. 307, fig. 5, p. 308, figs. 6, 7, p. 309, figs. 9, 10, p. 312, fig. 12, p. 314, p. 46, fig., p. 12, fig., p. 102, fig., p. 224, fig., p. 232, fig., p. 327

Robert E. Mates: Cat. no. 140

Robert E. Mates and Mary Donlon: Cat. nos. 11, 15, 21, 35, 43, 48, 56, 60, 62, 64, 67, 68, 76, 77, 81, 84-86, 100, 104, 106, 114, 115, 119, 129, 131, 134, 146, 152-155, 158, 159, 161, 162, 165, 168-170, 186
Fig. 3, p. 17, fig. 4, p. 308, fig. 6, p. 19, fig. 8, p. 310, fig. 5B, p. 41, figs. 5C, 6C, p. 45, fig., p. 240

Robert E. Mates and Paul Katz: Cat. nos. 42, 116, 118, 138, 190

Courtesy Muzeum Města, Prague: Fig. 1A, p. 38

Courtesy Metropolitan Museum of Art, New York: Cat. no. 176

Courtesy Meda Mladek: Fig. 2, p. 16, fig. 5, p. 18, fig. 7, p. 21, figs. 1A, 1B, p. 42, fig. 2B, p. 43, fig., p. 208, fig. 14, p. 36

Courtesy The Museum of Modern Art, New York: Cat. nos. 23, 30, 32, 33, 45, 53, 55, 61, 71, 88-91, 95
Fig. 5, p. 55, fig. 9, p. 59, fig. 11, p. 61, fig. 3A, p. 38, figs. 5A, p. 39, figs. 1B, 2B, 3B, p. 40, fig. 6B, p. 41, figs. 2C, 3C, p. 44, fig. 4C, p. 45, fig., p. 119

André Morain, Paris: Cat. nos. 102, 103, 117, 132, 174

Musée du Louvre: Fig. 10, p. 31

Courtesy Musée National des Techniques, Paris: Fig. 7, p. 57, fig., p. 92, fig., p. 175

Jiří Mucha: Fig. 14, p. 315

Courtesy Národní Galerie, Prague: Cat. nos. 1-3, 6-8, 13, 15, 17, 19, 21, 25-27, 34, 38, 39, 44, 80, 82, 92, 97, 108, 121, 125, 139, 141, 144, 149, 164, 167, 171, 173, 175, 179
Fig. 1, p. 16, fig. 4, p. 18, fig. 8, p. 21, fig. 9a, p. 28, fig. 9b, p. 29, fig. 4A, p. 39, fig. 4B, p. 40, figs. 2A, 3A, p. 42, figs. 3B, 4B, p. 43, fig. 1C, p. 44, fig. 13, p. 36, fig., p. 169, fig., p. 298

Photo Passet, Paris: Fig. 3, p. 52

Courtesy Philadelphia Museum of Art, Staff Photographer, A. J. Wyatt: Cat. no. 75

Photo Studios Ltd., London: Cat. no. 127

Courtesy P. P., Paris: Fig. 7A, p. 39, fig. 4A, p. 42

Eric Pollitzer, New York: Cat. nos. 177, 183

Fotostudio Otto, Vienna: Cat. no. 70

Courtesy Camille Renault, Paris: Cat. no. 123

Courtesy Galerie Denise René, Paris: Cat. no. 94

Rheinischer Bildarchiv, Cologne: Cat. no. 122

Walter Rosenblum, New York: Cat. no. 111

John D. Schiff, New York: Cat. nos. 87, 128, 181

Courtesy Mr. and Mrs. G. E. S.: Cat. no. 178

Courtesy Mr. and Mrs. Joseph Randall Shapiro: Cat. no. 143

Taylor and Dull, Inc., New York City: Fig., p. 248

Frank J. Thomas: Cat. no. 126

Sabine Weiss: Fig. 15, p. 316, fig. 16, p. 317

EKTACHROMES

Studio Lourmel 77, Paris: Cat. no. 133

Courtesy Cliché des Musées Nationaux, France: Cat. nos. 29, 46, 73

Courtesy Galerie Karl Flinker: Cat. no. 172

Robert E. Mates and Mary Donlon: Cat. nos. 59, 99, 105, 160

Courtesy P. P., Paris: Cat. no. 150

Kupka and Jacques Villon behind
Kupka's house, Puteaux, c. 1952.